JP AHONEN

VOLUME II

No Rest for the Wicked

FOREWORD *by Max Sarin*

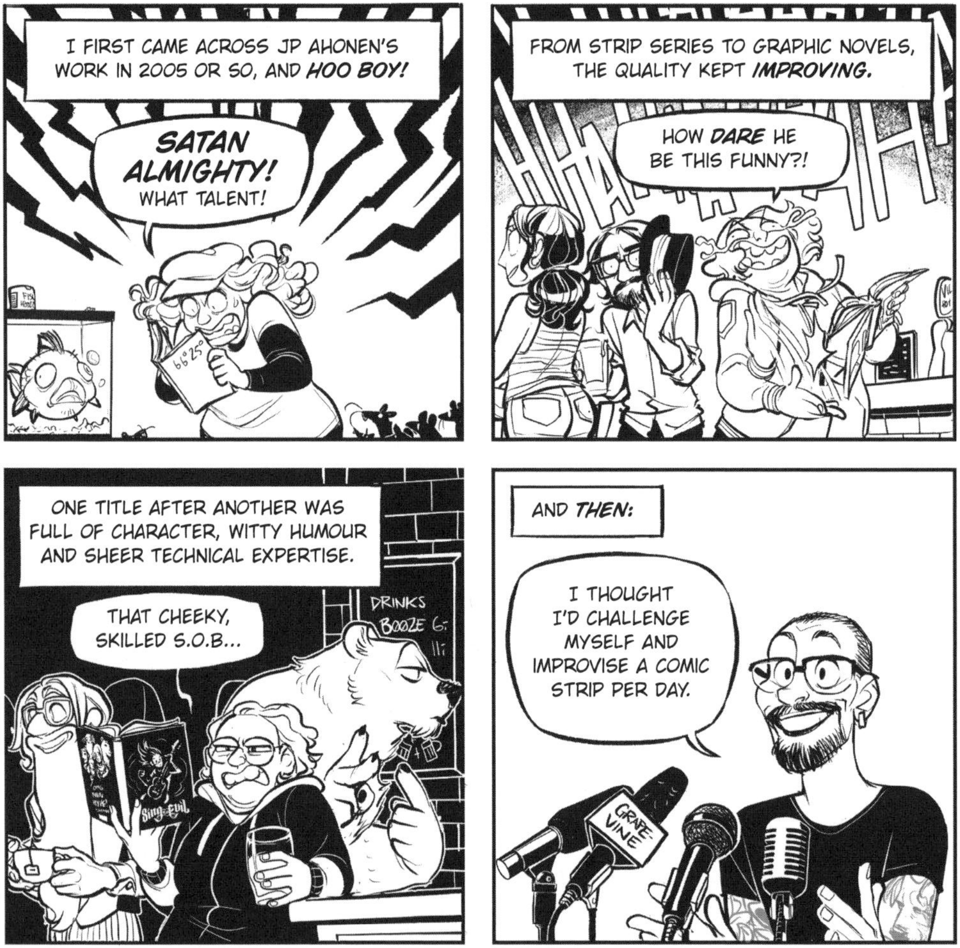
I FIRST CAME ACROSS JP AHONEN'S WORK IN 2005 OR SO, AND HOO BOY!
SATAN ALMIGHTY! WHAT TALENT!
FROM STRIP SERIES TO GRAPHIC NOVELS, THE QUALITY KEPT IMPROVING.
HOW DARE HE BE THIS FUNNY?!
ONE TITLE AFTER ANOTHER WAS FULL OF CHARACTER, WITTY HUMOUR AND SHEER TECHNICAL EXPERTISE.
THAT CHEEKY, SKILLED S.O.B...
DRINKS
BOOZE
AND THEN:
I THOUGHT I'D CHALLENGE MYSELF AND IMPROVISE A COMIC STRIP PER DAY.
GRAPE VINE

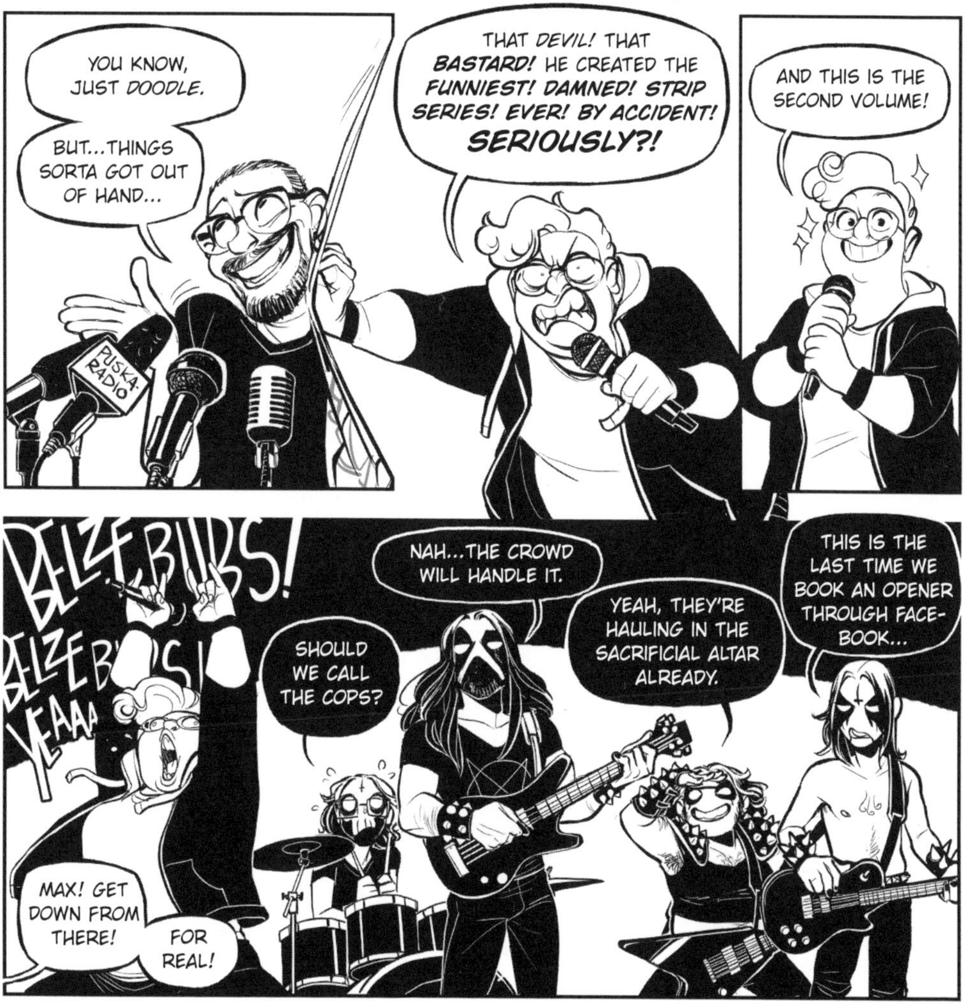

YOU KNOW, JUST DOODLE.
BUT...THINGS SORTA GOT OUT OF HAND...
THAT DEVIL! THAT BASTARD! HE CREATED THE FUNNIEST! DAMNED! STRIP SERIES! EVER! BY ACCIDENT! SERIOUSLY?!
PUSKA RADIO
AND THIS IS THE SECOND VOLUME!
BELZEBUBS!
YEAAA
SHOULD WE CALL THE COPS?
NAH...THE CROWD WILL HANDLE IT.
YEAH, THEY'RE HAULING IN THE SACRIFICIAL ALTAR ALREADY.
THIS IS THE LAST TIME WE BOOK AN OPENER THROUGH FACE-BOOK...
MAX! GET DOWN FROM THERE!
FOR REAL!

Belzebubs

VOLUME II

No Rest for the Wicked

by

JP AHONEN

Published by

TOP SHELF PRODUCTIONS

Dedicated to Maikki

Editor-in-Chief: Chris Staros.
Designed by JP Ahonen.

Published by Top Shelf Productions, an imprint of IDW Publishing, a division of Idea and Design Works, LLC. Offices: 14144 Ventura Blvd, Suite 210, Sherman Oaks, CA 91423. Top Shelf Productions®, the Top Shelf logo, Idea and Design Works®, and the IDW logo are registered trademarks of Idea and Design Works, LLC.

Visit our online catalog at WWW.TOPSHELFCOMIX.COM.

ISBN 978-1-60309-542-6
Printed in China.

28 27 26 25 24 1 2 3 4 5

Thanks to Chris, Janne-Matti, Terhi, Samppa, Inari, Lassi, Leo, Jenny, Max, Mikael, Oscar and Antje, Taike, SKR and Sarjakuvantekijät ry. Also, a massive thank you to the Belzebubs fans. You continue to rule!

And last but certainly not least, my family: Maikki, Aamos, Ukko & Mimmi,
I love you with all my heart. ❤ Thanks for sticking with me.

WWW.BELZEBUBS.COM | WWW.JPAHONEN.COM

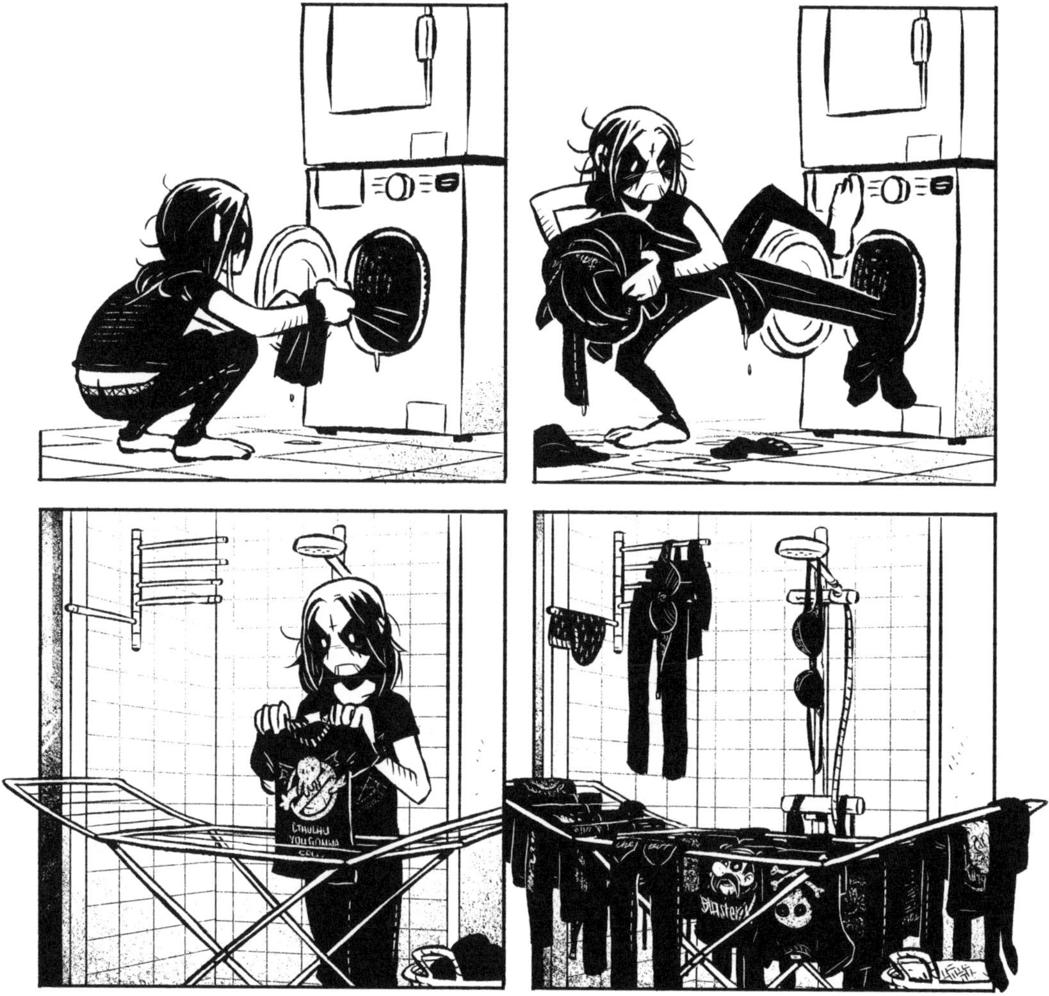
CTHULHU
YOU GONNA

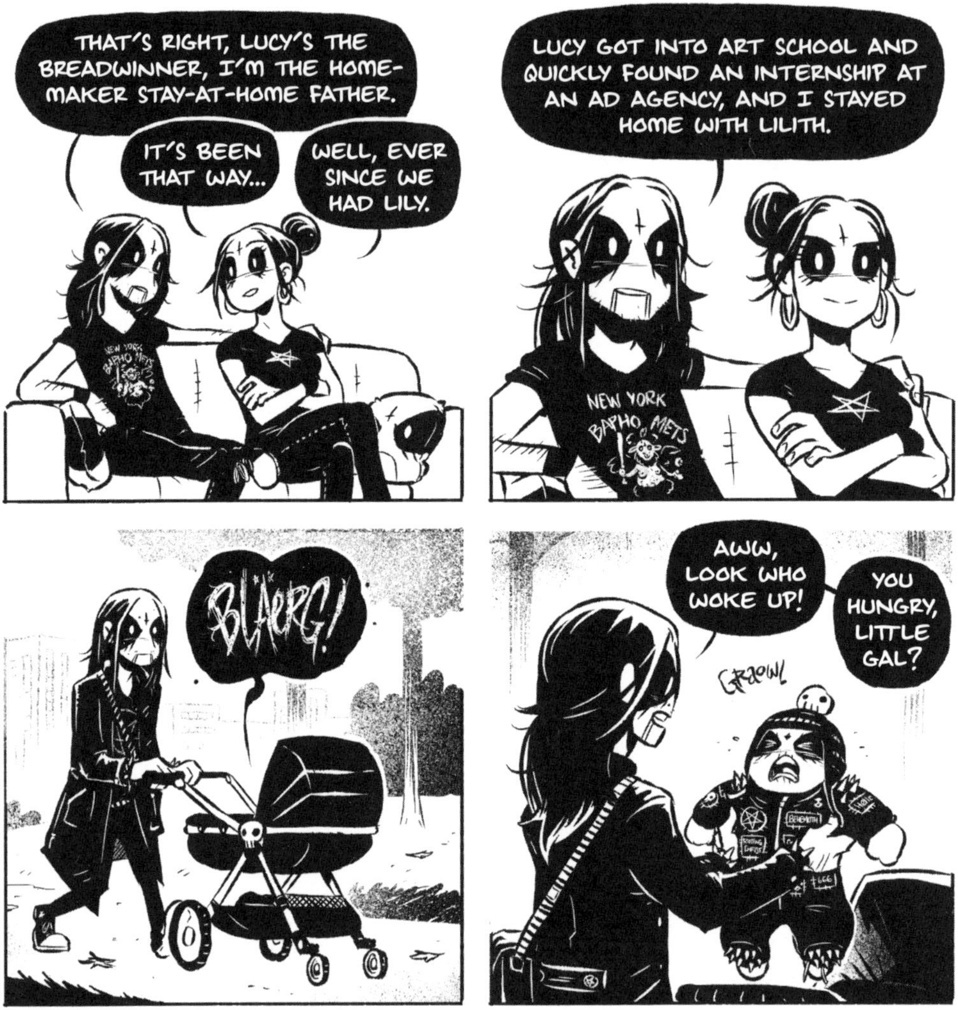
THAT'S RIGHT, LUCY'S THE BREADWINNER, I'M THE HOME-MAKER STAY-AT-HOME FATHER.
IT'S BEEN THAT WAY...
WELL, EVER SINCE WE HAD LILY.
NEW YORK BAPHO METS
LUCY GOT INTO ART SCHOOL AND QUICKLY FOUND AN INTERNSHIP AT AN AD AGENCY, AND I STAYED HOME WITH LILITH.
NEW YORK BAPHO METS
BLÆRG!
AWW, LOOK WHO WOKE UP!
YOU HUNGRY, LITTLE GAL?
GRAOWL

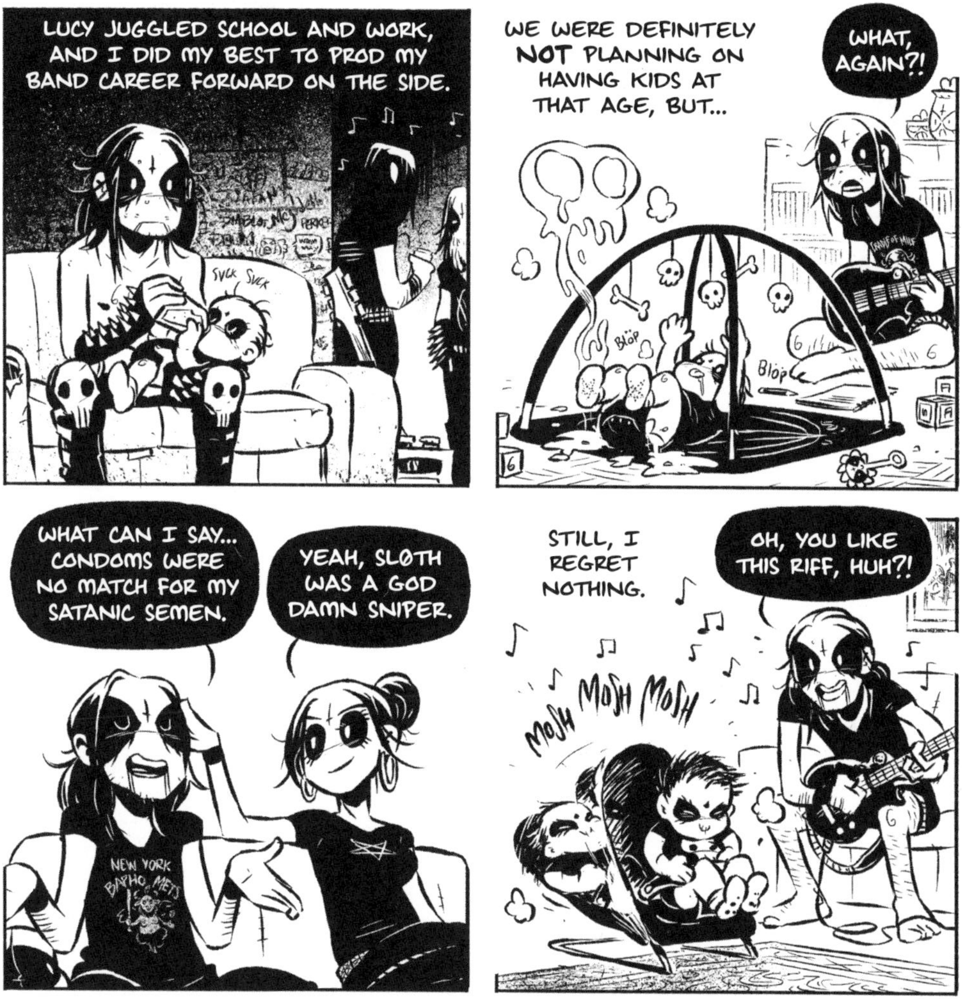
LUCY JUGGLED SCHOOL AND WORK, AND I DID MY BEST TO PROD MY BAND CAREER FORWARD ON THE SIDE.
SUCK SUCK
WE WERE DEFINITELY NOT PLANNING ON HAVING KIDS AT THAT AGE, BUT...
WHAT, AGAIN?!
BLOP
BLOP
WHAT CAN I SAY... CONDOMS WERE NO MATCH FOR MY SATANIC SEMEN.
YEAH, SLØTH WAS A GOD DAMN SNIPER.
NEW YORK BAPHO METS
STILL, I REGRET NOTHING.
OH, YOU LIKE THIS RIFF, HUH?!
MOSH MOSH MOSH

OK, LILITH. SPIT IT OUT.
WHAT?
COME ON, WHAT'S WITH THE SMIRK?
Ehh, LET'S JUST SAY SAM AND I HAVE REACHED A WHOLE NEW LEVEL IN OUR RELATIONSHIP...
NO! TELL ME ALL THE DIRTY LITTLE DETAILS!
WELL, WE HAD THE HOUSE TO OURSELVES FOR A WHILE, GOT A LITTLE TOO COMFY, AND...you know...

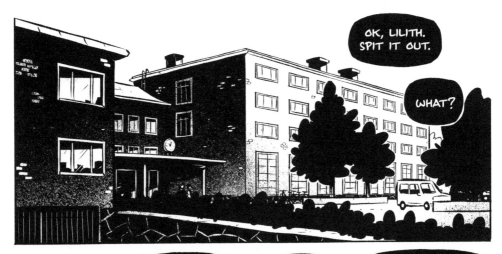

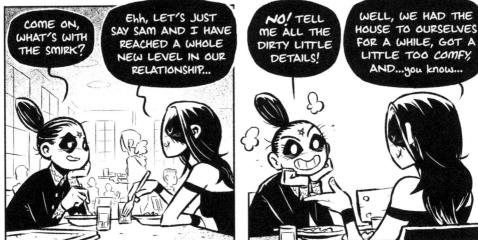

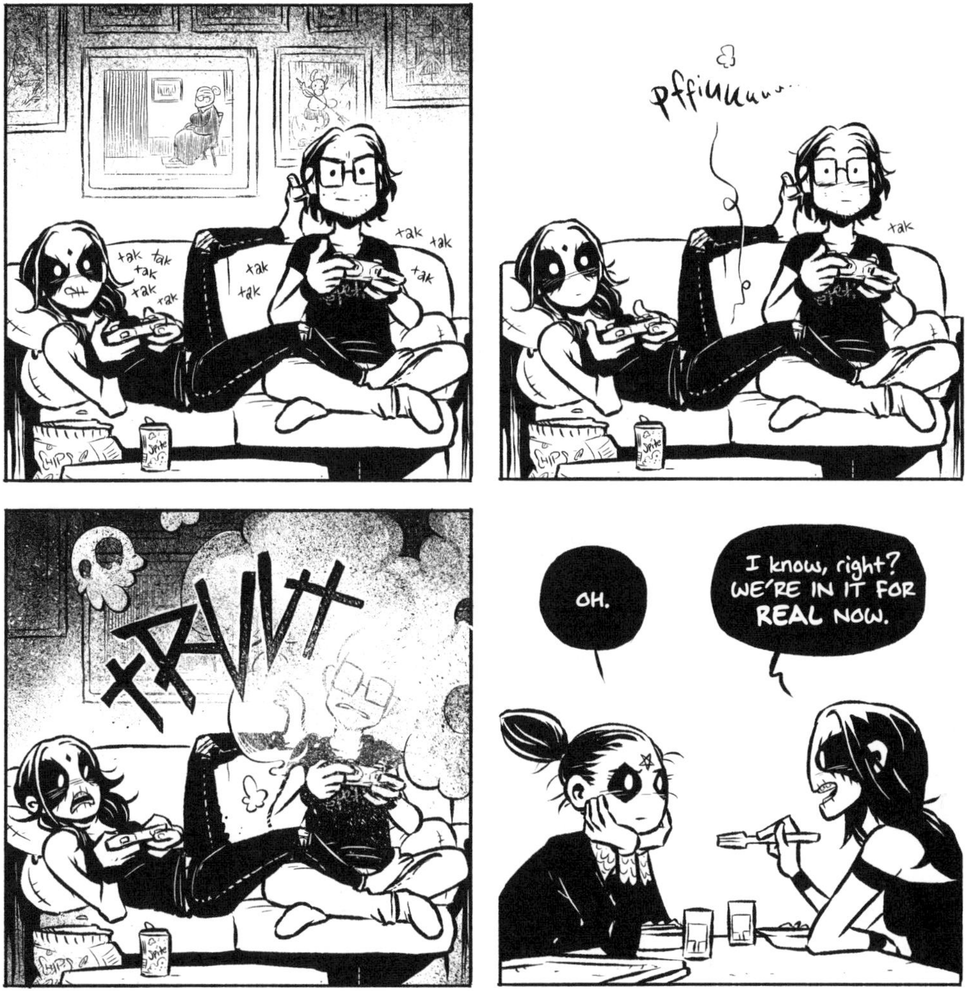
tak tak
tak
tak
tak
tak
tak
tak
tak
tak
tak
pffiuuuu...
tak
OH.
I know, right? WE'RE IN IT FOR REAL NOW.

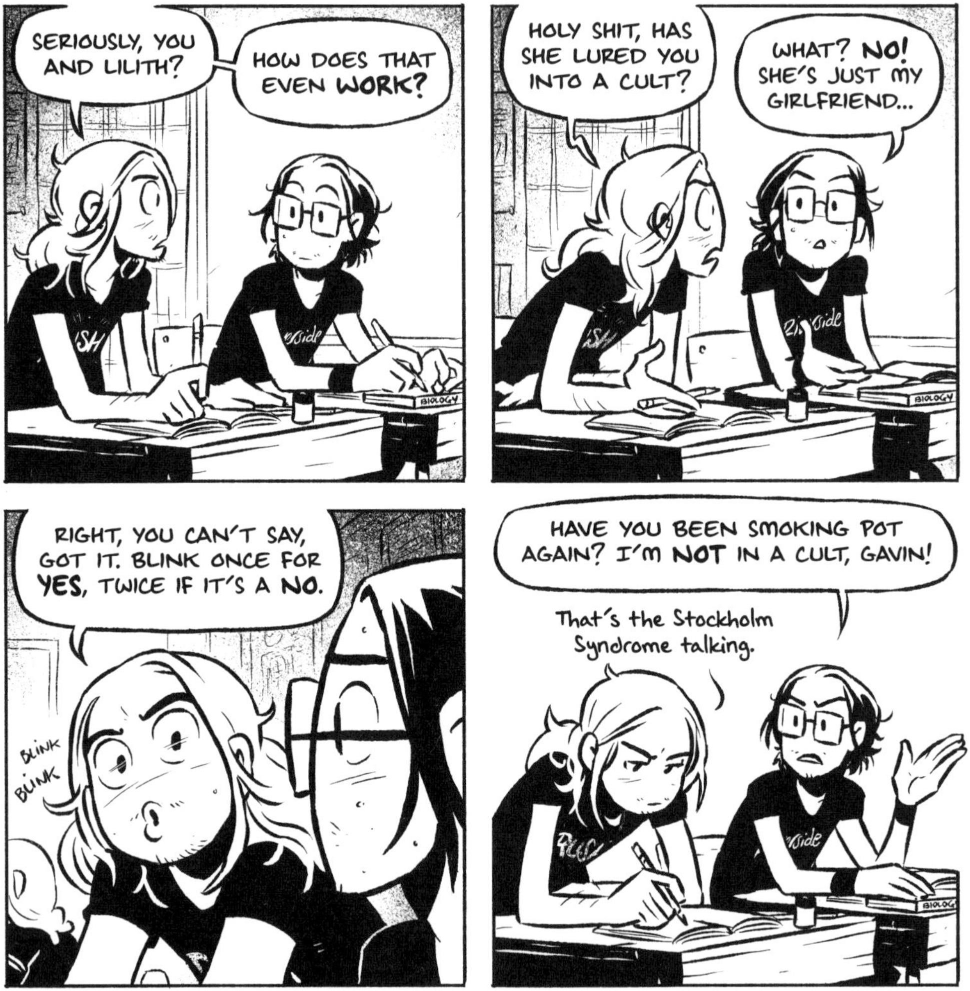
SERIOUSLY, YOU AND LILITH?
HOW DOES THAT EVEN WORK?
HOLY SHIT, HAS SHE LURED YOU INTO A CULT?
WHAT? NO! SHE'S JUST MY GIRLFRIEND...
BIOLOGY
RIGHT, YOU CAN'T SAY, GOT IT. BLINK ONCE FOR YES, TWICE IF IT'S A NO.
BLINK
BLINK
HAVE YOU BEEN SMOKING POT AGAIN? I'M NOT IN A CULT, GAVIN!
That's the Stockholm Syndrome talking.

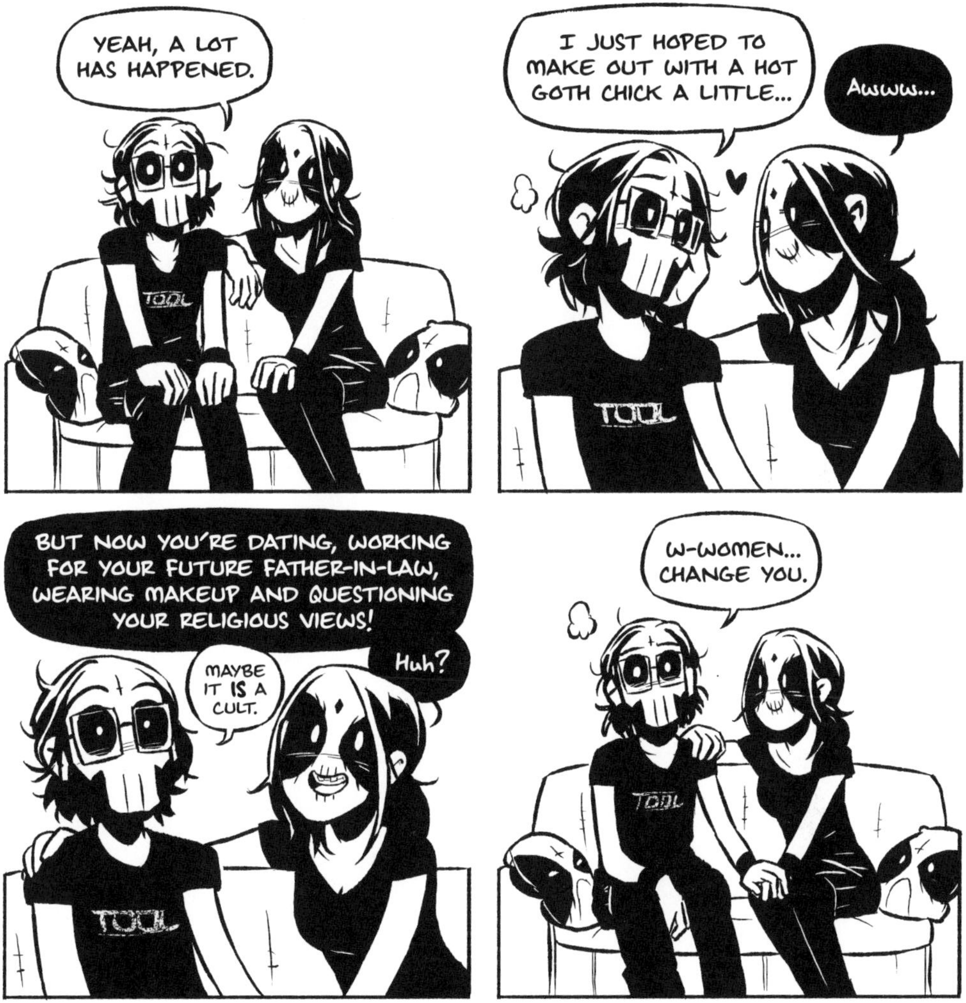
YEAH, A LOT HAS HAPPENED.
I JUST HOPED TO MAKE OUT WITH A HOT GOTH CHICK A LITTLE...
Awww...
TOOL
BUT NOW YOU'RE DATING, WORKING FOR YOUR FUTURE FATHER-IN-LAW, WEARING MAKEUP AND QUESTIONING YOUR RELIGIOUS VIEWS!
Huh?
MAYBE IT IS A CULT.
W-WOMEN... CHANGE YOU.

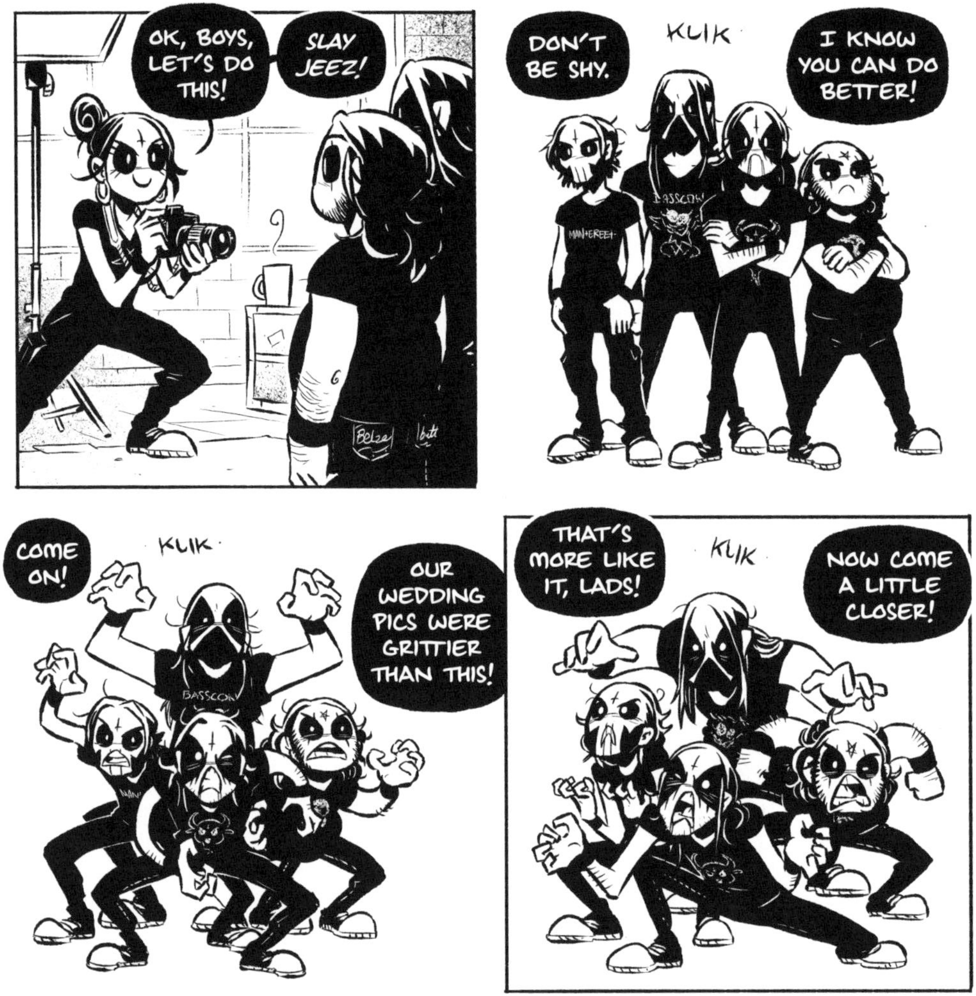
OK, BOYS, LET'S DO THIS!
SLAY JEEZ!
DON'T BE SHY.
KLIK
I KNOW YOU CAN DO BETTER!
COME ON!
KLIK
OUR WEDDING PICS WERE GRITTIER THAN THIS!
THAT'S MORE LIKE IT, LADS!
KLIK
NOW COME A LITTLE CLOSER!

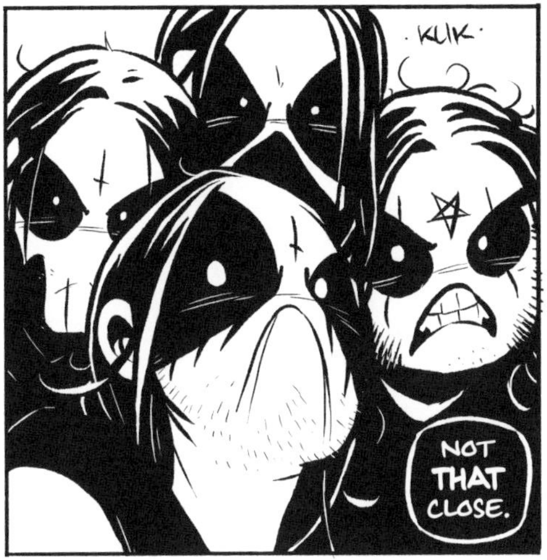
KLIK
NOT THAT CLOSE.

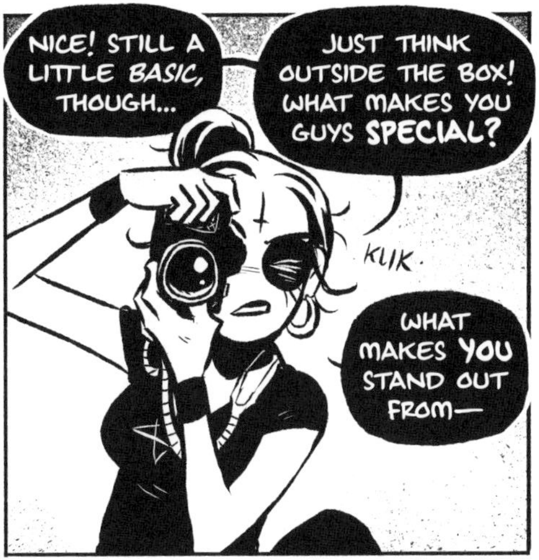
NICE! STILL A LITTLE BASIC, THOUGH...
JUST THINK OUTSIDE THE BOX! WHAT MAKES YOU GUYS SPECIAL?
KLIK
WHAT MAKES YOU STAND OUT FROM—

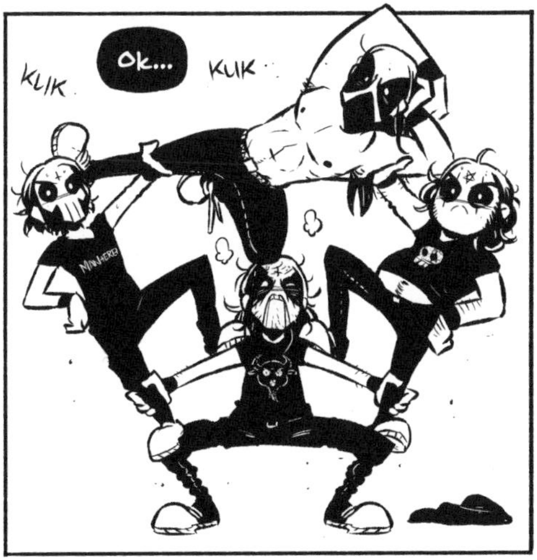
KLIK
Ok...
KLIK

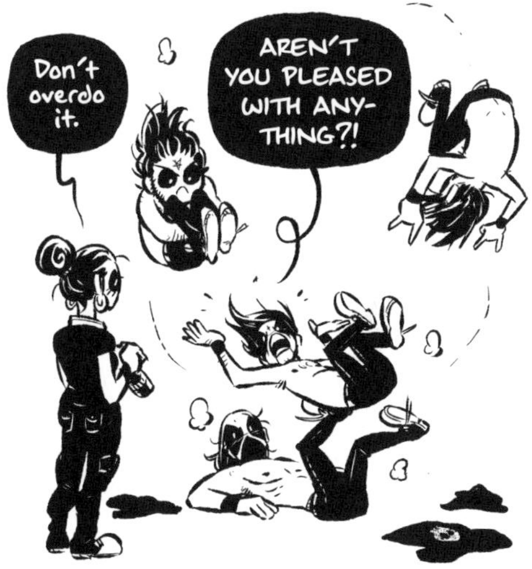
Don't overdo it.
AREN'T YOU PLEASED WITH ANY-THING?!

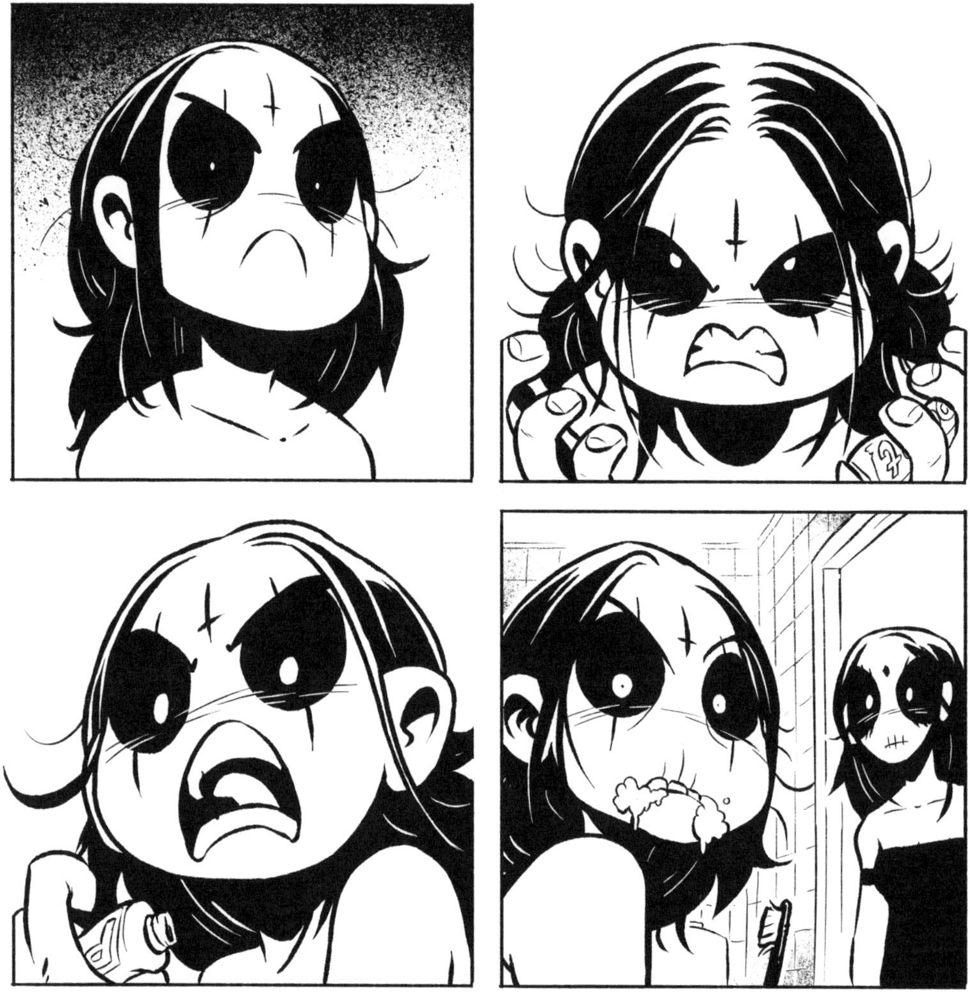

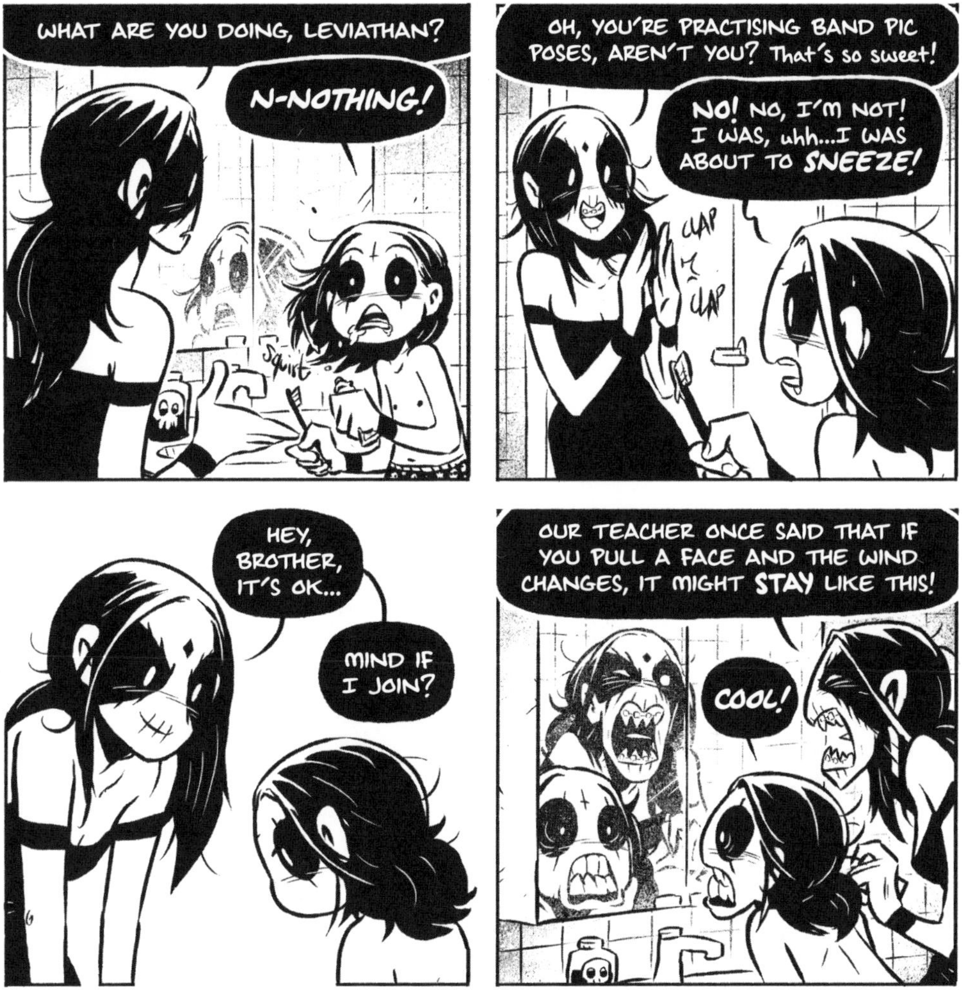
WHAT ARE YOU DOING, LEVIATHAN?
N-NOTHING!
Squirt
OH, YOU'RE PRACTISING BAND PIC POSES, AREN'T YOU? That's so sweet!
NO! NO, I'M NOT! I WAS, uhh...I WAS ABOUT TO SNEEZE!
CLAP CLAP
HEY, BROTHER, IT'S OK...
MIND IF I JOIN?
OUR TEACHER ONCE SAID THAT IF YOU PULL A FACE AND THE WIND CHANGES, IT MIGHT STAY LIKE THIS!
COOL!

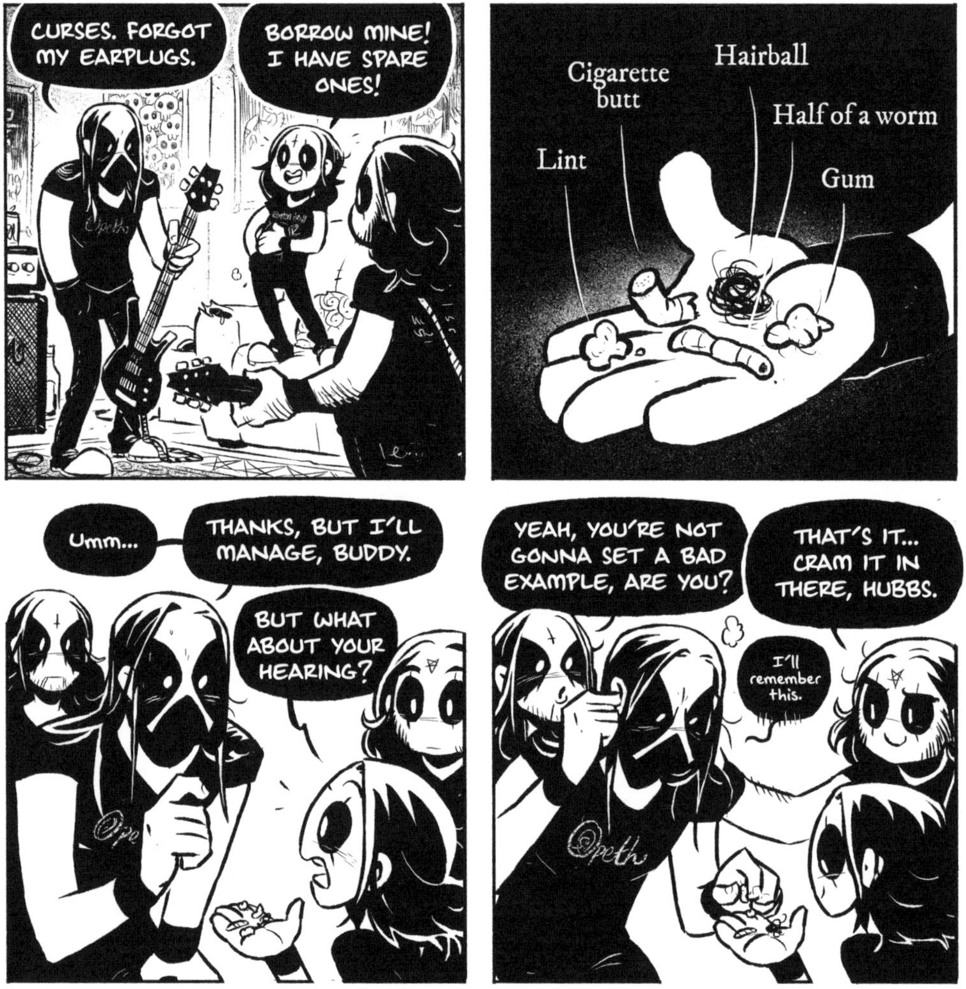
CURSES. FORGOT MY EARPLUGS.
BORROW MINE! I HAVE SPARE ONES!
Cigarette butt
Hairball
Half of a worm
Lint
Gum
Umm...
THANKS, BUT I'LL MANAGE, BUDDY.
BUT WHAT ABOUT YOUR HEARING?
YEAH, YOU'RE NOT GONNA SET A BAD EXAMPLE, ARE YOU?
THAT'S IT... CRAM IT IN THERE, HUBBS.
I'll remember this.
Opeth

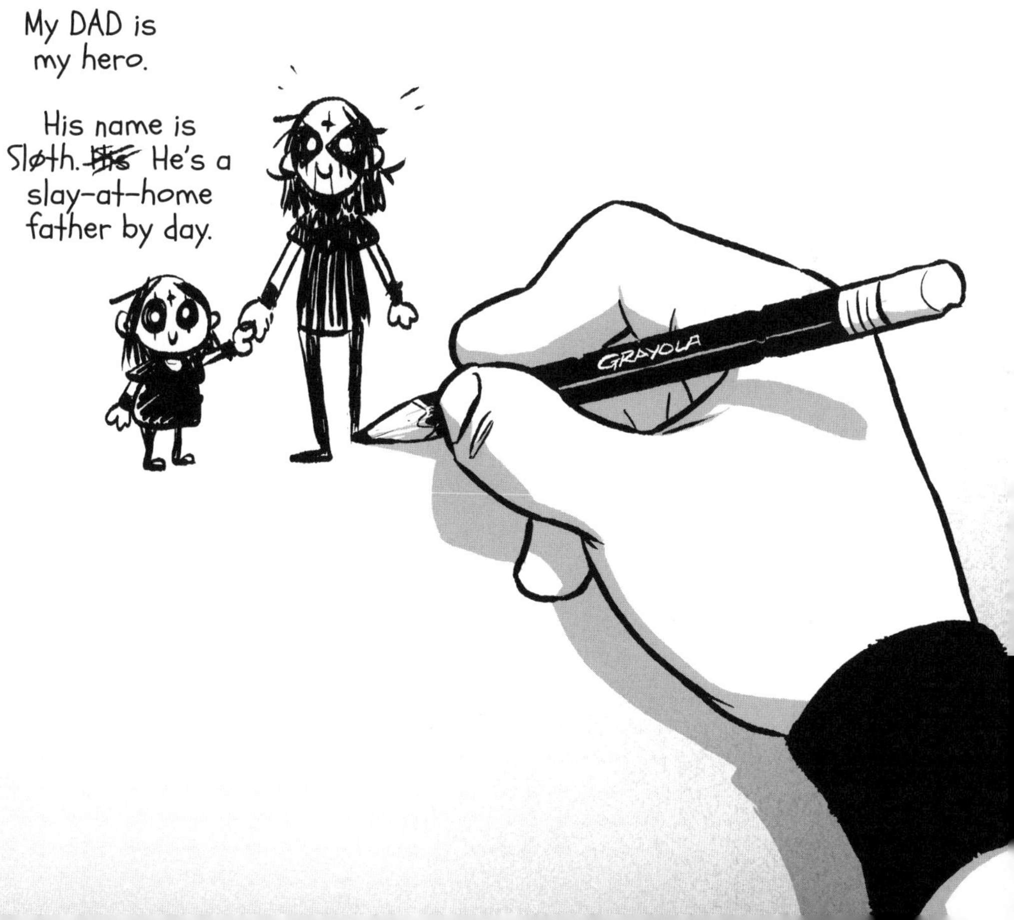
My DAD is my hero.
His name is Sløth. ~~His~~ He's a slay-at-home father by day.
GRAYOLA

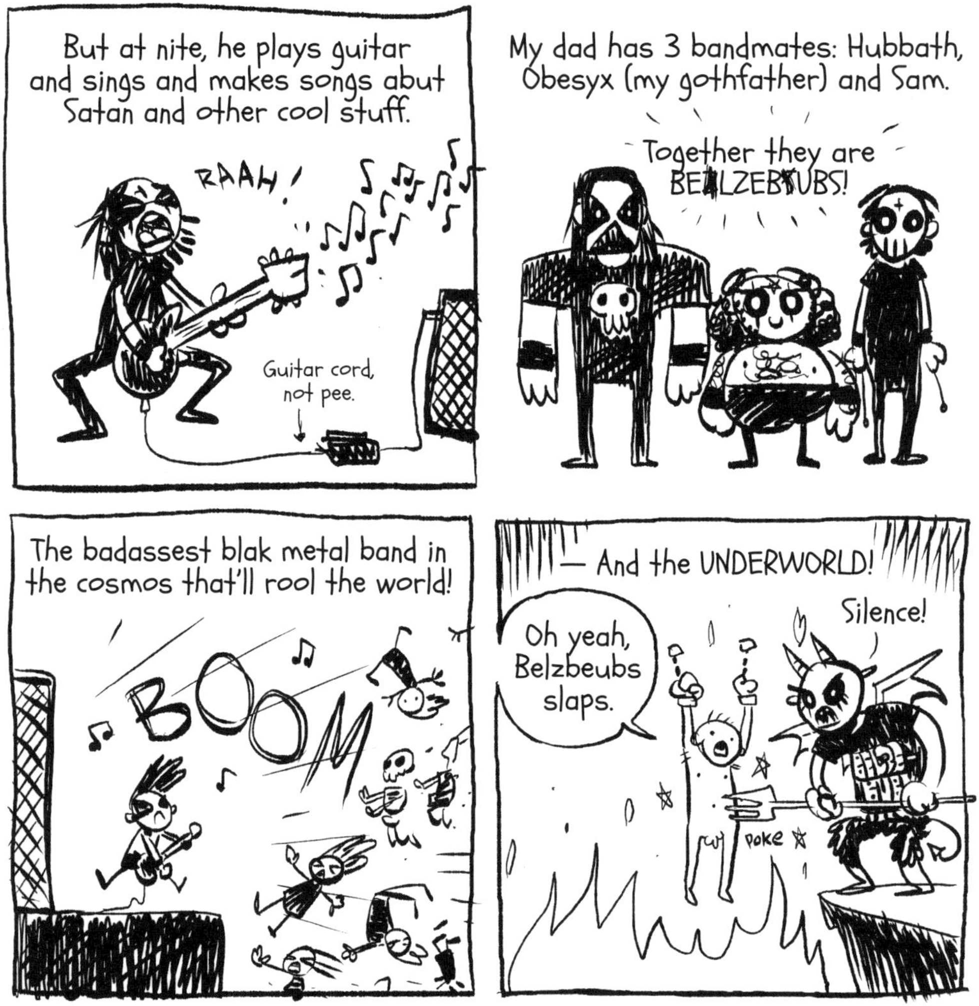
But at nite, he plays guitar and sings and makes songs abut Satan and other cool stuff.
RAAH!
Guitar cord, not pee.
My dad has 3 bandmates: Hubbath, Obesyx (my gothfather) and Sam.
Together they are BELZEBUBS!
The badassest blak metal band in the cosmos that'll rool the world!
BOOM
— And the UNDERWORLD!
Oh yeah, Belzbeubs slaps.
Silence!
POKE

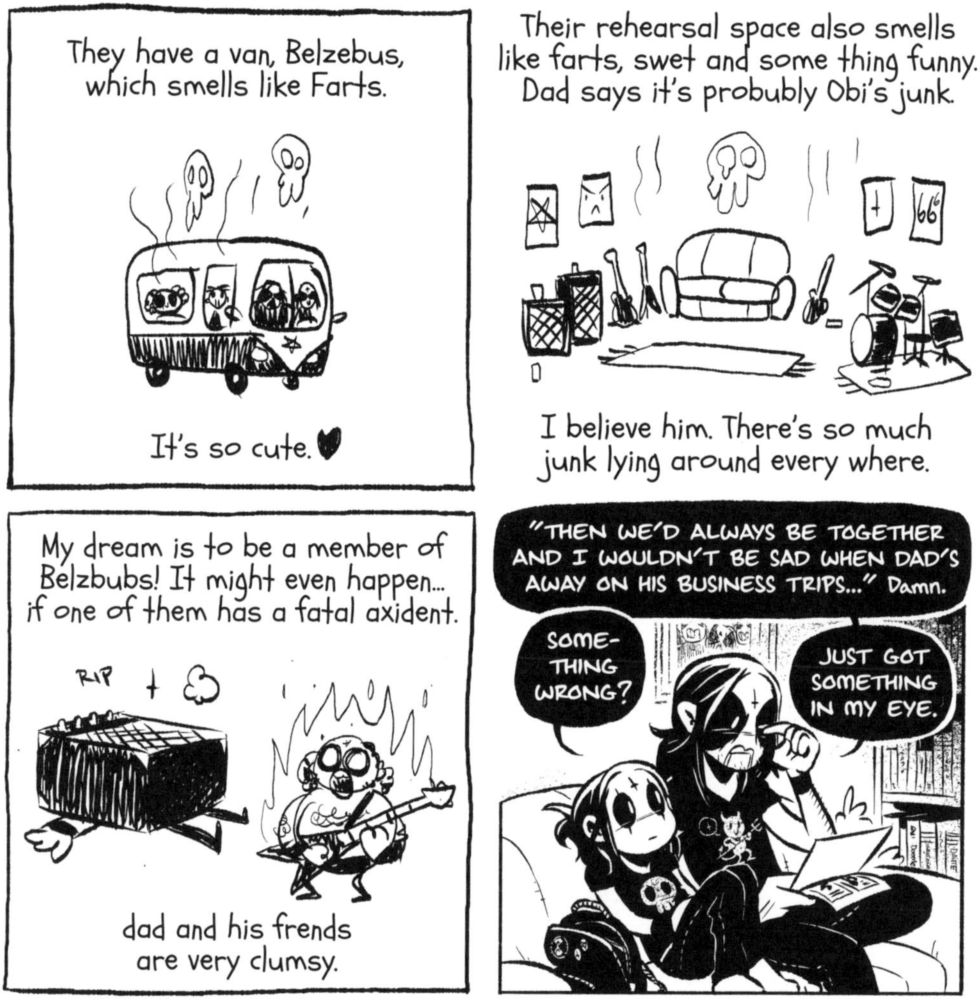
They have a van, Belzebus, which smells like Farts.
It's so cute.
Their rehearsal space also smells like farts, swet and some thing funny. Dad says it's probubly Obi's junk.
666
I believe him. There's so much junk lying around every where.
My dream is to be a member of Belzbubs! It might even happen... if one of them has a fatal axident.
RIP
dad and his frends are very clumsy.
"THEN WE'D ALWAYS BE TOGETHER AND I WOULDN'T BE SAD WHEN DAD'S AWAY ON HIS BUSINESS TRIPS..." Damn.
SOME-THING WRONG?
JUST GOT SOMETHING IN MY EYE.

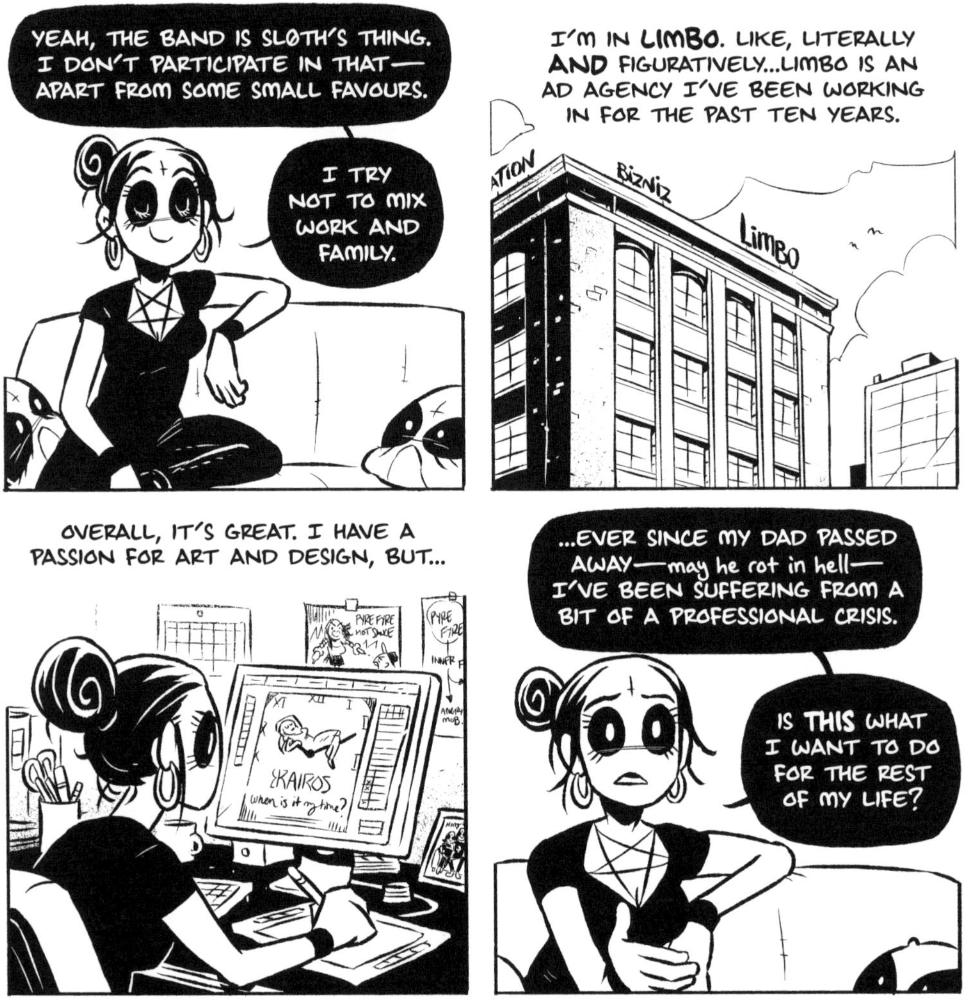
YEAH, THE BAND IS SLØTH'S THING. I DON'T PARTICIPATE IN THAT— APART FROM SOME SMALL FAVOURS.
I TRY NOT TO MIX WORK AND FAMILY.
I'M IN **LIMBO**. LIKE, LITERALLY **AND** FIGURATIVELY...LIMBO IS AN AD AGENCY I'VE BEEN WORKING IN FOR THE PAST TEN YEARS.
ATION
BizNiz
LimBO
OVERALL, IT'S GREAT. I HAVE A PASSION FOR ART AND DESIGN, BUT...
KAIROS
when is it my time?
...EVER SINCE MY DAD PASSED AWAY—may he rot in hell— I'VE BEEN SUFFERING FROM A BIT OF A PROFESSIONAL CRISIS.
IS **THIS** WHAT I WANT TO DO FOR THE REST OF MY LIFE?

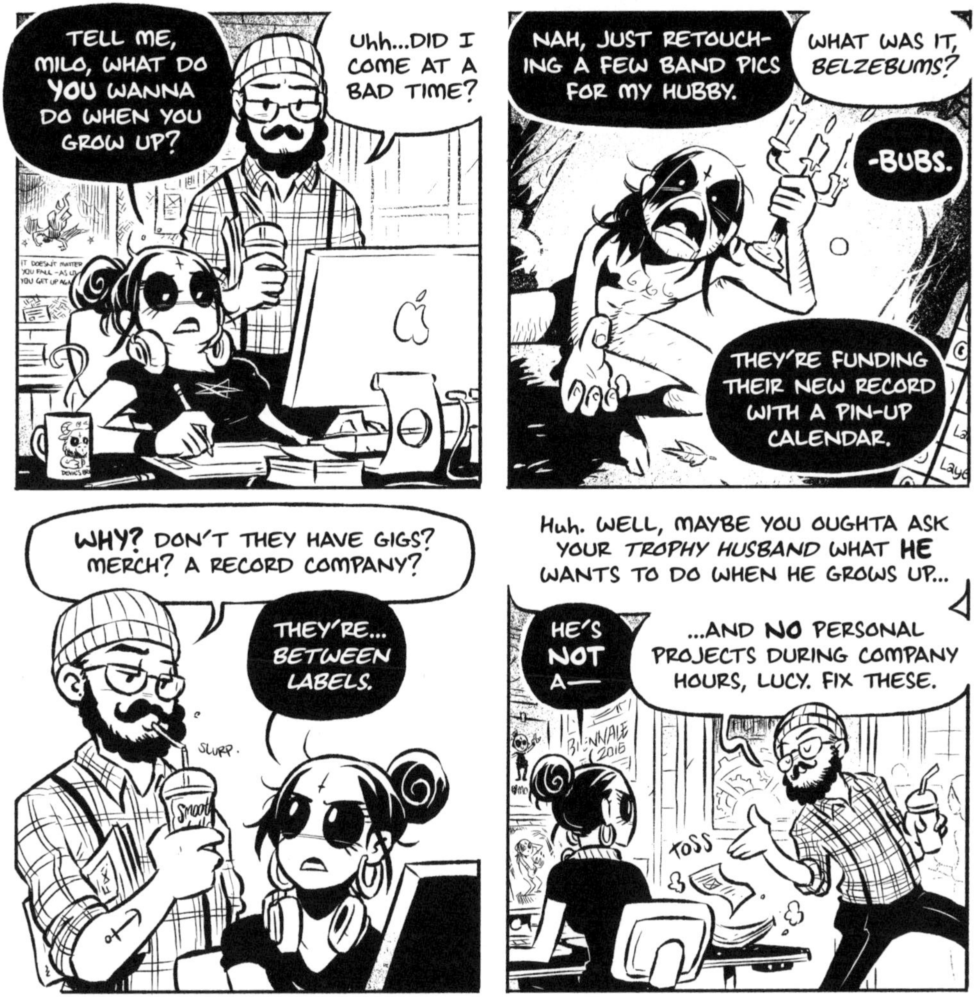
TELL ME, MILO, WHAT DO YOU WANNA DO WHEN YOU GROW UP?
Uhh...DID I COME AT A BAD TIME?
NAH, JUST RETOUCH-ING A FEW BAND PICS FOR MY HUBBY.
WHAT WAS IT, BELZEBUMS?
-BUBS.
THEY'RE FUNDING THEIR NEW RECORD WITH A PIN-UP CALENDAR.
WHY? DON'T THEY HAVE GIGS? MERCH? A RECORD COMPANY?
THEY'RE... BETWEEN LABELS.
SLURP.
Huh. WELL, MAYBE YOU OUGHTA ASK YOUR TROPHY HUSBAND WHAT HE WANTS TO DO WHEN HE GROWS UP...
HE'S NOT A—
...AND NO PERSONAL PROJECTS DURING COMPANY HOURS, LUCY. FIX THESE.
TOSS

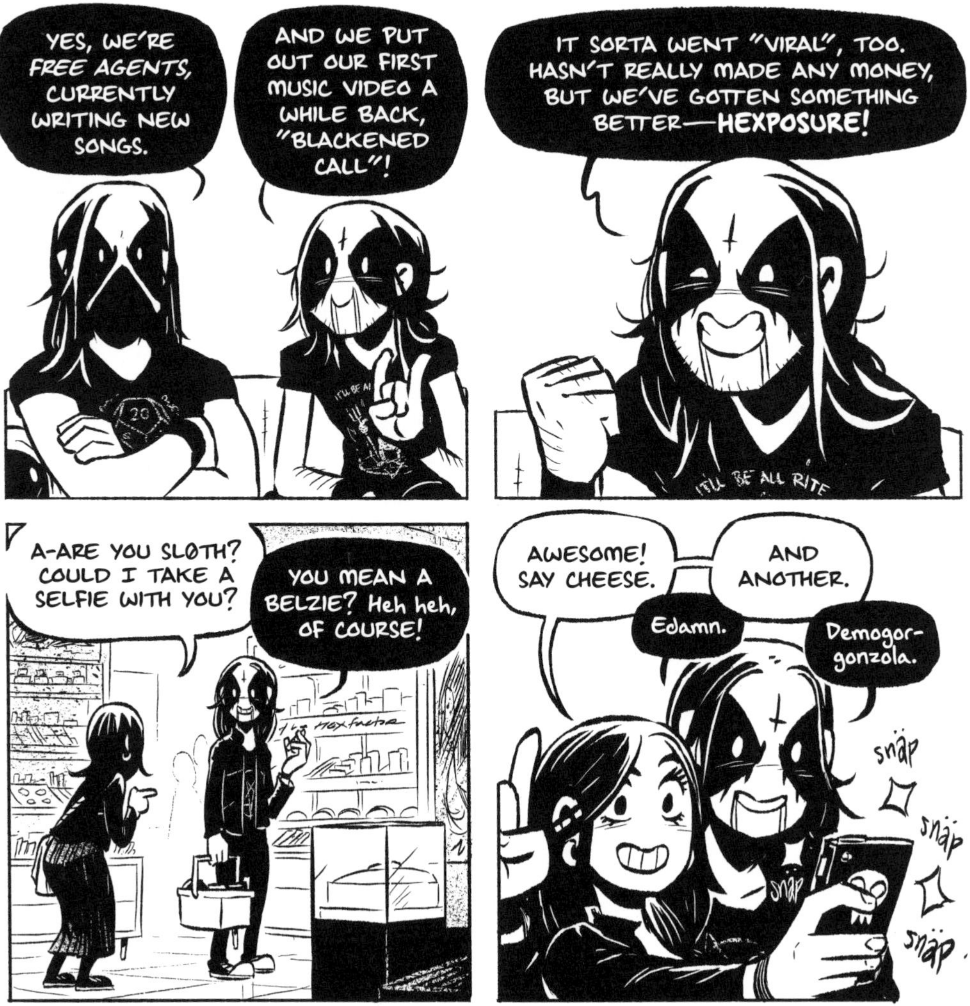
YES, WE'RE FREE AGENTS, CURRENTLY WRITING NEW SONGS.
AND WE PUT OUT OUR FIRST MUSIC VIDEO A WHILE BACK, "BLACKENED CALL"!
IT SORTA WENT "VIRAL", TOO. HASN'T REALLY MADE ANY MONEY, BUT WE'VE GOTTEN SOMETHING BETTER—HEXPOSURE!
IT'LL BE ALL RITE
A-ARE YOU SLØTH? COULD I TAKE A SELFIE WITH YOU?
YOU MEAN A BELZIE? Heh heh, OF COURSE!
AWESOME! SAY CHEESE.
Edamn.
AND ANOTHER.
Demogorgonzola.
snap
snap
snap

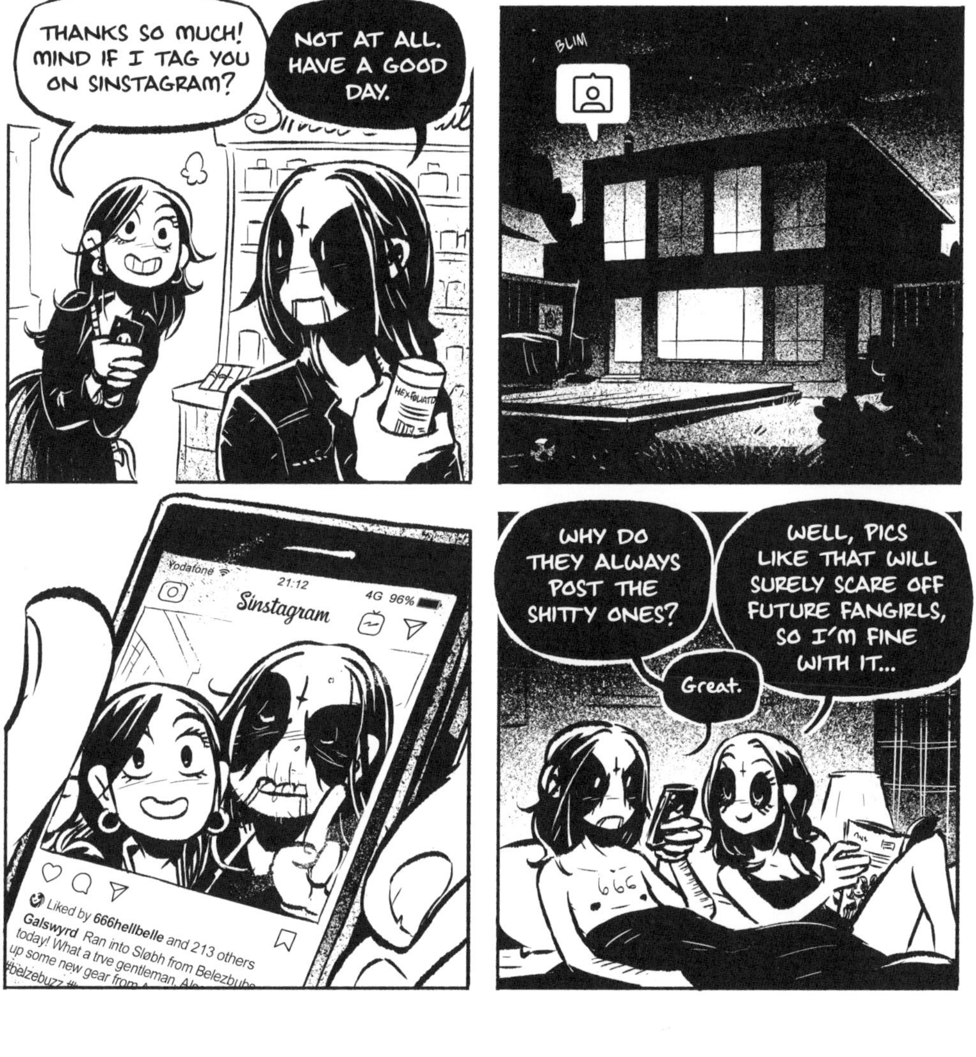
THANKS SO MUCH! MIND IF I TAG YOU ON SINSTAGRAM?
NOT AT ALL. HAVE A GOOD DAY.
BLIM
Yodafone
21:12
4G 96%
Sinstagram
Liked by 666hellbelle and 213 others
Galswyrd Ran into Sløbh from Belezbubs
today! What a trve gentleman.
WHY DO THEY ALWAYS POST THE SHITTY ONES?
WELL, PICS LIKE THAT WILL SURELY SCARE OFF FUTURE FANGIRLS, SO I'M FINE WITH IT...
Great.
666

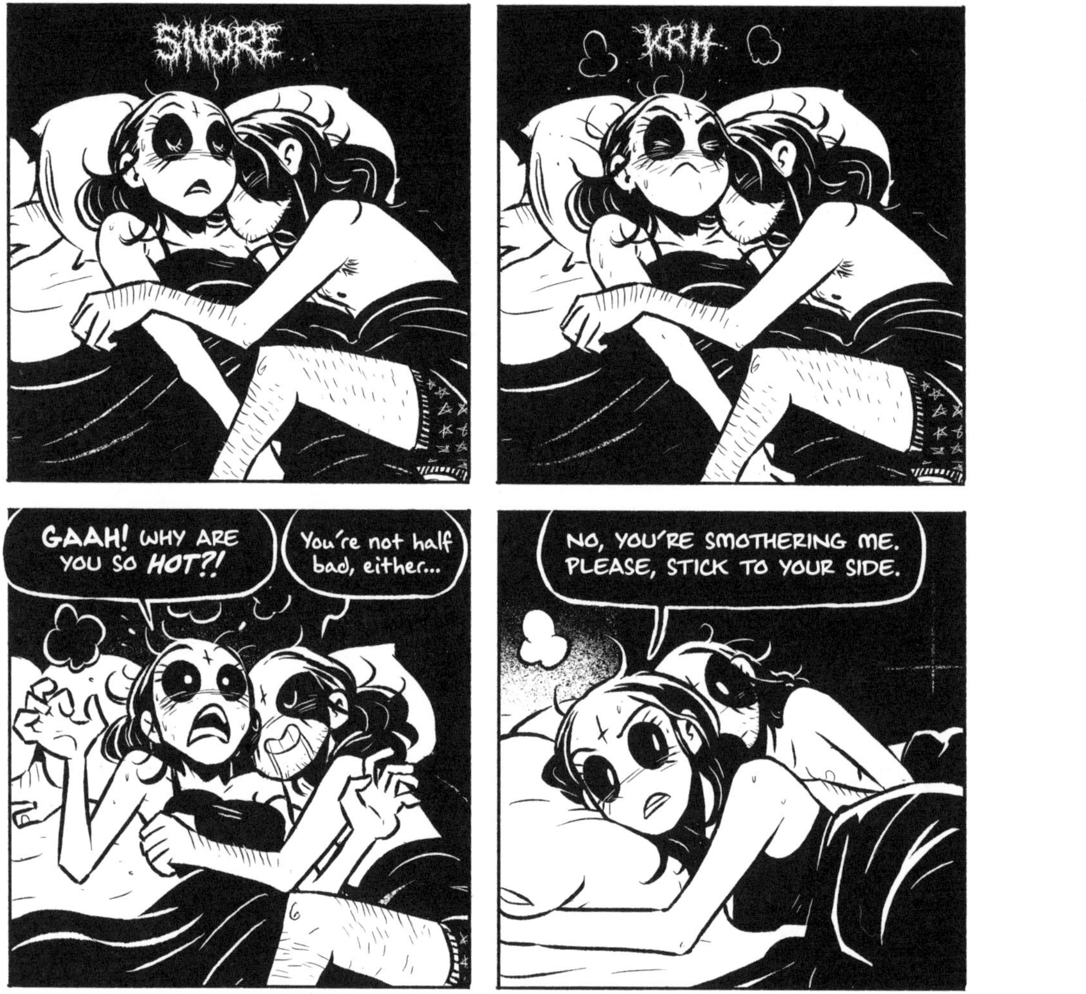
SNORE
KRH
GAAH! WHY ARE YOU SO HOT?!
You're not half bad, either...
NO, YOU'RE SMOTHERING ME. PLEASE, STICK TO YOUR SIDE.

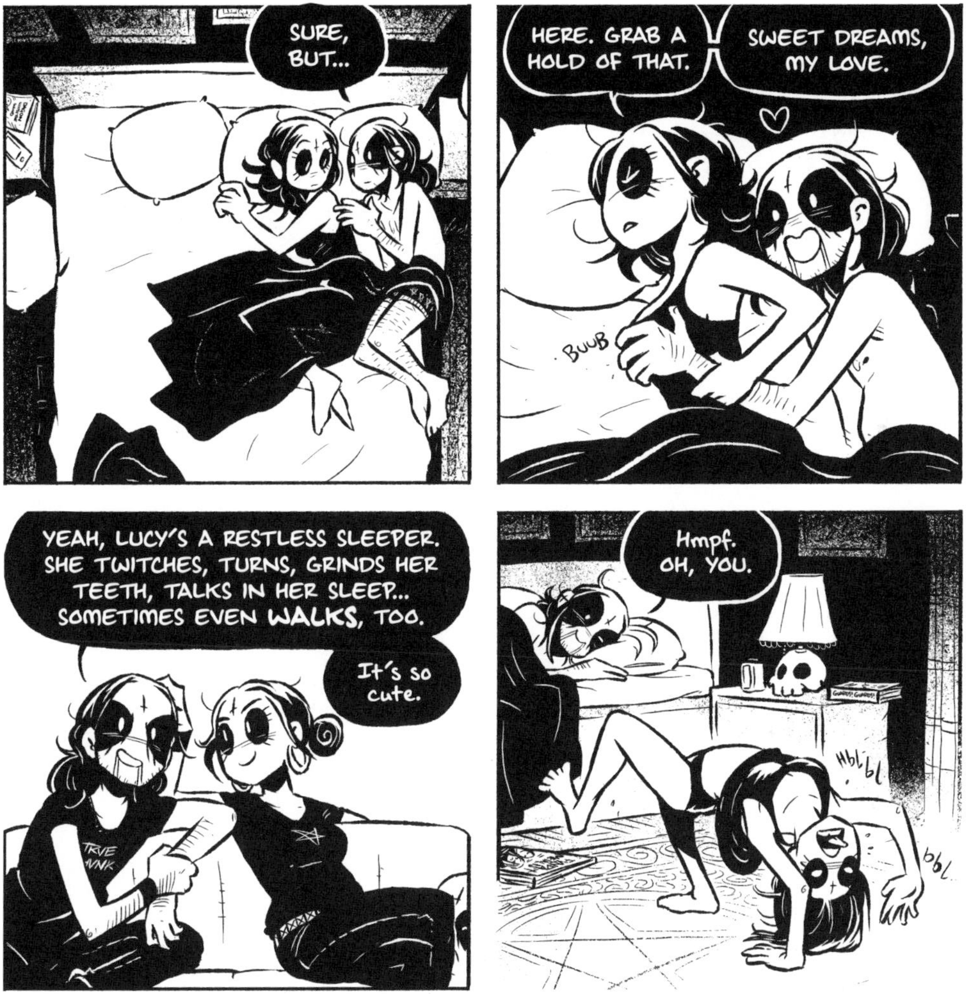
SURE, BUT...
HERE. GRAB A HOLD OF THAT.
SWEET DREAMS, MY LOVE.
BUUB
YEAH, LUCY'S A RESTLESS SLEEPER. SHE TWITCHES, TURNS, GRINDS HER TEETH, TALKS IN HER SLEEP... SOMETIMES EVEN WALKS, TOO.
It's so cute.
TRVE KVLT
Hmpf. OH, YOU.
Hbl bl
bbl

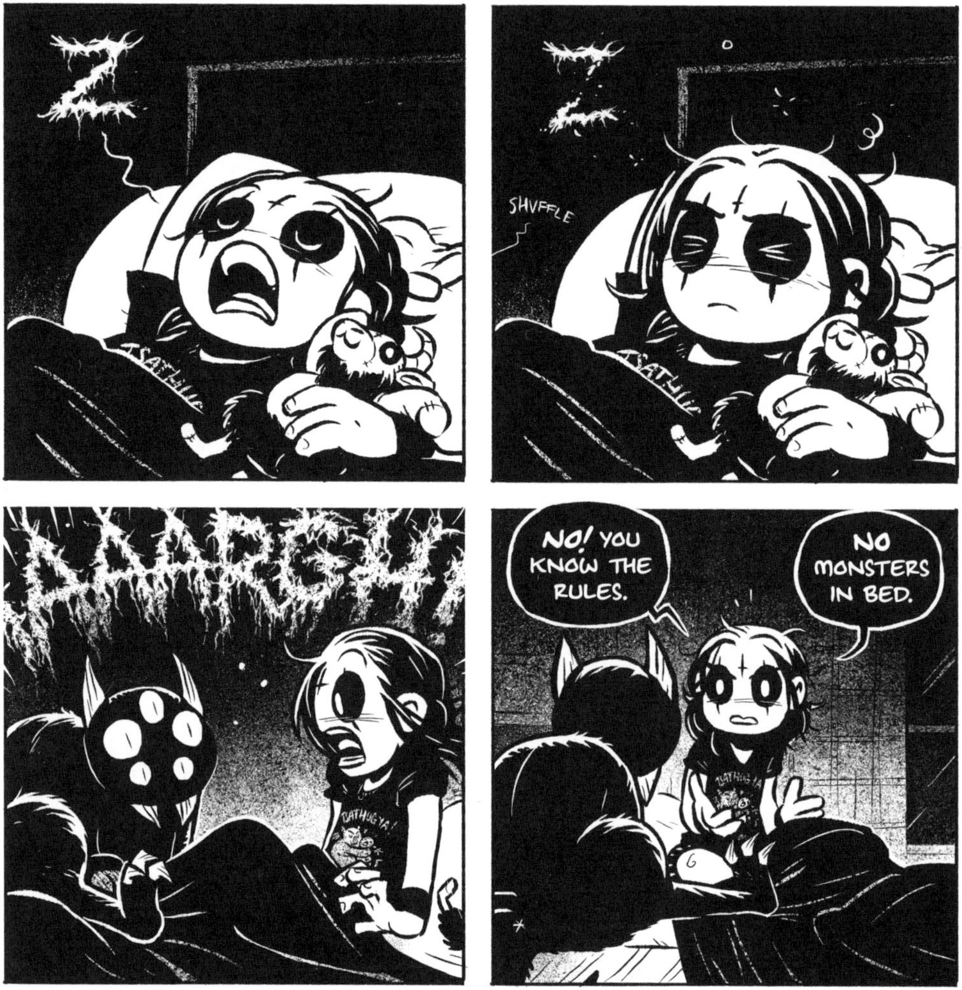
Z
Z
SHUFFLE
NO! YOU KNOW THE RULES.
NO MONSTERS IN BED.

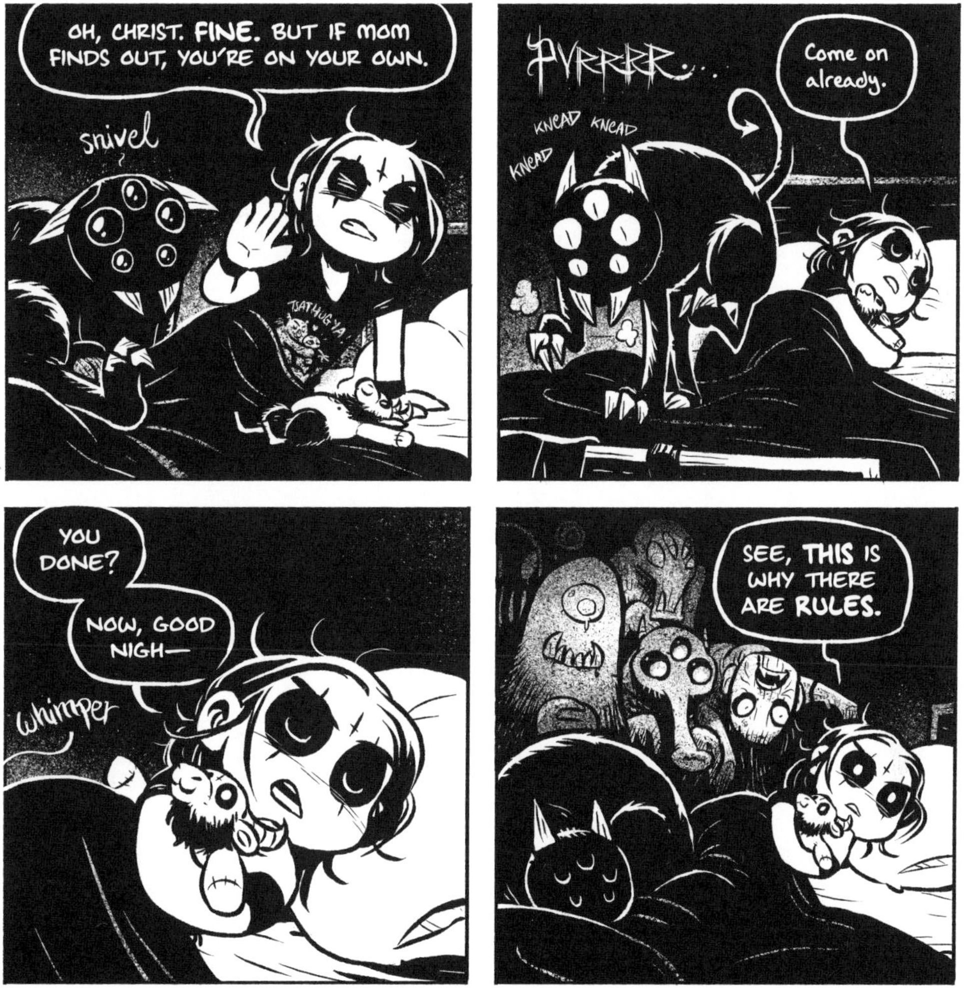
OH, CHRIST. FINE. BUT IF MOM FINDS OUT, YOU'RE ON YOUR OWN.
snivel
TSATHUG-YA
PVRRRR...
Come on already.
KNEAD KNEAD
KNEAD
YOU DONE?
NOW, GOOD NIGH—
whimper
SEE, THIS IS WHY THERE ARE RULES.

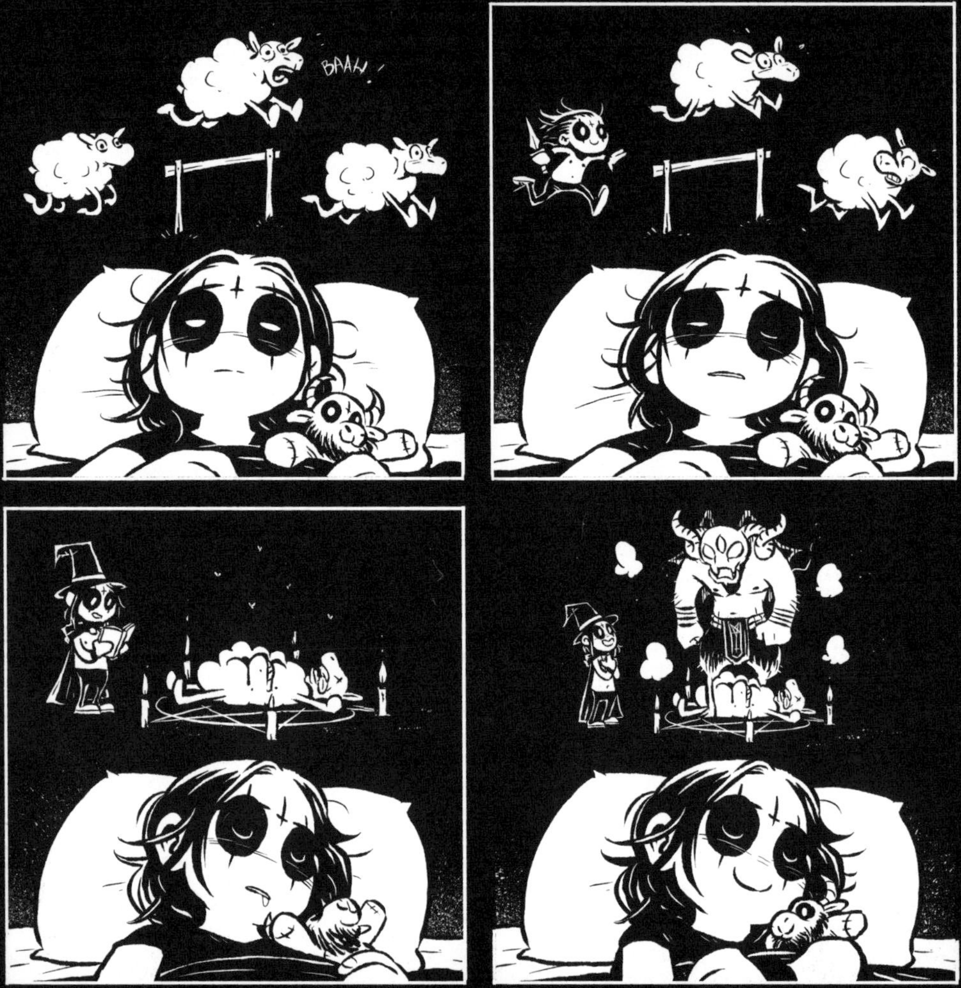
BAAH!

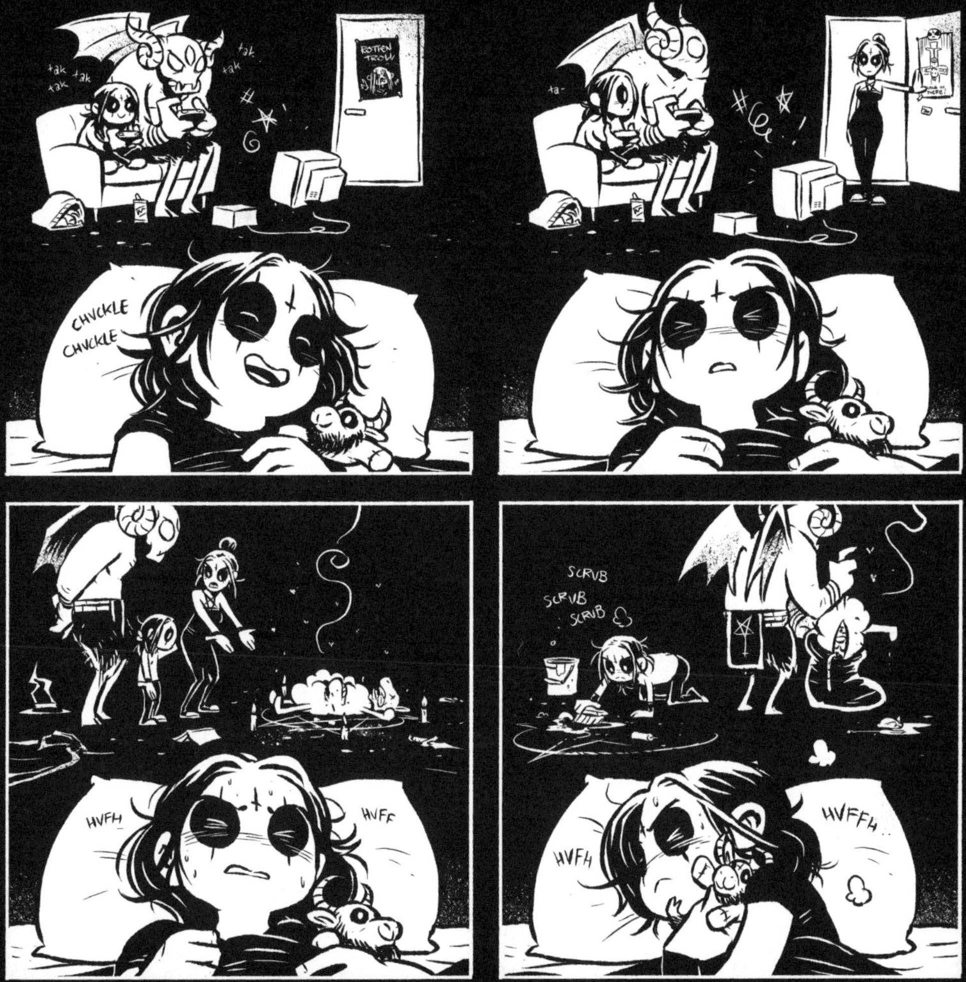
tak tak
tak tak
tak
tak
ROTTEN TROLL
ta-
CHUCKLE
CHUCKLE
SCRUB
SCRUB
SCRUB
HUFH
HUFF
HUFH
HUFFH..

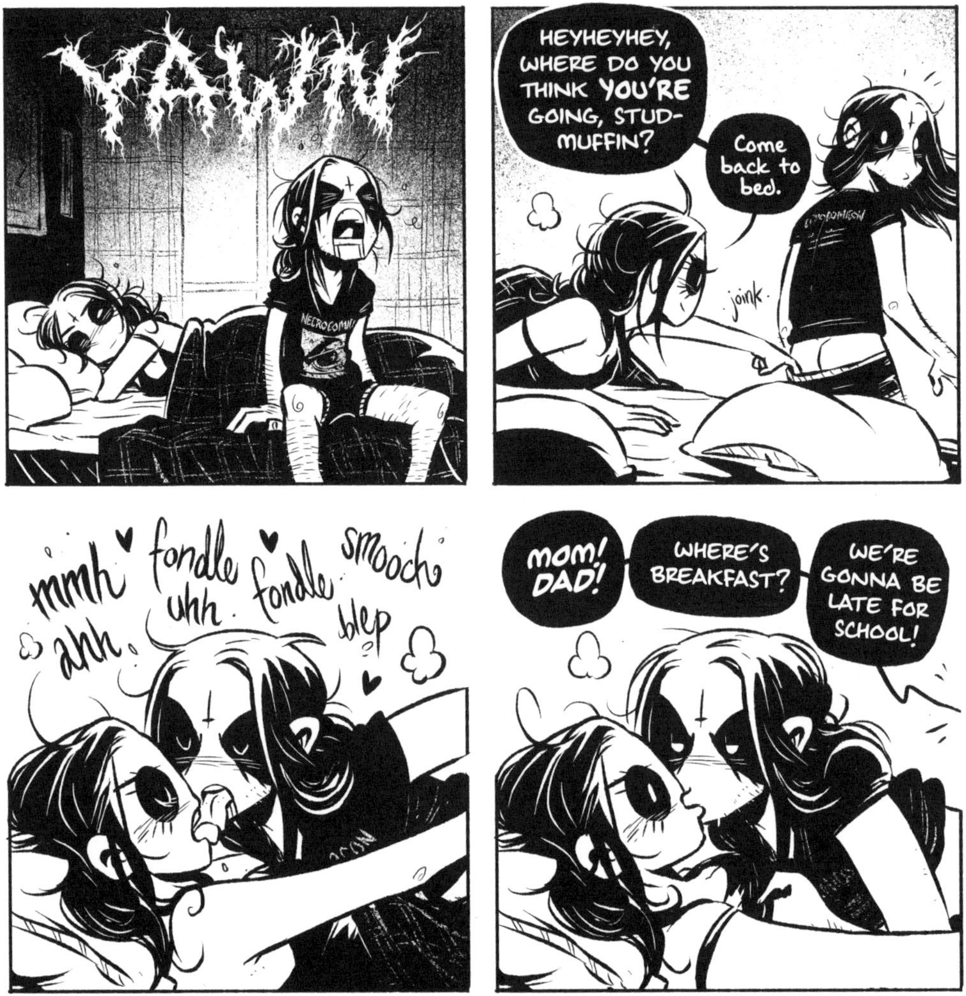
YAWN
HEYHEYHEY, WHERE DO YOU THINK YOU'RE GOING, STUD-MUFFIN?
Come back to bed.
joink.
mmh
fondle
fondle
smooch
ahh
uhh
blep
MOM! DAD!
WHERE'S BREAKFAST?
WE'RE GONNA BE LATE FOR SCHOOL!

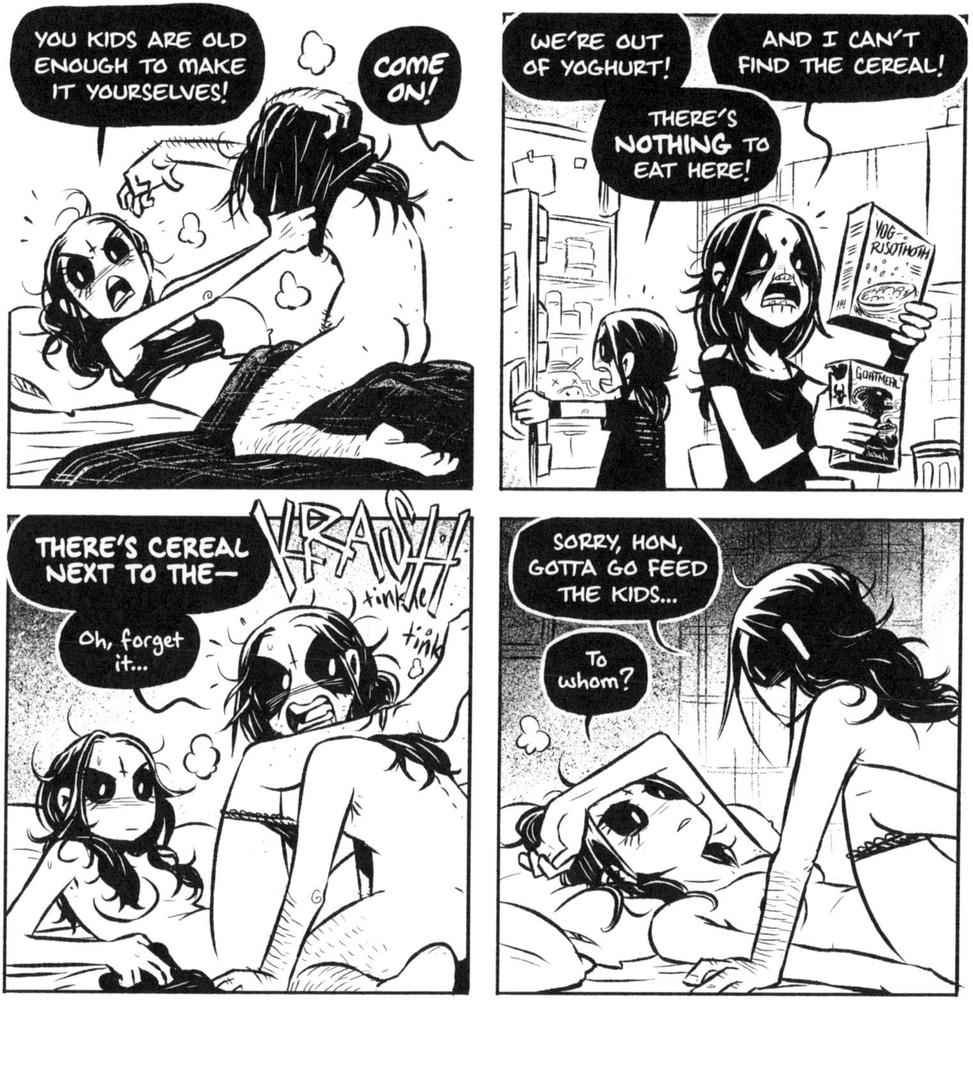
YOU KIDS ARE OLD ENOUGH TO MAKE IT YOURSELVES!
COME ON!
WE'RE OUT OF YOGHURT!
AND I CAN'T FIND THE CEREAL!
THERE'S NOTHING TO EAT HERE!
YOG-RISOTHOTH
GOATMEAL
THERE'S CEREAL NEXT TO THE—
KRASH
tinkle!
tink
Oh, forget it...
SORRY, HON, GOTTA GO FEED THE KIDS...
To whom?

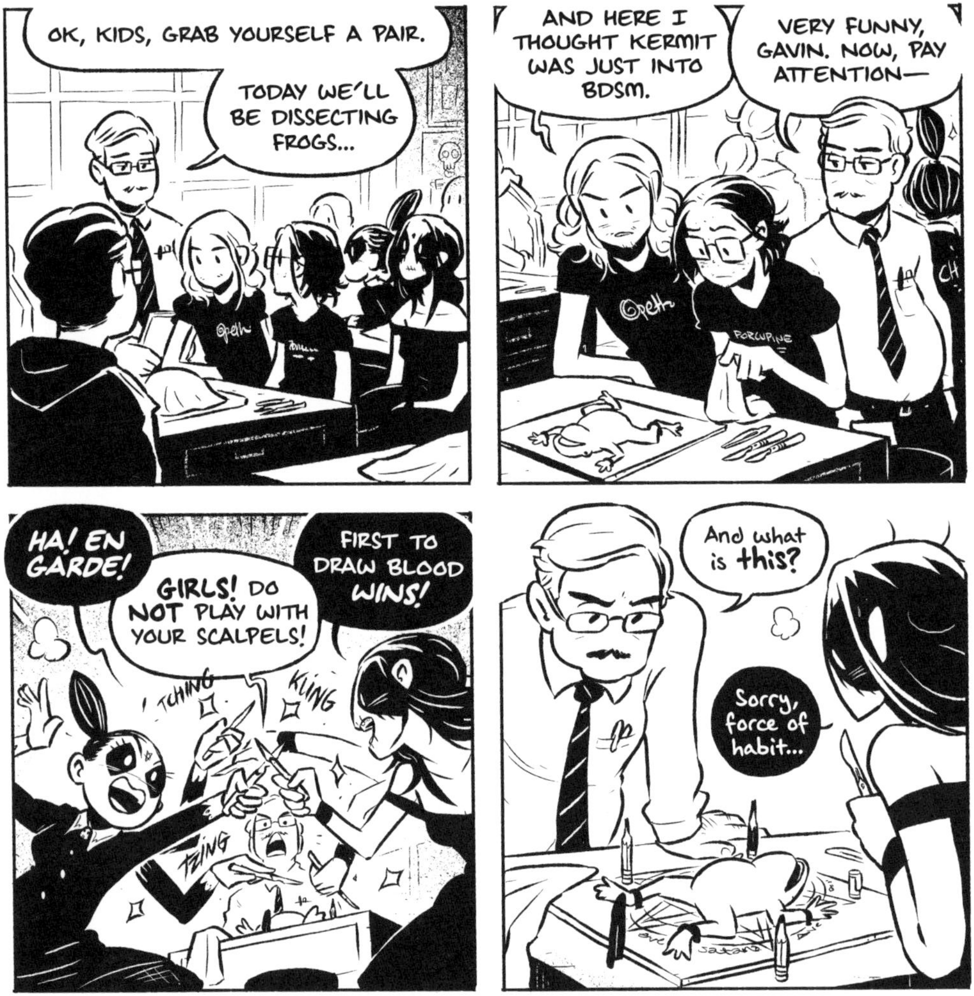
OK, KIDS, GRAB YOURSELF A PAIR.
TODAY WE'LL BE DISSECTING FROGS...
AND HERE I THOUGHT KERMIT WAS JUST INTO BDSM.
VERY FUNNY, GAVIN. NOW, PAY ATTENTION—
HA! EN GARDE!
GIRLS! DO NOT PLAY WITH YOUR SCALPELS!
FIRST TO DRAW BLOOD WINS!
TCHING
KLING
TZING
And what is this?
Sorry, force of habit...

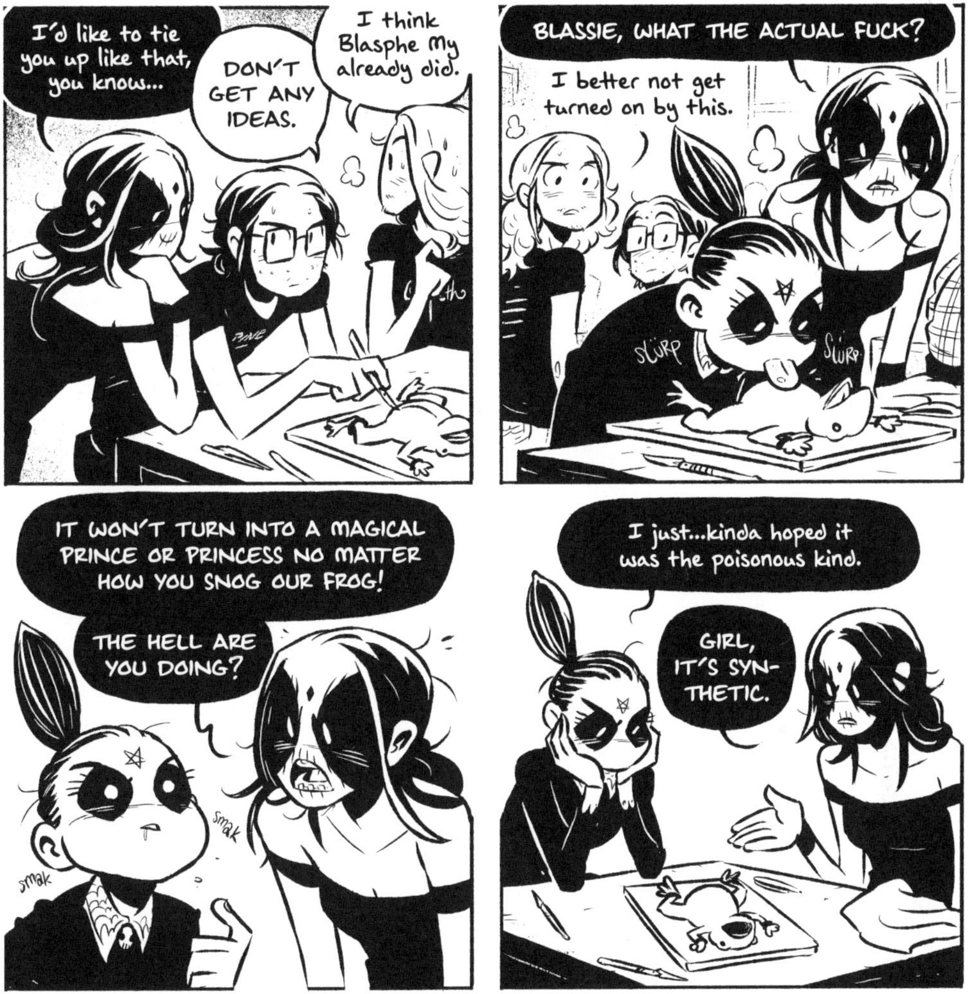
I'd like to tie you up like that, you know...
DON'T GET ANY IDEAS.
I think Blasphe my already did.
BLASSIE, WHAT THE ACTUAL FUCK?
I better not get turned on by this.
SLURP
SLURP
IT WON'T TURN INTO A MAGICAL PRINCE OR PRINCESS NO MATTER HOW YOU SNOG OUR FROG!
THE HELL ARE YOU DOING?
smak
smak
I just...kinda hoped it was the poisonous kind.
GIRL, IT'S SYN-THETIC.

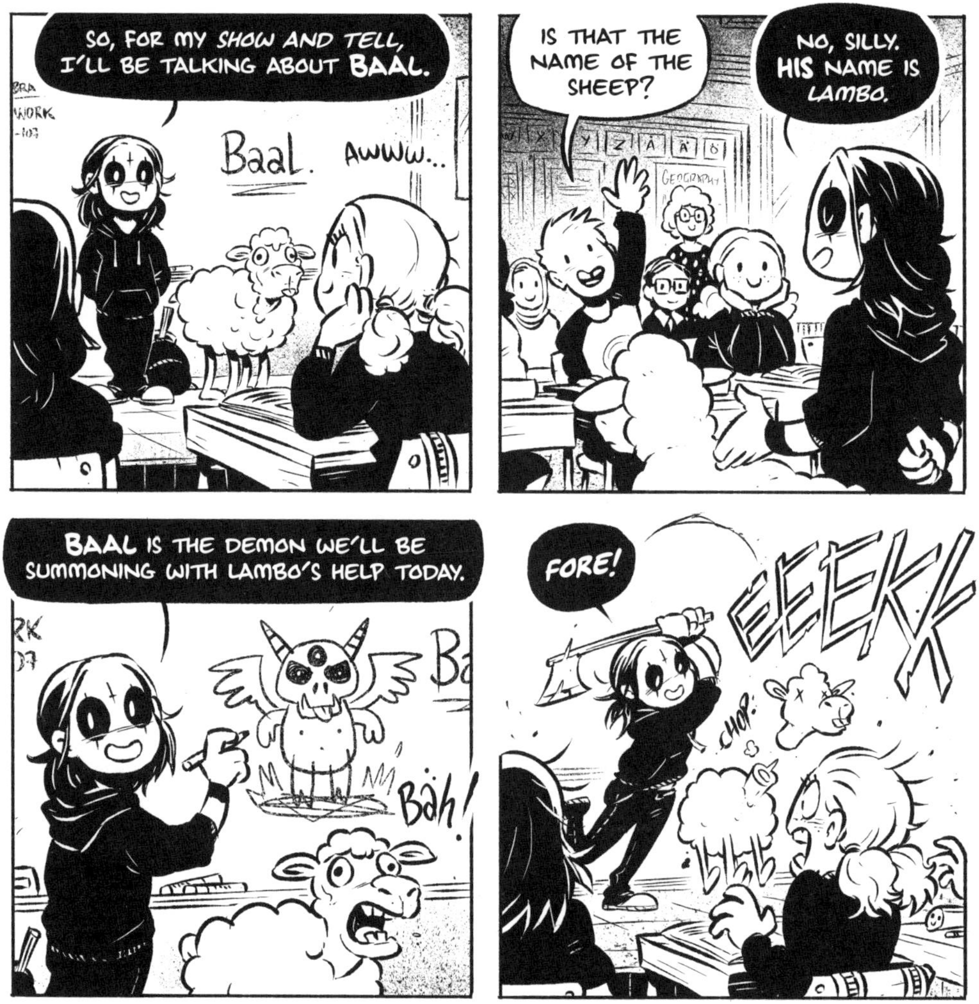
SO, FOR MY SHOW AND TELL, I'LL BE TALKING ABOUT BAAL.
Baal.
AWWW...
IS THAT THE NAME OF THE SHEEP?
NO, SILLY. HIS NAME IS LAMBO.
GEOGRAPHY
BAAL IS THE DEMON WE'LL BE SUMMONING WITH LAMBO'S HELP TODAY.
Bäh!
FORE!
EEEKK
CHOP

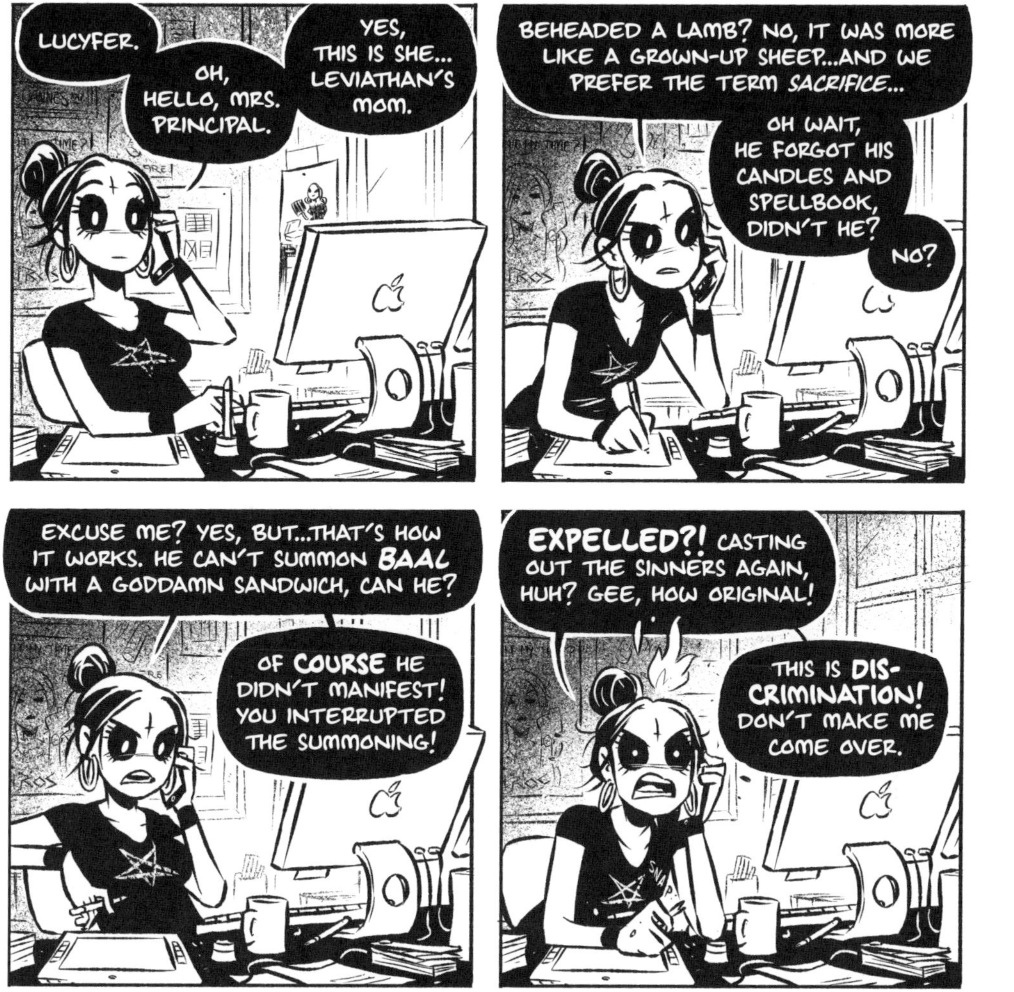
LUCYFER.
OH, HELLO, MRS. PRINCIPAL.
YES, THIS IS SHE... LEVIATHAN'S MOM.
BEHEADED A LAMB? NO, IT WAS MORE LIKE A GROWN-UP SHEEP...AND WE PREFER THE TERM *SACRIFICE*...
OH WAIT, HE FORGOT HIS CANDLES AND SPELLBOOK, DIDN'T HE?
NO?
EXCUSE ME? YES, BUT...THAT'S HOW IT WORKS. HE CAN'T SUMMON **BAAL** WITH A GODDAMN SANDWICH, CAN HE?
OF **COURSE** HE DIDN'T MANIFEST! YOU INTERRUPTED THE SUMMONING!
EXPELLED?! CASTING OUT THE SINNERS AGAIN, HUH? GEE, HOW ORIGINAL!
THIS IS **DIS-CRIMINATION!** DON'T MAKE ME COME OVER.
SNAP!

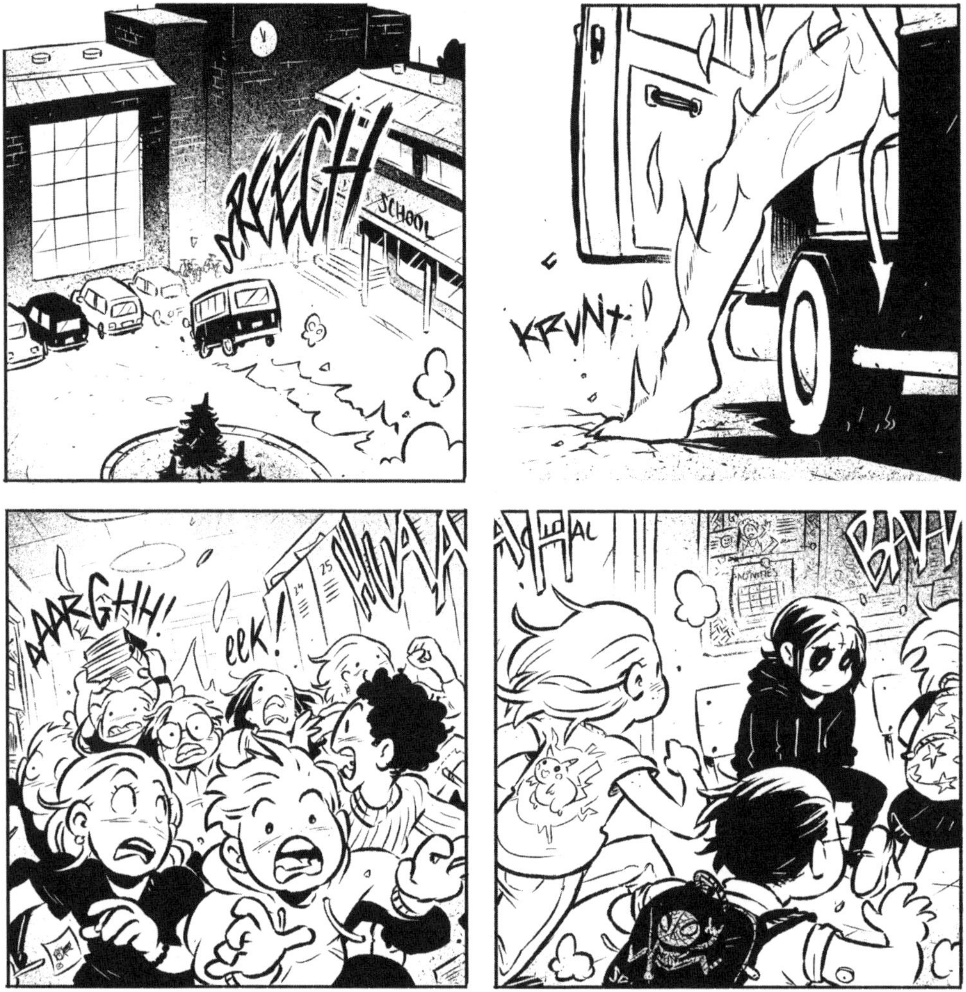
SCREECH
SCHOOL
KRUNT
AAARGHH!
eek!
ACTIVITIES

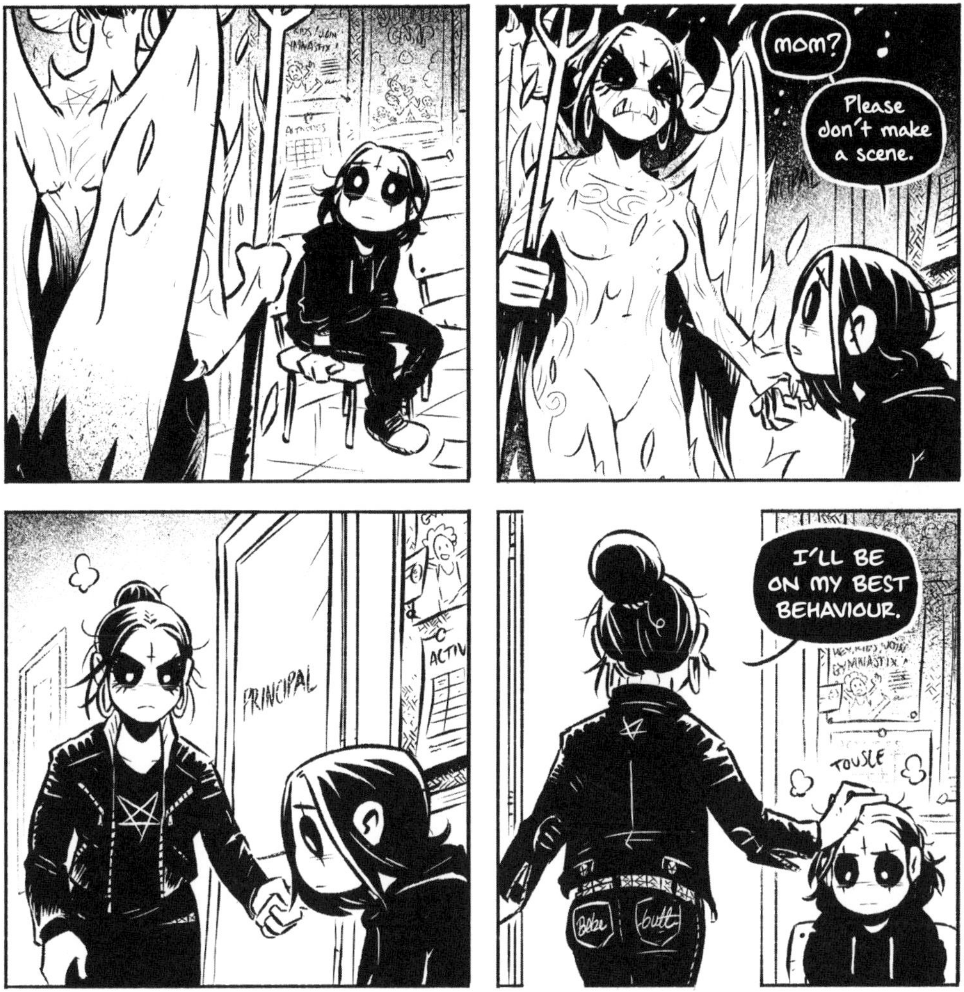
mom?
Please don't make a scene.
PRINCIPAL
I'LL BE ON MY BEST BEHAVIOUR.
TOUSLE

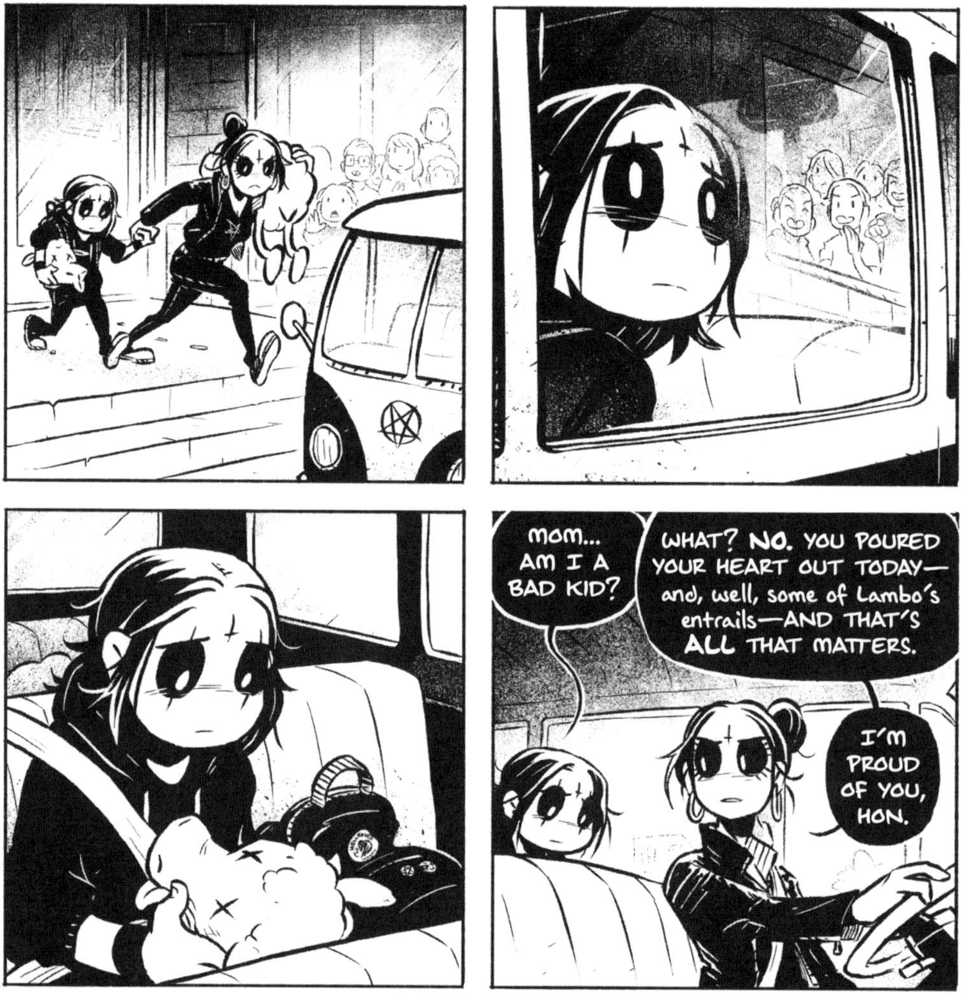
MOM... AM I A BAD KID?
WHAT? NO. YOU POURED YOUR HEART OUT TODAY—and, well, some of Lambo's entrails—AND THAT'S ALL THAT MATTERS.
I'M PROUD OF YOU, HON.

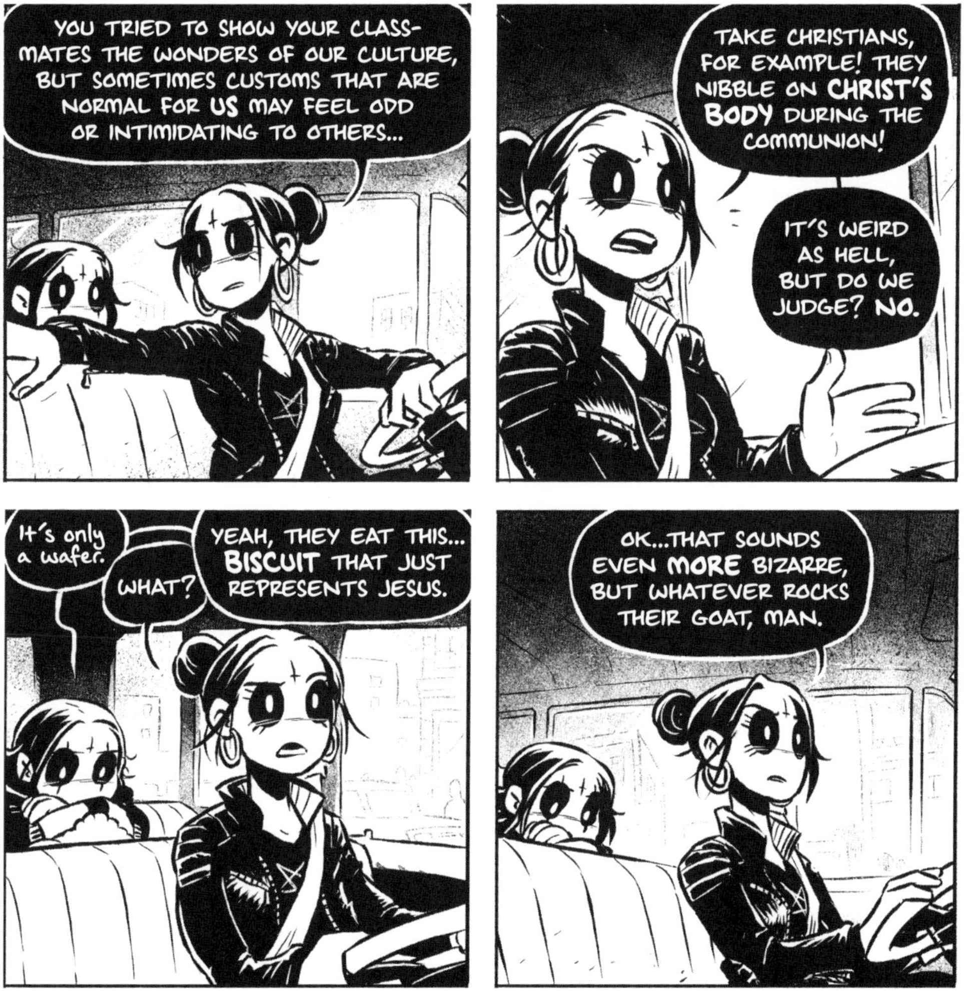
YOU TRIED TO SHOW YOUR CLASSMATES THE WONDERS OF OUR CULTURE, BUT SOMETIMES CUSTOMS THAT ARE NORMAL FOR US MAY FEEL ODD OR INTIMIDATING TO OTHERS...
TAKE CHRISTIANS, FOR EXAMPLE! THEY NIBBLE ON CHRIST'S BODY DURING THE COMMUNION!
IT'S WEIRD AS HELL, BUT DO WE JUDGE? NO.
It's only a wafer.
WHAT?
YEAH, THEY EAT THIS... BISCUIT THAT JUST REPRESENTS JESUS.
OK...THAT SOUNDS EVEN MORE BIZARRE, BUT WHATEVER ROCKS THEIR GOAT, MAN.

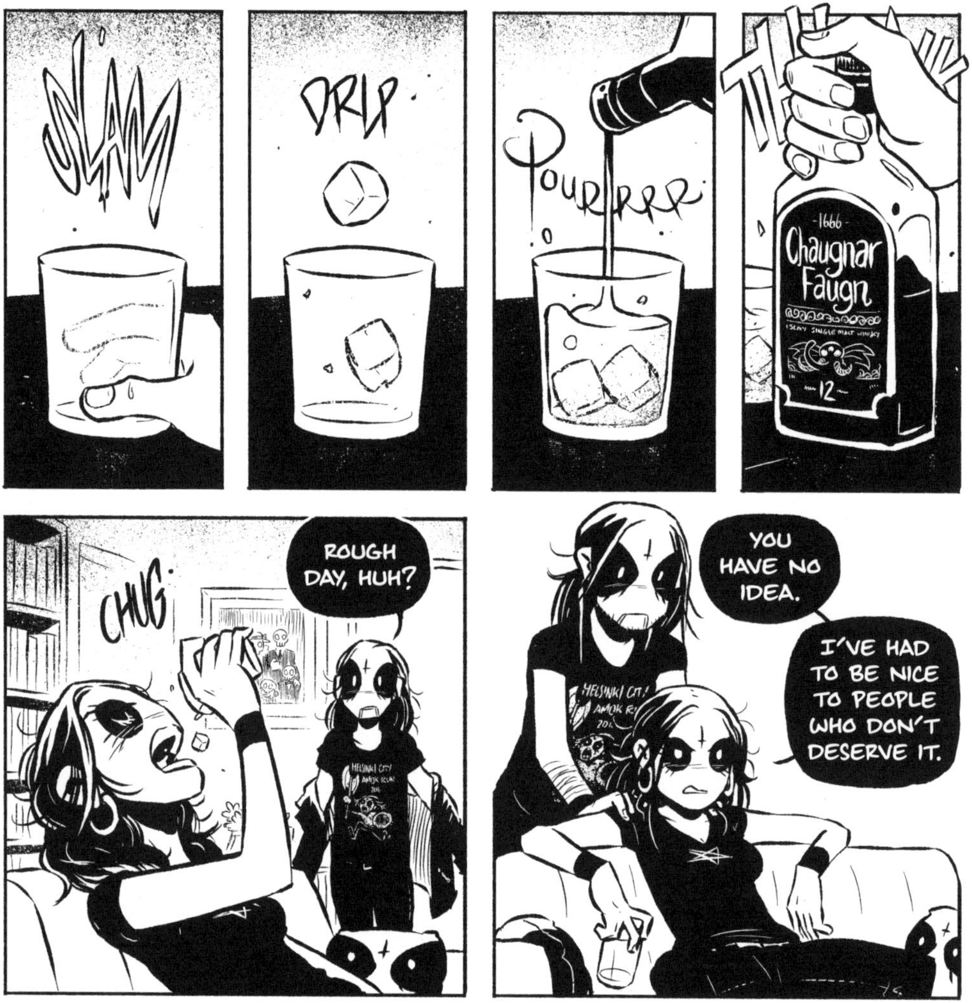
SLAM
DRIP
POURRRR
1666
Chaugnar Faugn
ISLAY SINGLE MALT WHISKY
12
CHUG
ROUGH DAY, HUH?
YOU HAVE NO IDEA.
I'VE HAD TO BE NICE TO PEOPLE WHO DON'T DESERVE IT.

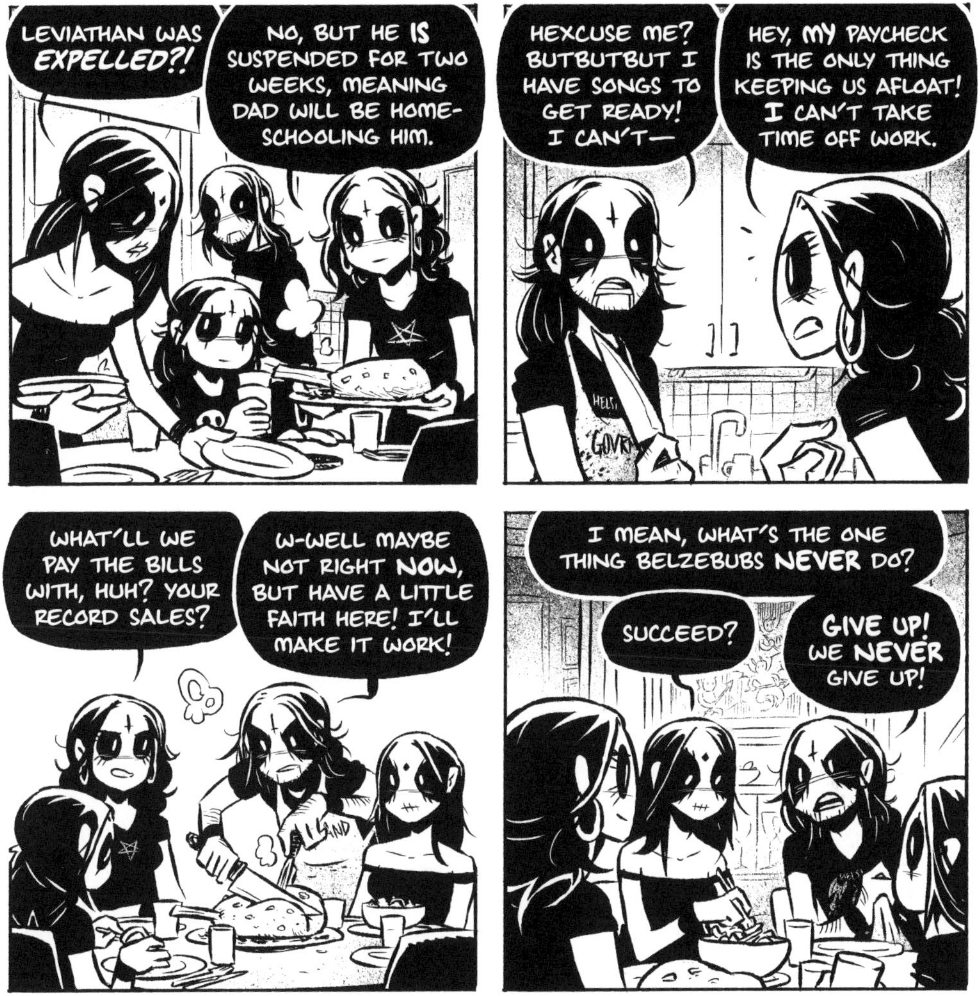
LEVIATHAN WAS *EXPELLED?!*
NO, BUT HE **IS** SUSPENDED FOR TWO WEEKS, MEANING DAD WILL BE HOME-SCHOOLING HIM.
HEXCUSE ME? BUTBUTBUT I HAVE SONGS TO GET READY! I CAN'T—
HEY, **MY** PAYCHECK IS THE ONLY THING KEEPING US AFLOAT! **I** CAN'T TAKE TIME OFF WORK.
WHAT'LL WE PAY THE BILLS WITH, HUH? YOUR RECORD SALES?
W-WELL MAYBE NOT RIGHT **NOW**, BUT HAVE A LITTLE FAITH HERE! I'LL MAKE IT WORK!
I MEAN, WHAT'S THE ONE THING BELZEBUBS **NEVER** DO?
SUCCEED?
GIVE UP! WE **NEVER** GIVE UP!

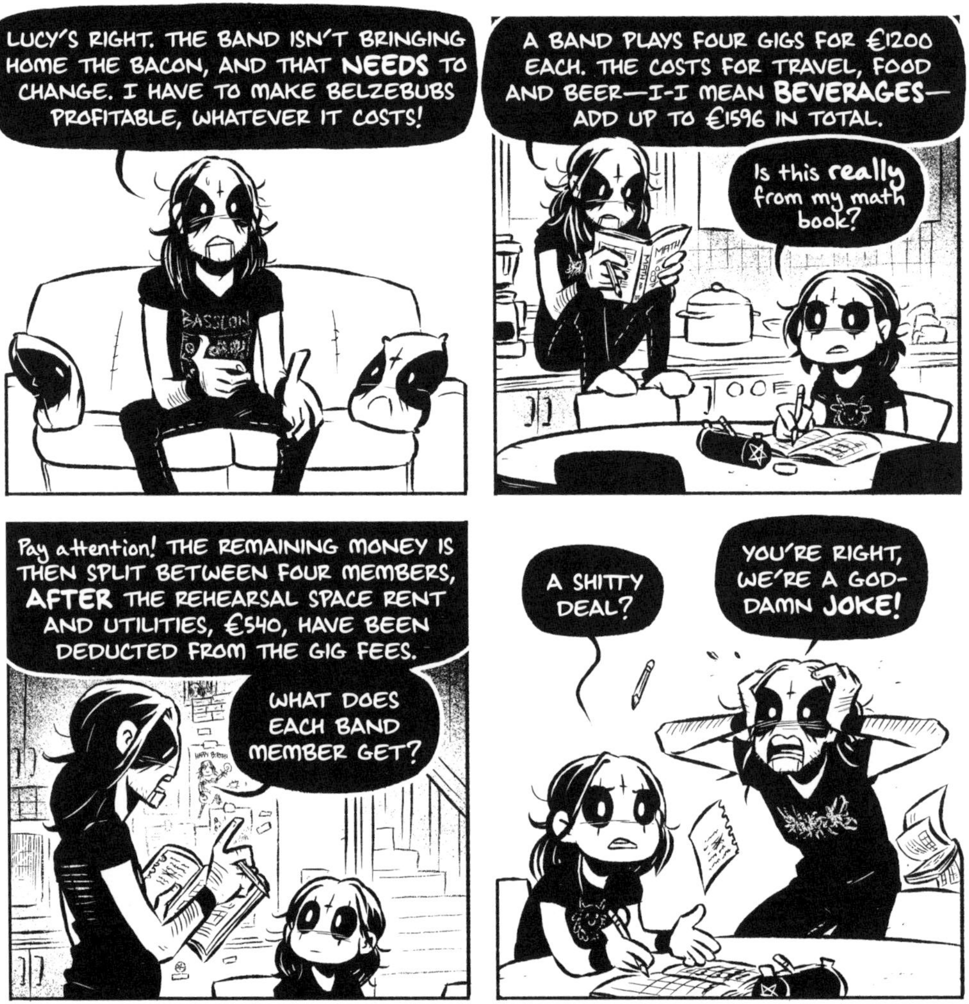
LUCY'S RIGHT. THE BAND ISN'T BRINGING HOME THE BACON, AND THAT NEEDS TO CHANGE. I HAVE TO MAKE BELZEBUBS PROFITABLE, WHATEVER IT COSTS!
BASSLON
A BAND PLAYS FOUR GIGS FOR €1200 EACH. THE COSTS FOR TRAVEL, FOOD AND BEER—I-I MEAN BEVERAGES—ADD UP TO €1596 IN TOTAL.
Is this really from my math book?
MATH
Pay attention! THE REMAINING MONEY IS THEN SPLIT BETWEEN FOUR MEMBERS, AFTER THE REHEARSAL SPACE RENT AND UTILITIES, €540, HAVE BEEN DEDUCTED FROM THE GIG FEES.
WHAT DOES EACH BAND MEMBER GET?
A SHITTY DEAL?
YOU'RE RIGHT, WE'RE A GOD-DAMN JOKE!

Help the black metal band out of the woods!

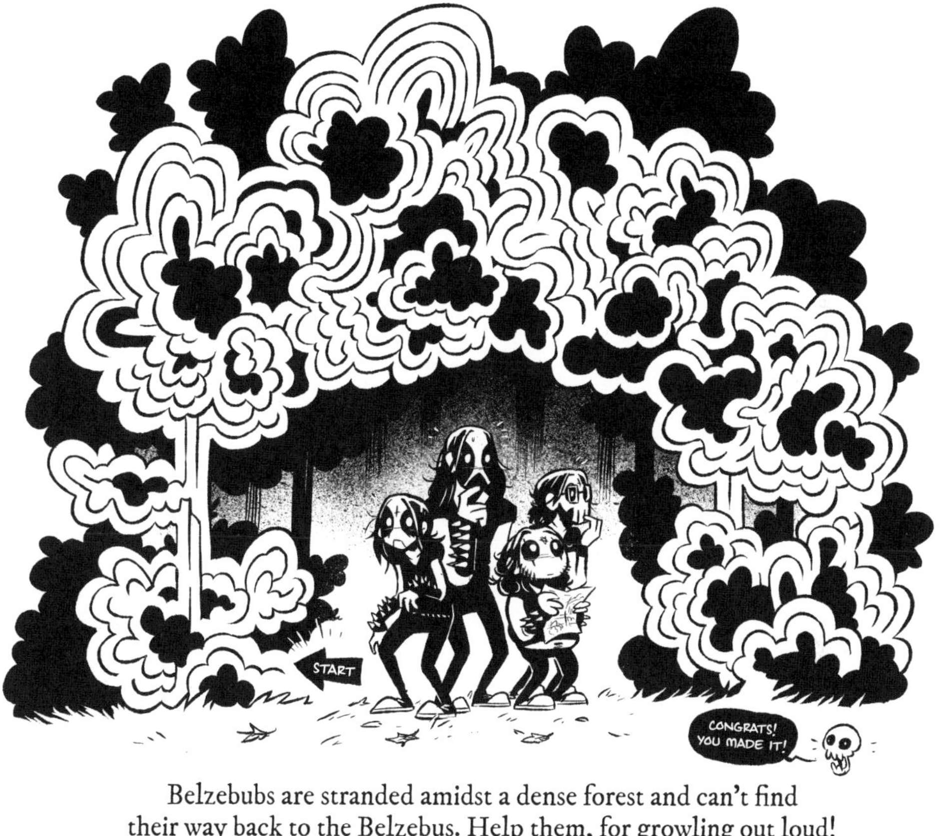
START
CONGRATS! YOU MADE IT!

Belzebubs are stranded amidst a dense forest and can't find their way back to the Belzebus. Help them, for growling out loud!

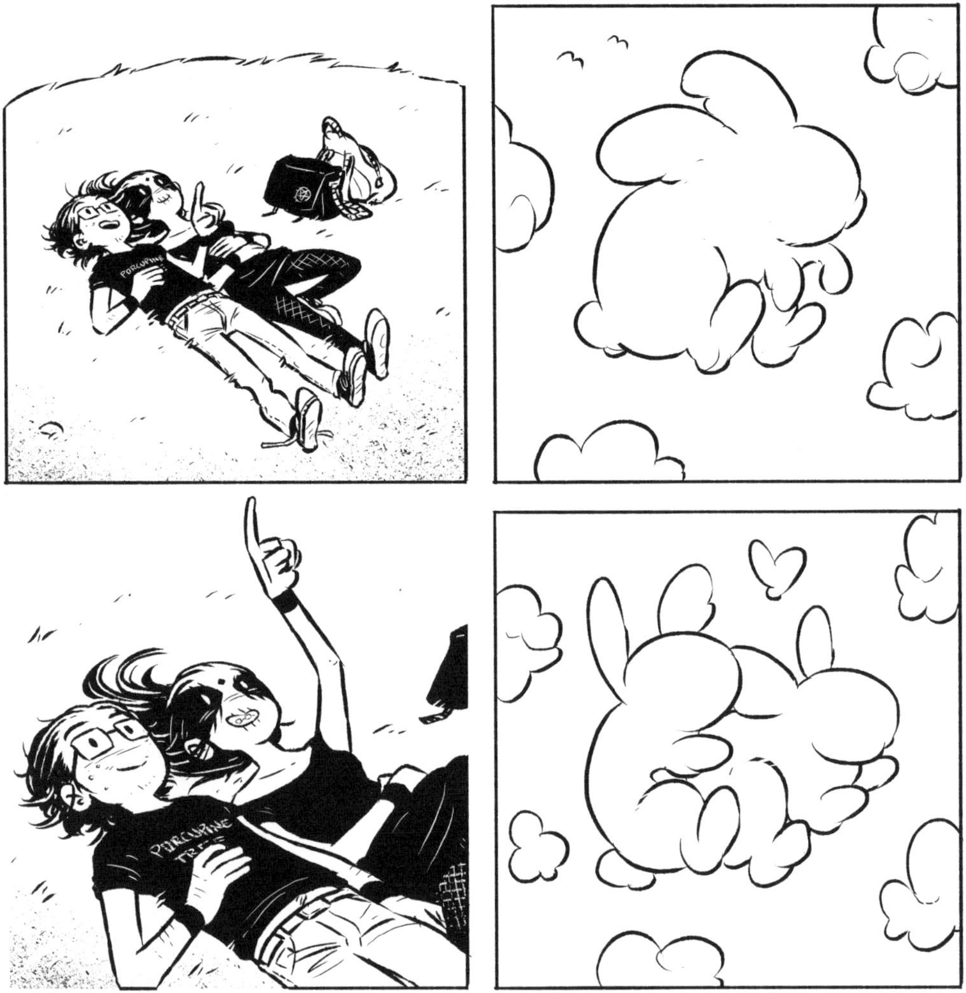
PORCUPINE

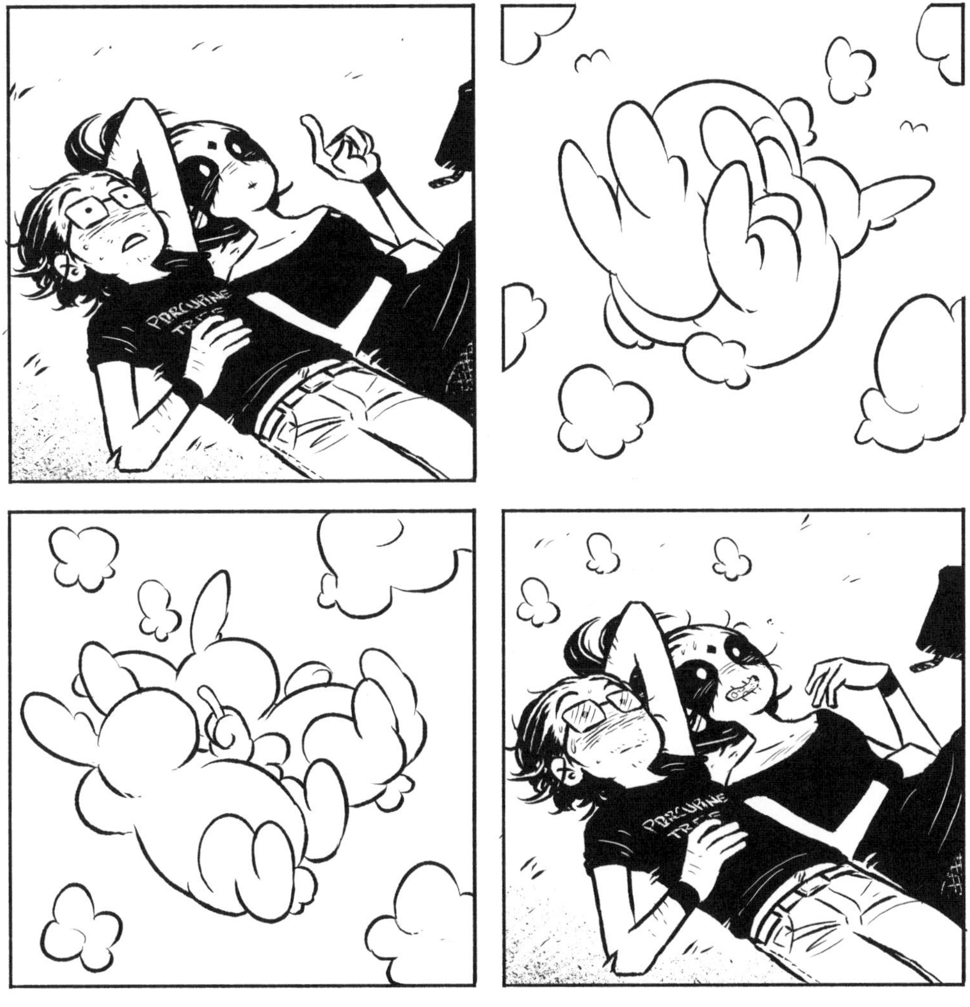
PORCUPINE
PORCUPINE

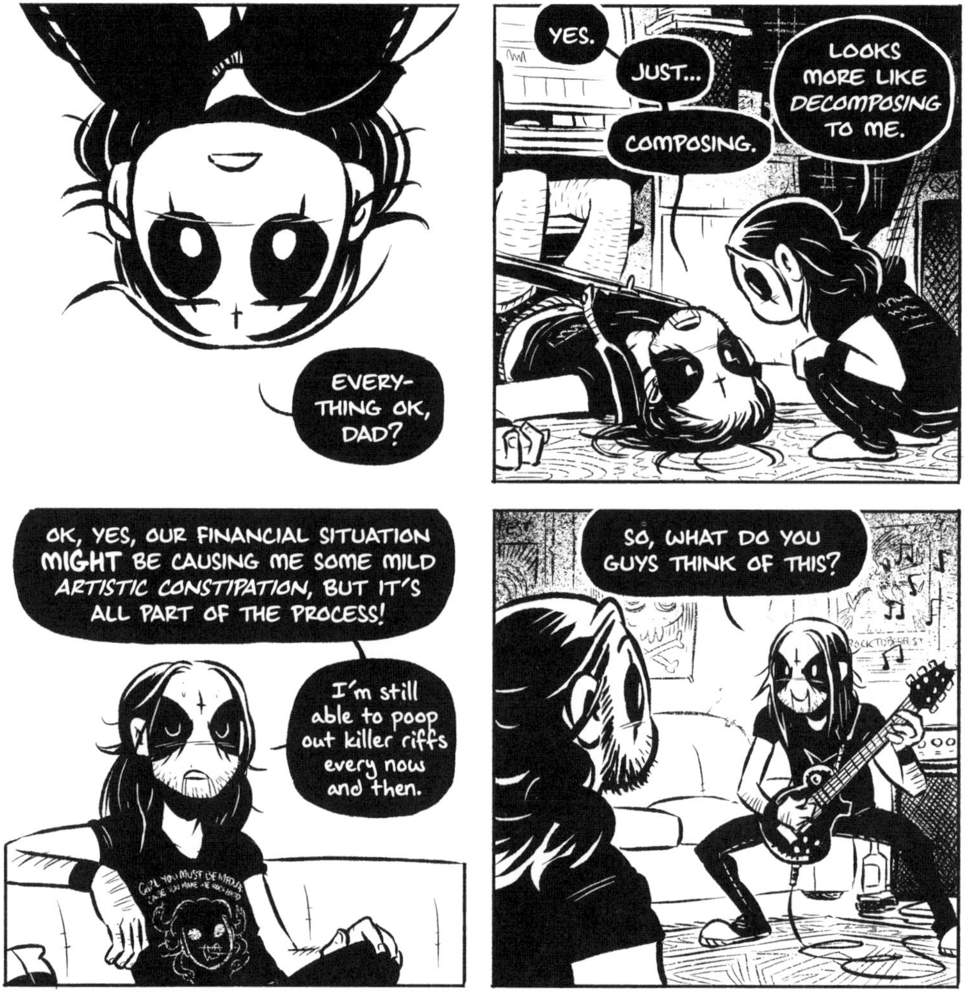
EVERY-THING OK, DAD?
YES.
JUST...
COMPOSING.
LOOKS MORE LIKE DECOMPOSING TO ME.
OK, YES, OUR FINANCIAL SITUATION **MIGHT** BE CAUSING ME SOME MILD *ARTISTIC CONSTIPATION*, BUT IT'S ALL PART OF THE PROCESS!
I'm still able to poop out killer riffs every now and then.
SO, WHAT DO YOU GUYS THINK OF THIS?

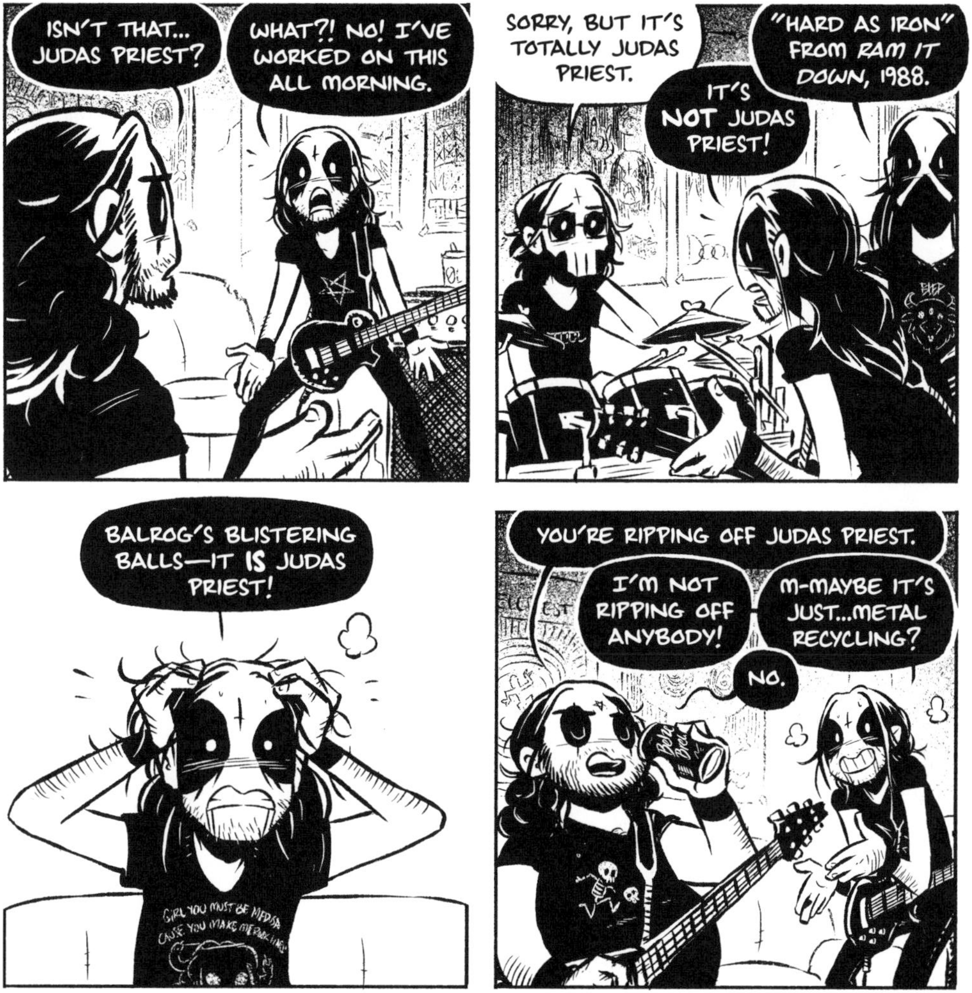
ISN'T THAT... JUDAS PRIEST?
WHAT?! NO! I'VE WORKED ON THIS ALL MORNING.
SORRY, BUT IT'S TOTALLY JUDAS PRIEST.
IT'S **NOT** JUDAS PRIEST!
"HARD AS IRON" FROM *RAM IT DOWN*, 1988.
BALROG'S BLISTERING BALLS—IT **IS** JUDAS PRIEST!
YOU'RE RIPPING OFF JUDAS PRIEST.
I'M NOT RIPPING OFF ANYBODY!
M-MAYBE IT'S JUST...METAL RECYCLING?
NO.

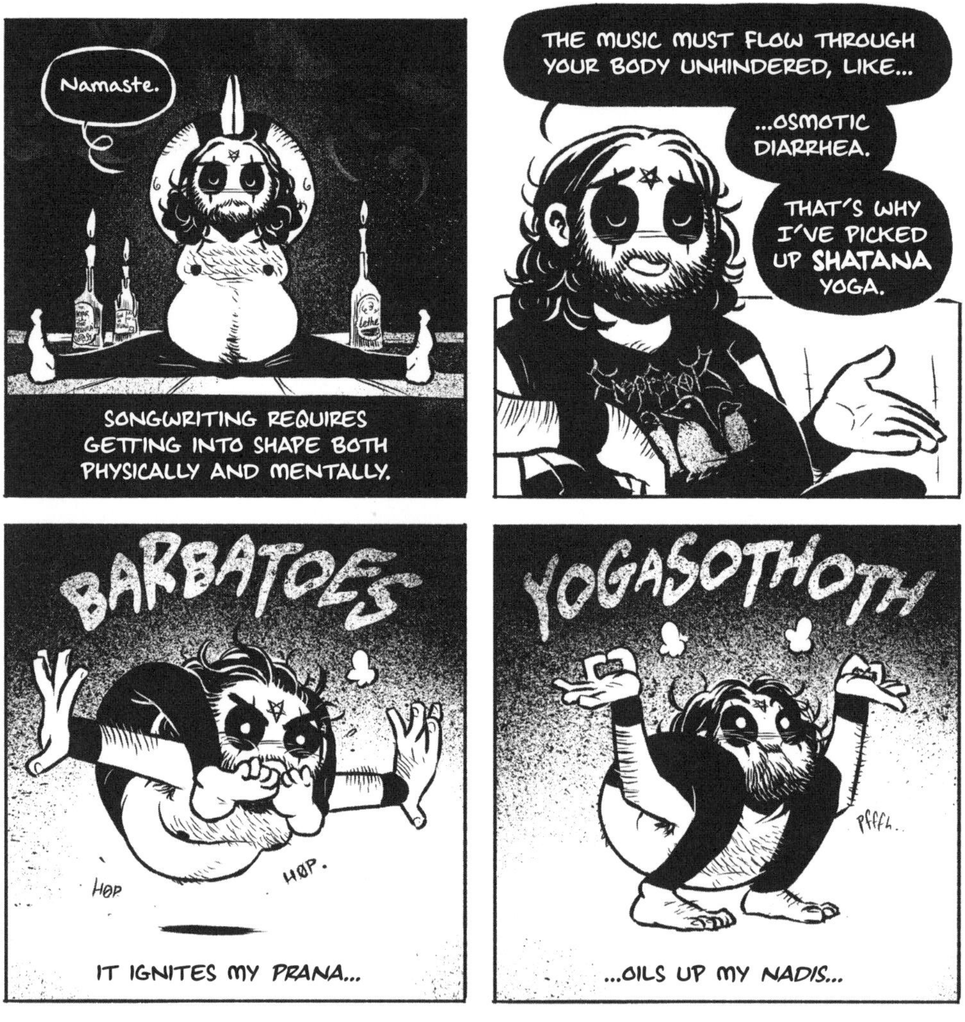
Namaste.
SONGWRITING REQUIRES GETTING INTO SHAPE BOTH PHYSICALLY AND MENTALLY.
THE MUSIC MUST FLOW THROUGH YOUR BODY UNHINDERED, LIKE...
...OSMOTIC DIARRHEA.
THAT'S WHY I'VE PICKED UP SHATANA YOGA.
BARBATOES
HØP
HØP.
IT IGNITES MY PRANA...
YOGASOTHOTH
PFFFH.
...OILS UP MY NADIS...

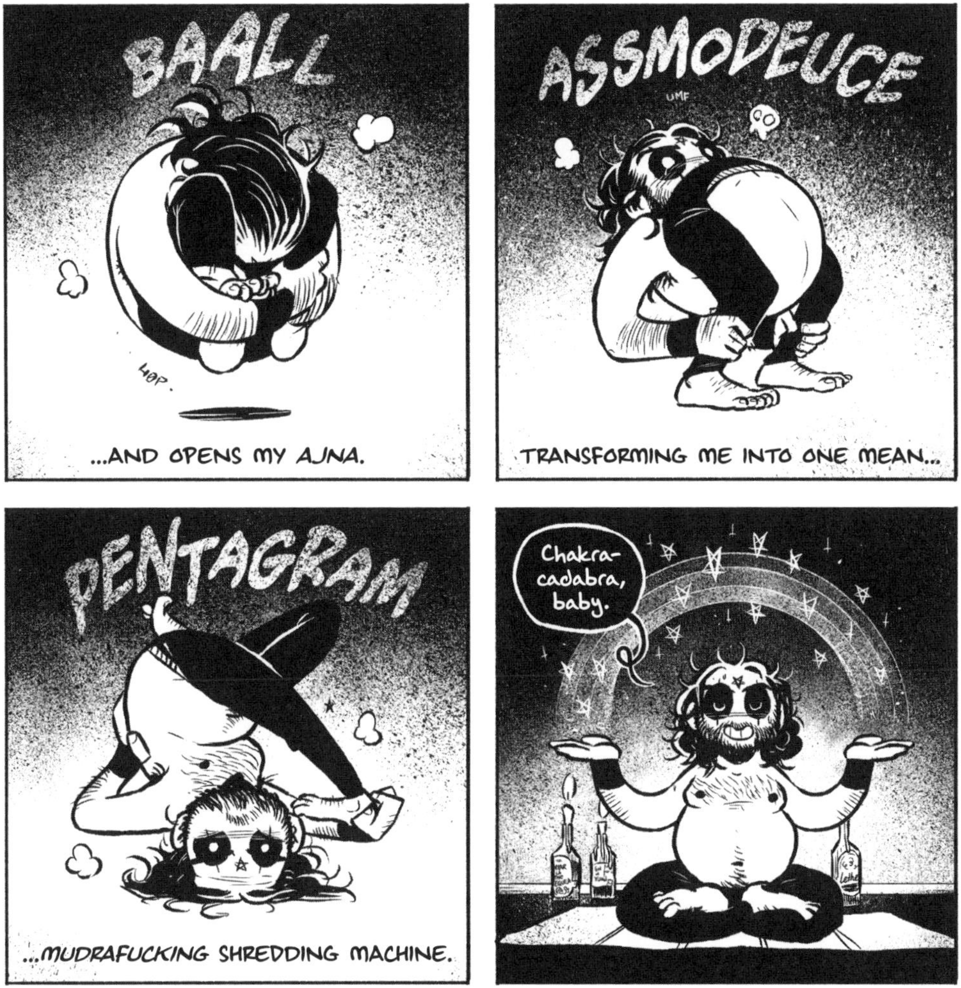
BAALL
HOP.
...AND OPENS MY AJNA.
ASSMODEUCE
UMF
TRANSFORMING ME INTO ONE MEAN...
PENTAGRAM
...MUDRAFUCKING SHREDDING MACHINE.
Chakra-cadabra, baby.

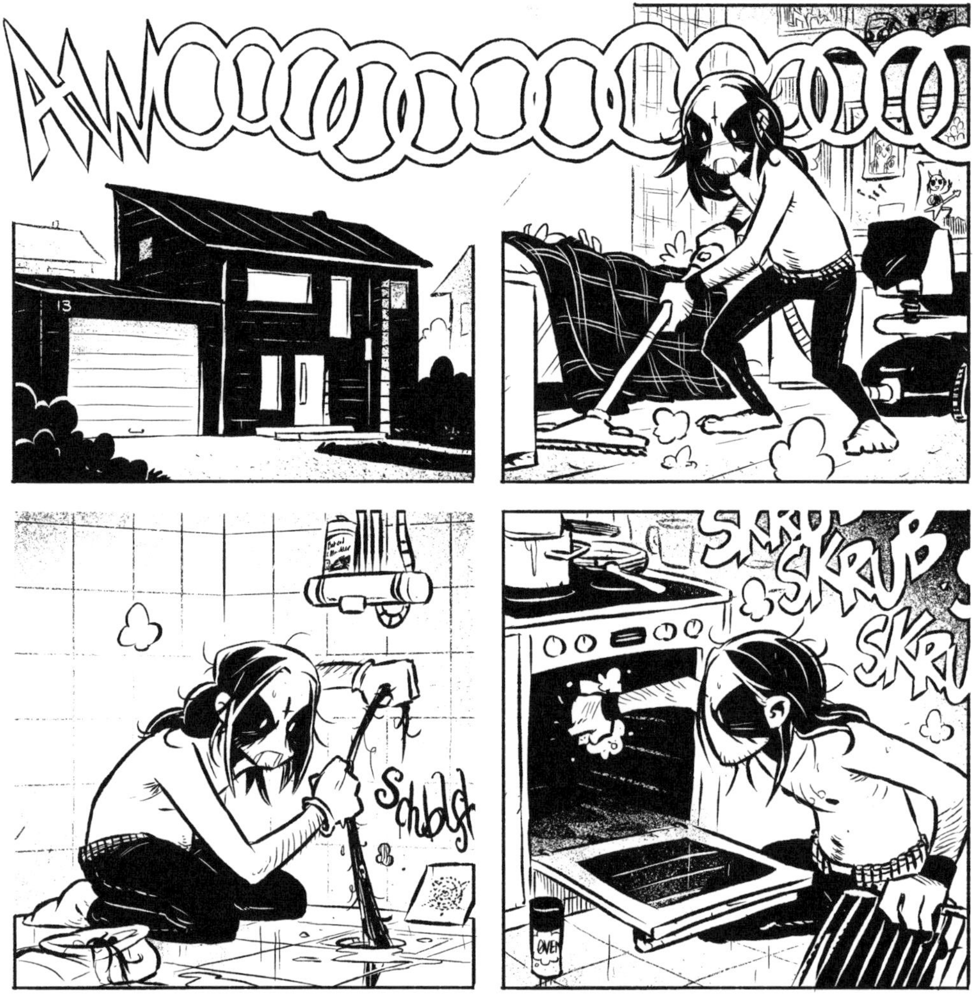
AWOOOOOOOOOOOOO
13
Schblgt
SKRUB
SKRUB
SKRU
OVEN

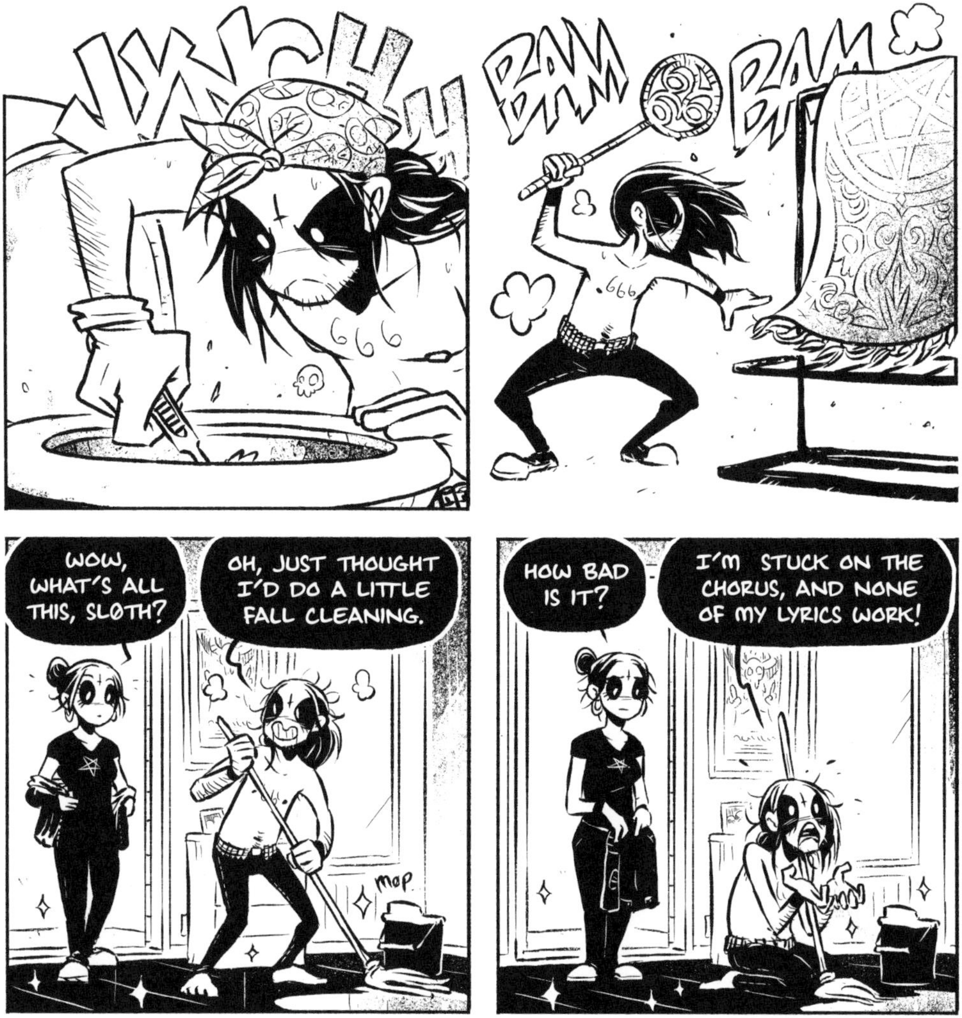
WOW, WHAT'S ALL THIS, SLØTH?
OH, JUST THOUGHT I'D DO A LITTLE FALL CLEANING.
mop
HOW BAD IS IT?
I'M STUCK ON THE CHORUS, AND NONE OF MY LYRICS WORK!

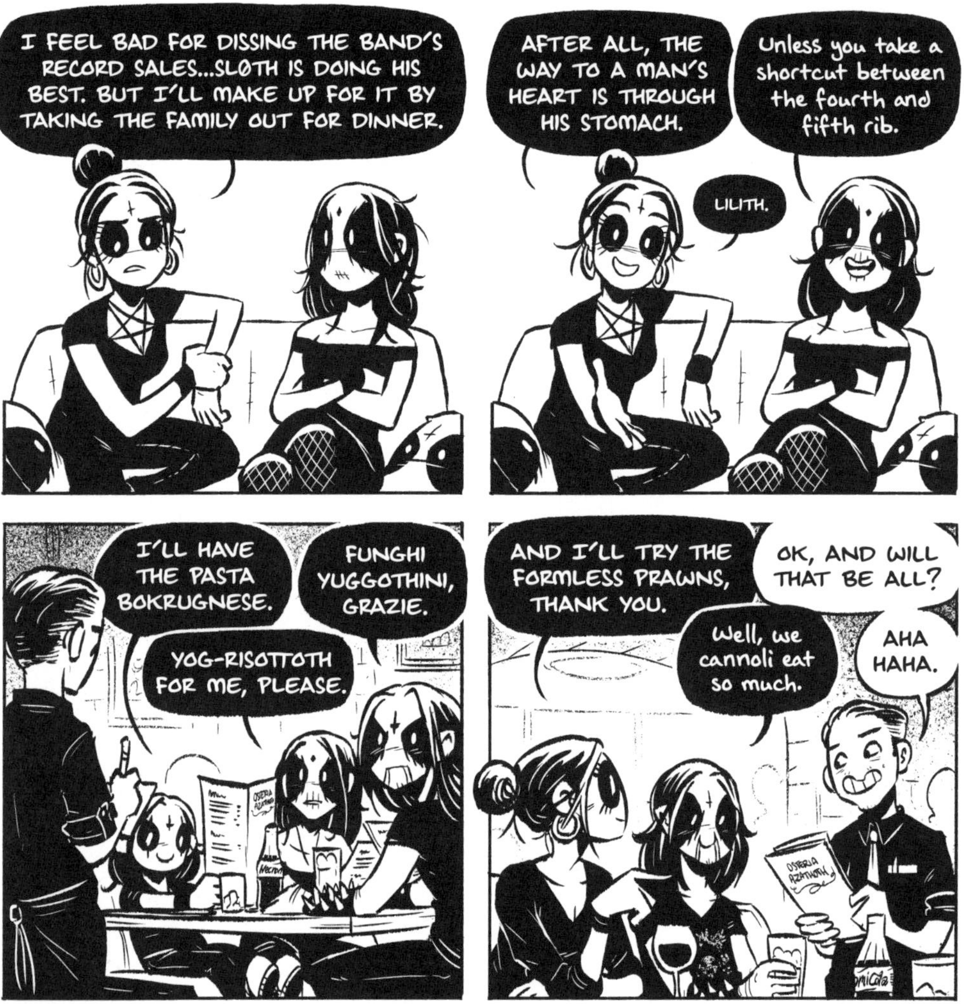
I FEEL BAD FOR DISSING THE BAND'S RECORD SALES...SLØTH IS DOING HIS BEST. BUT I'LL MAKE UP FOR IT BY TAKING THE FAMILY OUT FOR DINNER.
AFTER ALL, THE WAY TO A MAN'S HEART IS THROUGH HIS STOMACH.
LILITH.
Unless you take a shortcut between the fourth and fifth rib.
I'LL HAVE THE PASTA BOKRUGNESE.
FUNGHI YUGGOTHINI, GRAZIE.
YOG-RISOTTOTH FOR ME, PLEASE.
AND I'LL TRY THE FORMLESS PRAWNS, THANK YOU.
OK, AND WILL THAT BE ALL?
Well, we cannoli eat so much.
AHA HAHA.

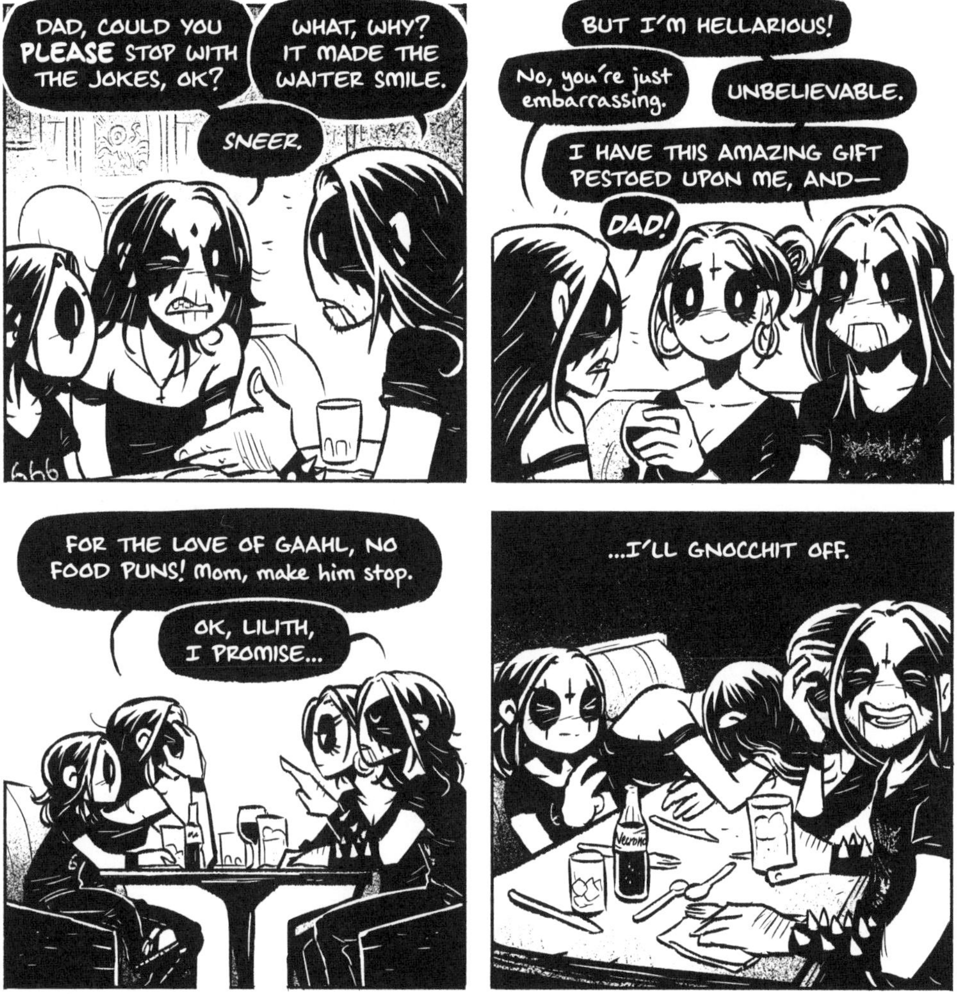
DAD, COULD YOU PLEASE STOP WITH THE JOKES, OK?
WHAT, WHY? IT MADE THE WAITER SMILE.
SNEER.
BUT I'M HELLARIOUS!
No, you're just embarrassing.
UNBELIEVABLE.
I HAVE THIS AMAZING GIFT PESTOED UPON ME, AND—
DAD!
FOR THE LOVE OF GAAHL, NO FOOD PUNS! Mom, make him stop.
OK, LILITH, I PROMISE...
...I'LL GNOCCHIT OFF.

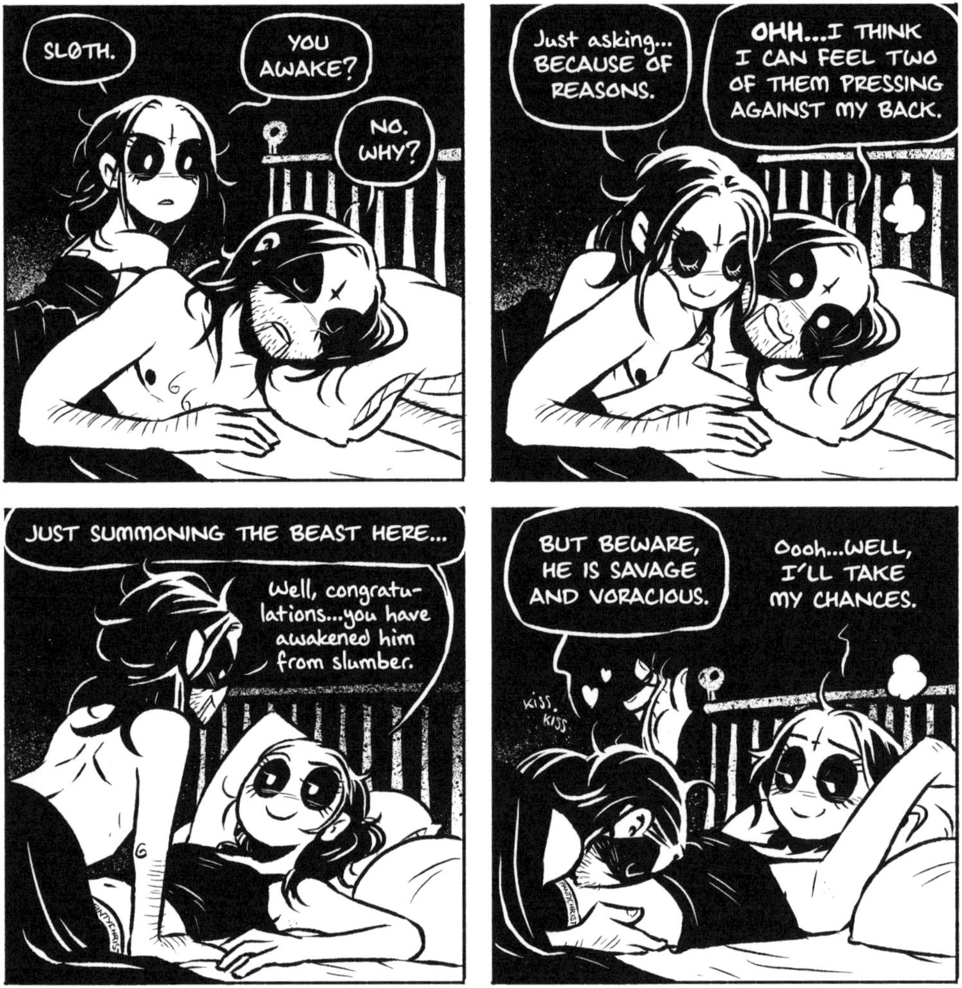
SLOTH.
YOU AWAKE?
NO. WHY?
Just asking... BECAUSE OF REASONS.
OHH...I THINK I CAN FEEL TWO OF THEM PRESSING AGAINST MY BACK.
JUST SUMMONING THE BEAST HERE...
Well, congratu-lations...you have awakened him from slumber.
BUT BEWARE, HE IS SAVAGE AND VORACIOUS.
Oooh...WELL, I'LL TAKE MY CHANCES.
KISS. KISS.

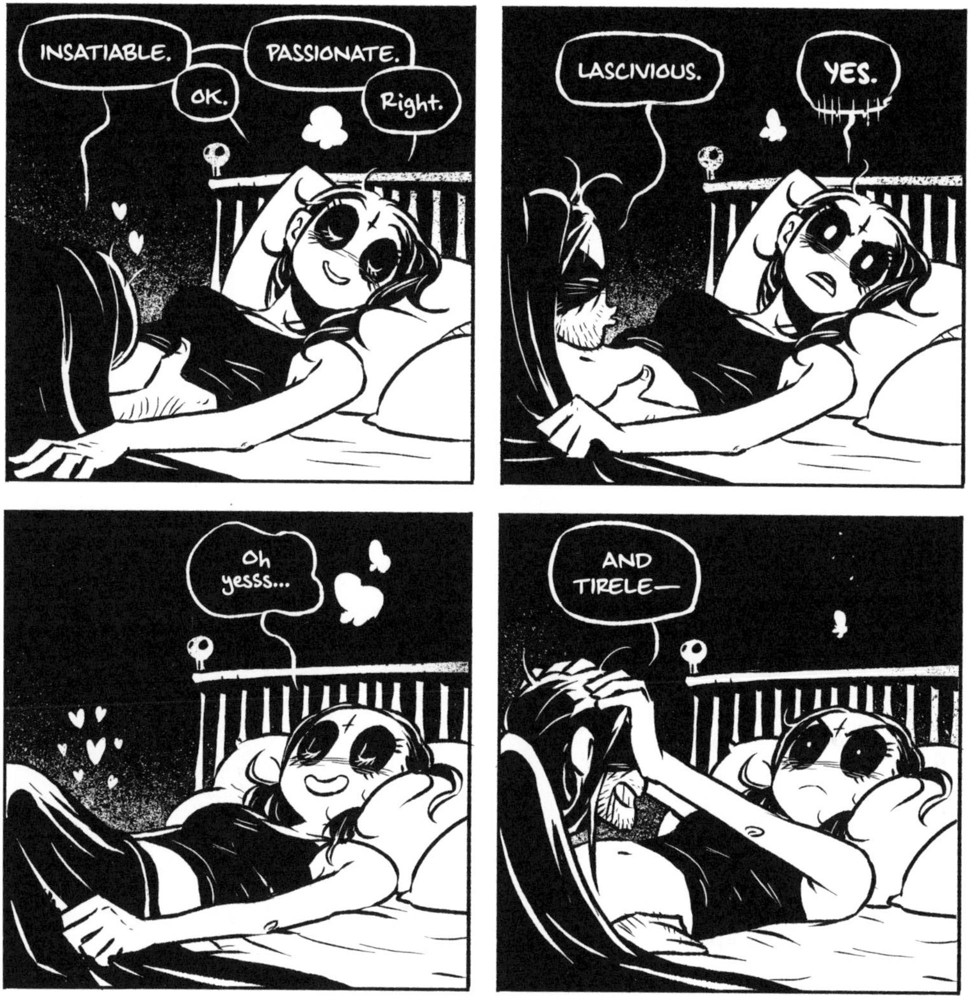
INSATIABLE.
OK.
PASSIONATE.
Right.
LASCIVIOUS.
YES.
Oh yesss...
AND TIRELE—

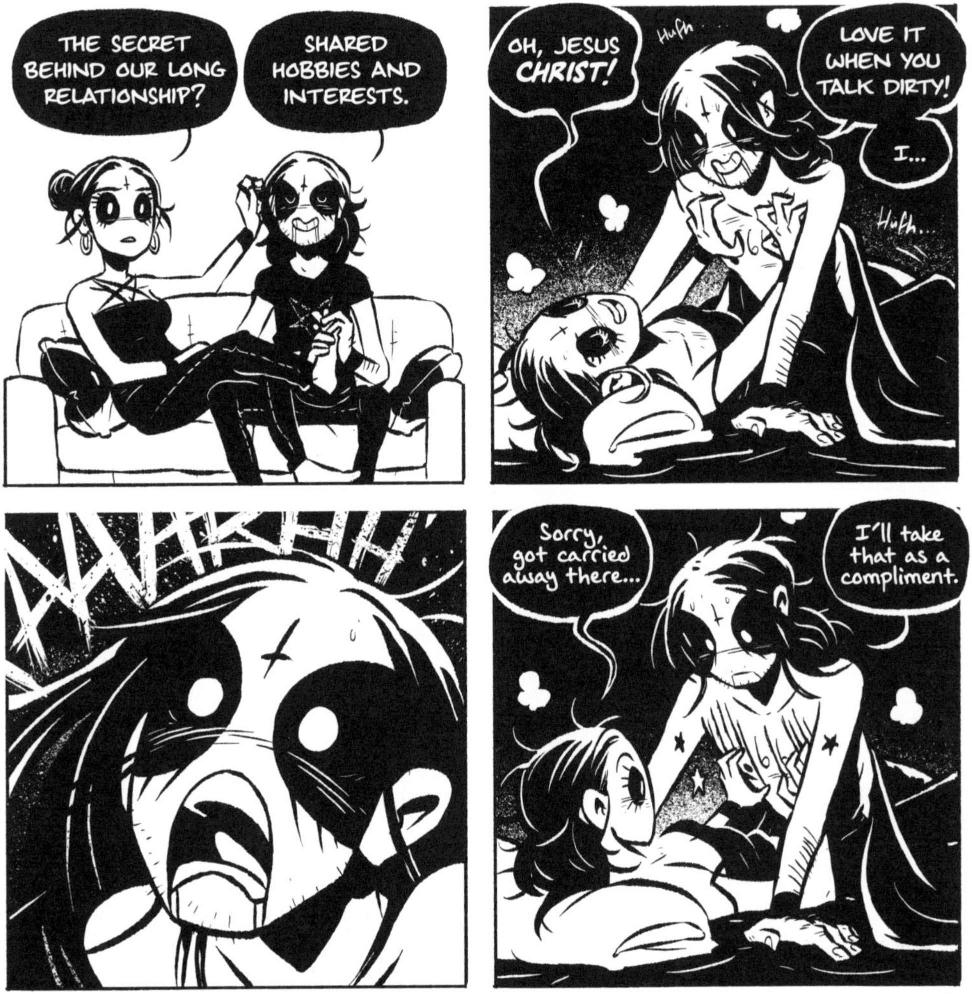
THE SECRET BEHIND OUR LONG RELATIONSHIP?
SHARED HOBBIES AND INTERESTS.
OH, JESUS CHRIST!
Hufh...
LOVE IT WHEN YOU TALK DIRTY!
I...
Hufh...
Sorry, got carried away there...
I'll take that as a compliment.

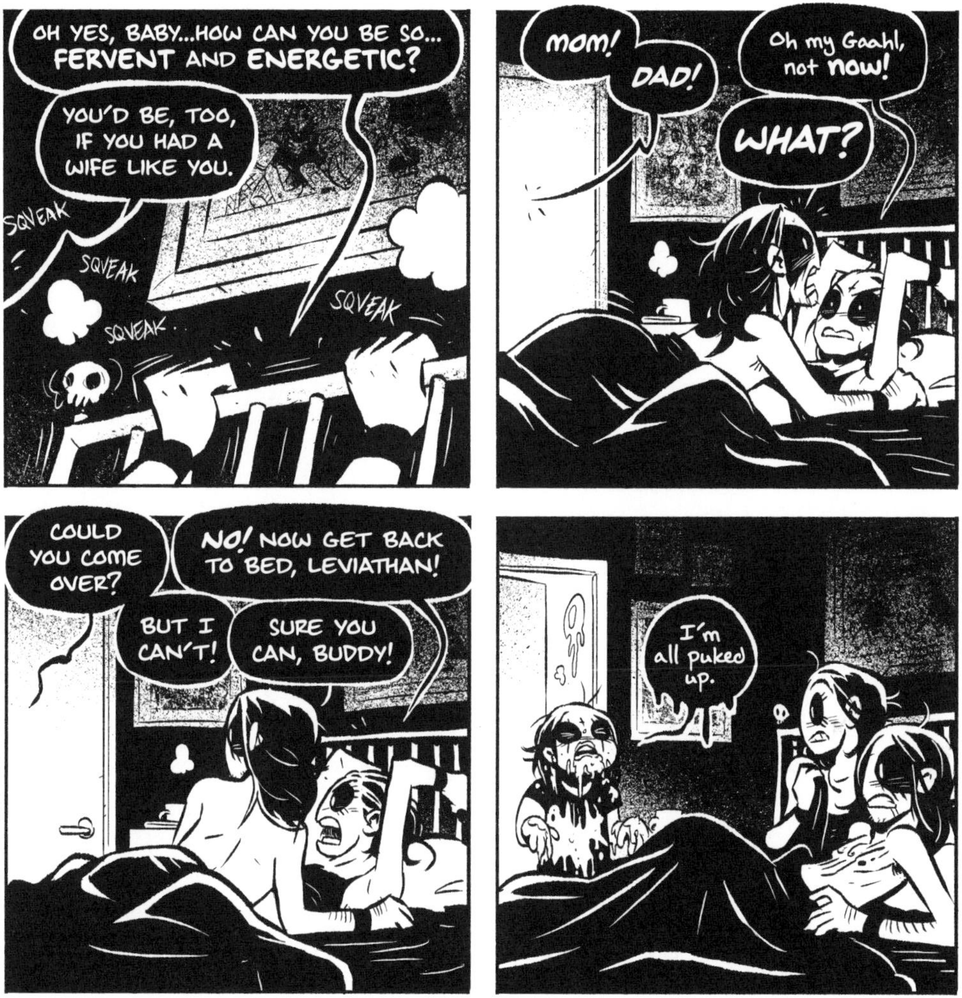
OH YES, BABY...HOW CAN YOU BE SO... FERVENT AND ENERGETIC?
YOU'D BE, TOO, IF YOU HAD A WIFE LIKE YOU.
SQVEAK
SQVEAK
SQVEAK
SQVEAK
MOM!
DAD!
Oh my Gaahl, not now!
WHAT?
COULD YOU COME OVER?
NO! NOW GET BACK TO BED, LEVIATHAN!
BUT I CAN'T!
SURE YOU CAN, BUDDY!
I'm all puked up.

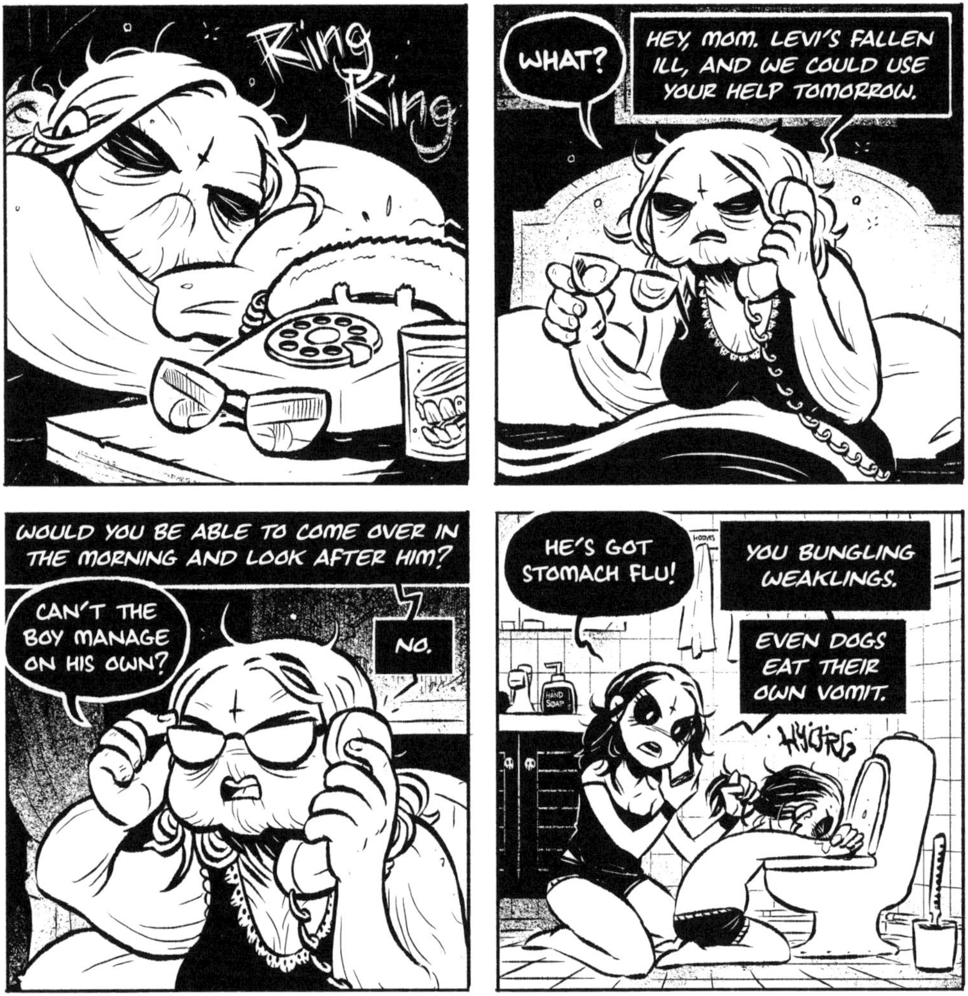
Ring
Ring
WHAT?
HEY, MOM. LEVI'S FALLEN ILL, AND WE COULD USE YOUR HELP TOMORROW.
WOULD YOU BE ABLE TO COME OVER IN THE MORNING AND LOOK AFTER HIM?
CAN'T THE BOY MANAGE ON HIS OWN?
NO.
HE'S GOT STOMACH FLU!
YOU BUNGLING WEAKLINGS.
EVEN DOGS EAT THEIR OWN VOMIT.
HAND SOAP
HYÖRG

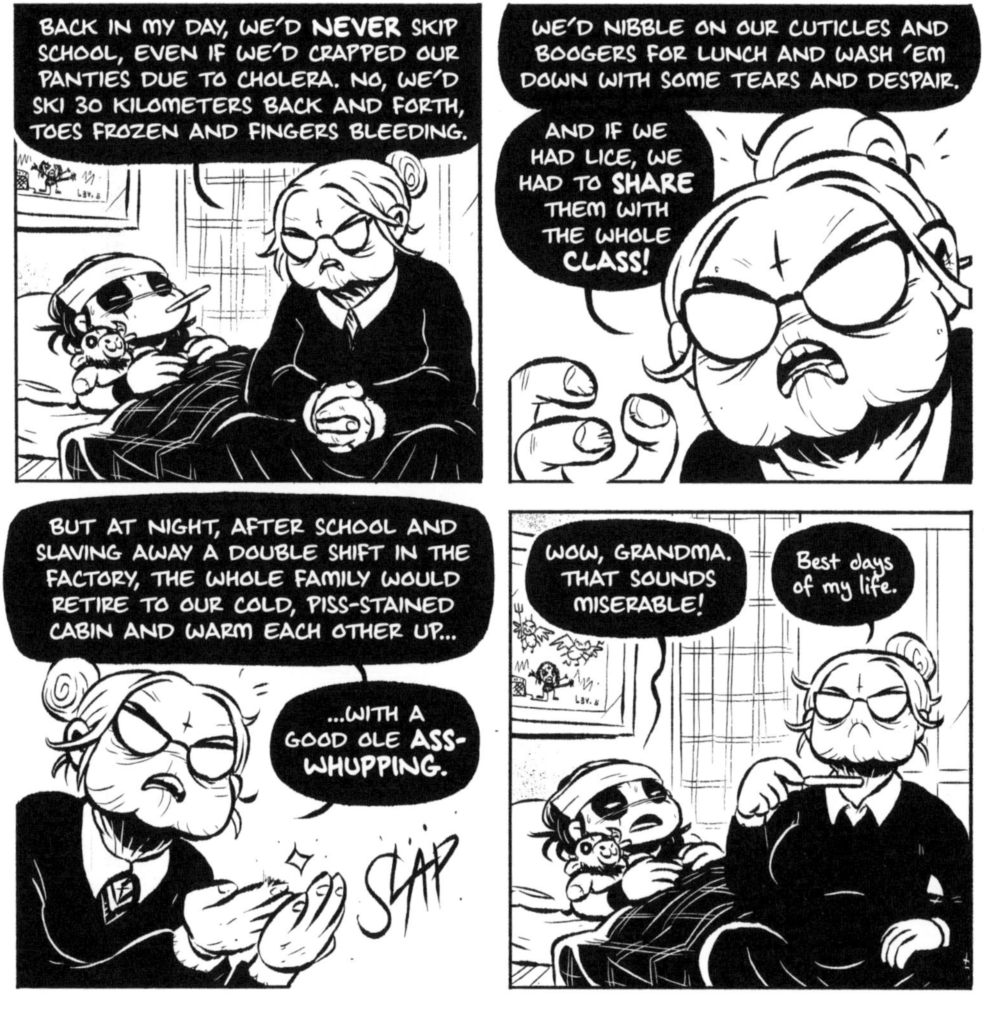
BACK IN MY DAY, WE'D NEVER SKIP SCHOOL, EVEN IF WE'D CRAPPED OUR PANTIES DUE TO CHOLERA. NO, WE'D SKI 30 KILOMETERS BACK AND FORTH, TOES FROZEN AND FINGERS BLEEDING.
WE'D NIBBLE ON OUR CUTICLES AND BOOGERS FOR LUNCH AND WASH 'EM DOWN WITH SOME TEARS AND DESPAIR.
AND IF WE HAD LICE, WE HAD TO SHARE THEM WITH THE WHOLE CLASS!
BUT AT NIGHT, AFTER SCHOOL AND SLAVING AWAY A DOUBLE SHIFT IN THE FACTORY, THE WHOLE FAMILY WOULD RETIRE TO OUR COLD, PISS-STAINED CABIN AND WARM EACH OTHER UP...
...WITH A GOOD OLE ASS-WHUPPING.
SLAP
WOW, GRANDMA. THAT SOUNDS MISERABLE!
Best days of my life.

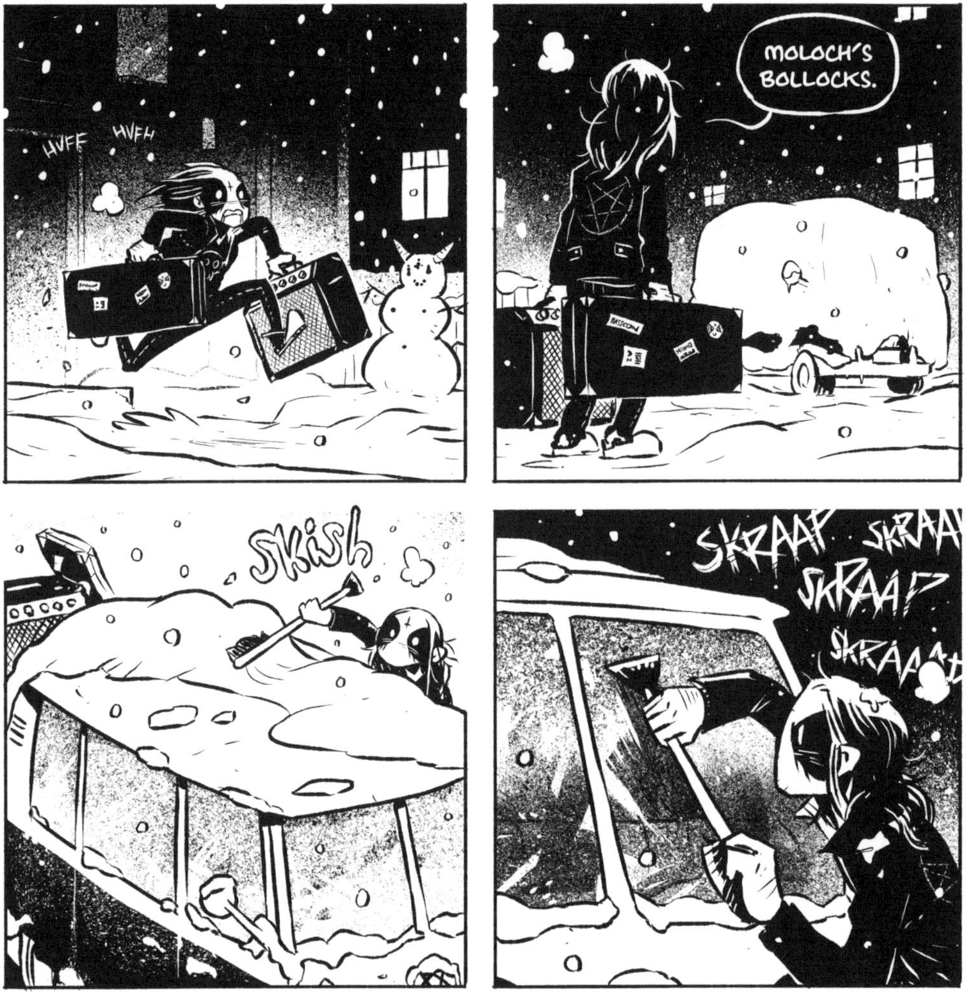
HUFF HUFH
MOLOCH'S BOLLOCKS.
SKISH
SKRAAP
SKRAA
SKRAAP
SKRAA

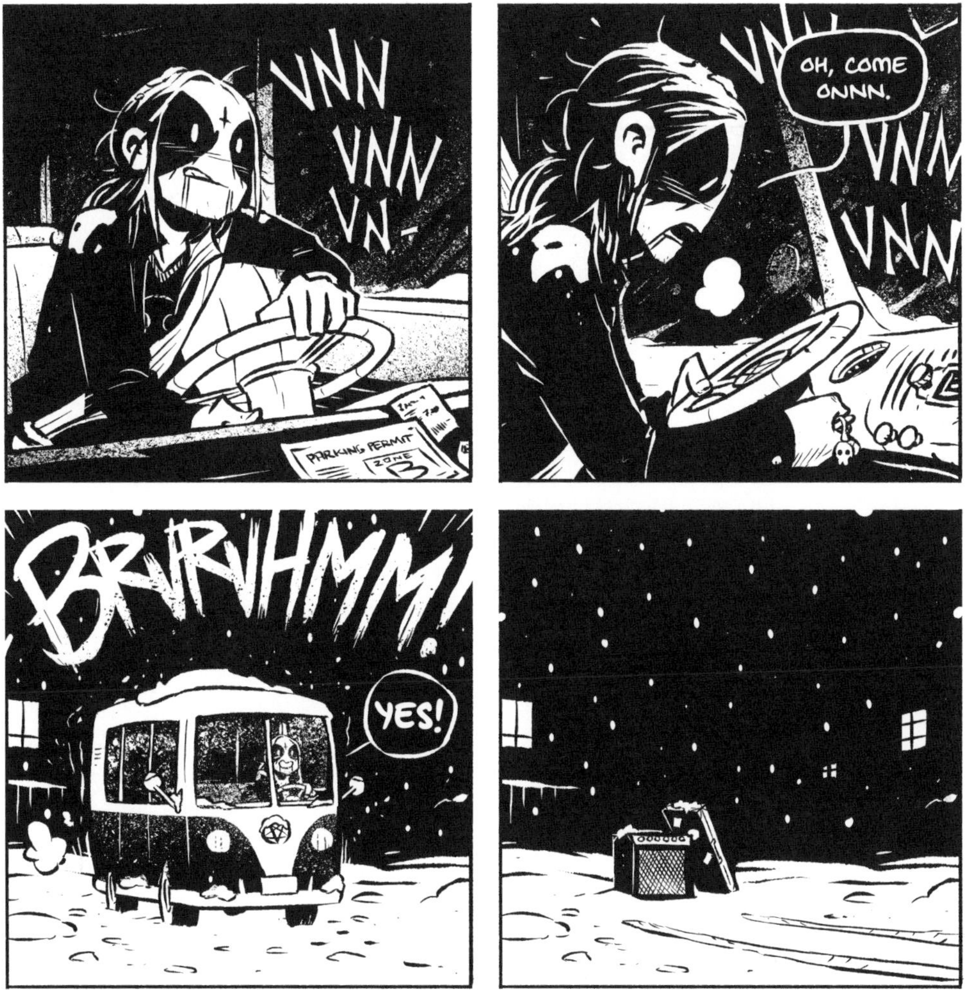
VNN VNN VN
PARKING PERMIT
ZONE B
OH, COME ONNN.
VNN VNN
BRRRHMM!
YES!

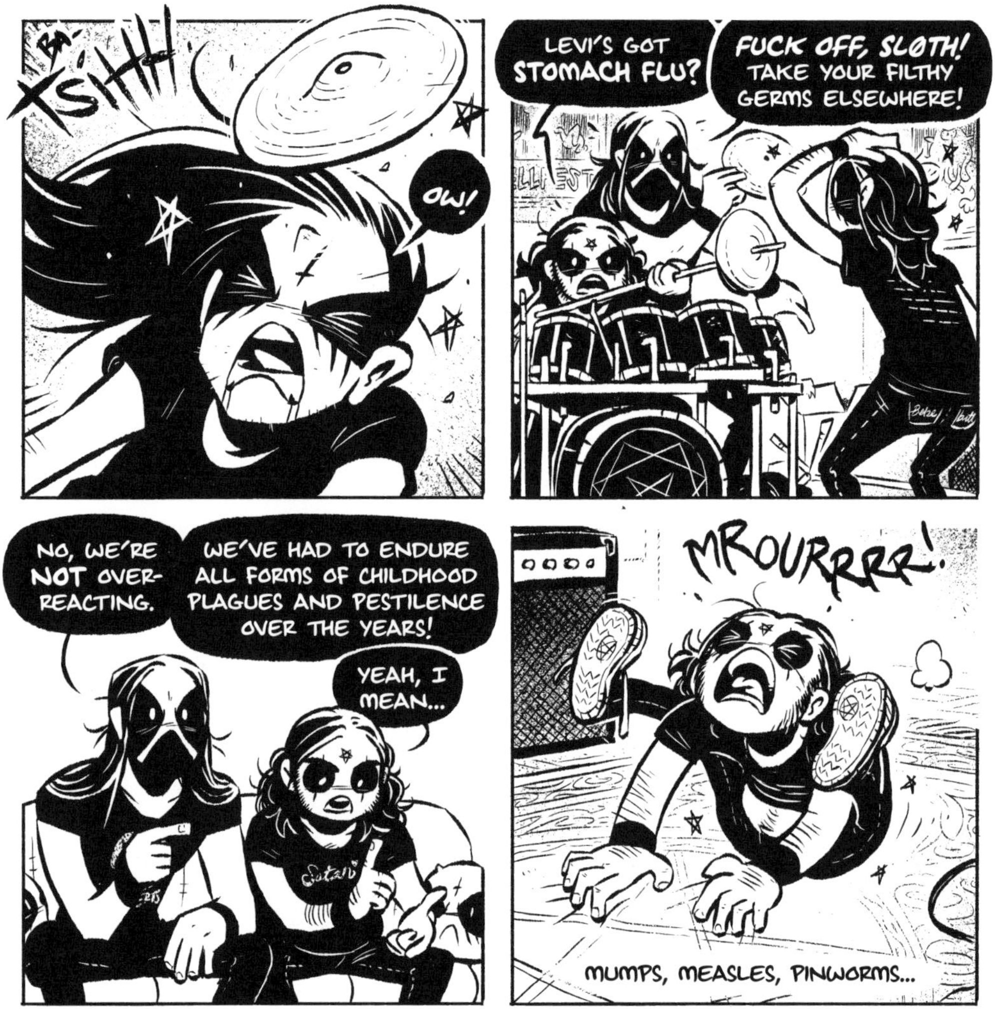
BA-TSHH!
OW!
LEVI'S GOT STOMACH FLU?
FUCK OFF, SLØTH! TAKE YOUR FILTHY GERMS ELSEWHERE!
NO, WE'RE NOT OVER-REACTING.
WE'VE HAD TO ENDURE ALL FORMS OF CHILDHOOD PLAGUES AND PESTILENCE OVER THE YEARS!
YEAH, I MEAN...
MROURRRR!
MUMPS, MEASLES, PINWORMS...

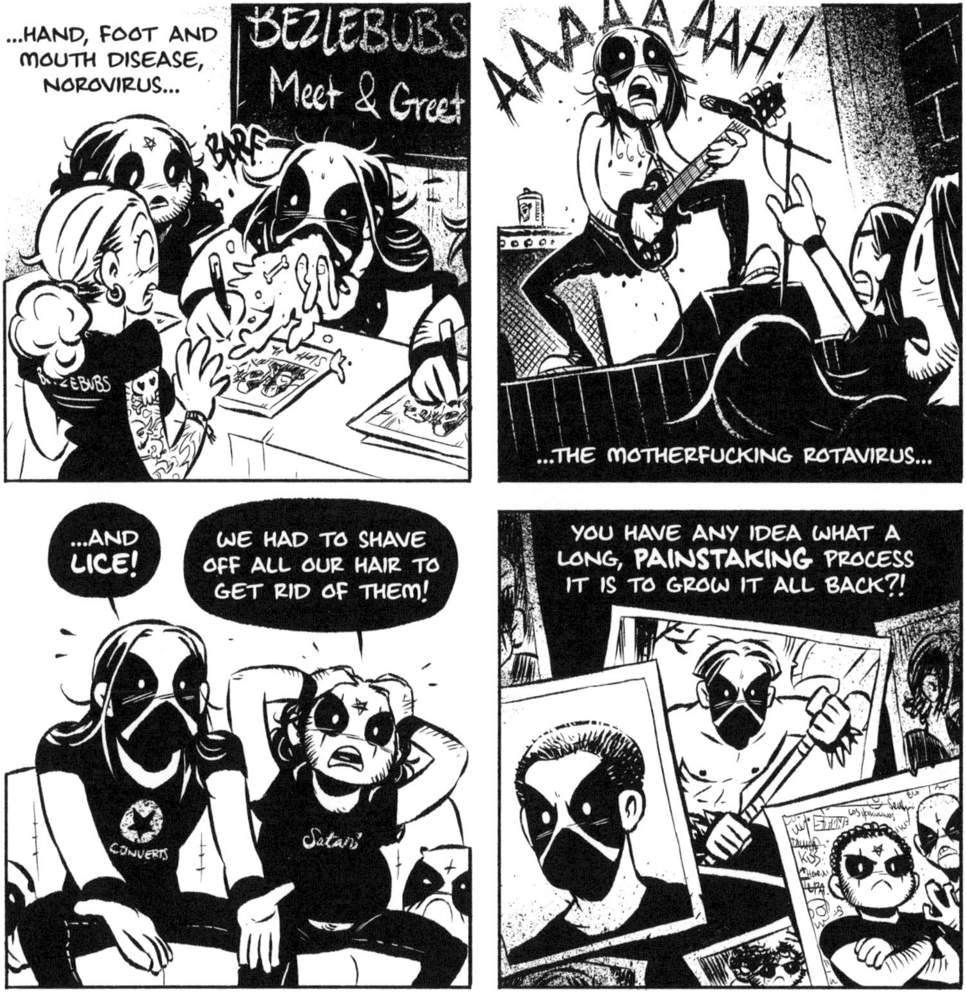
...HAND, FOOT AND MOUTH DISEASE, NOROVIRUS...
BEZLEBUBS
Meet & Greet
BARF
AAAAAAAH!
...THE MOTHERFUCKING ROTAVIRUS...
...AND LICE!
WE HAD TO SHAVE OFF ALL OUR HAIR TO GET RID OF THEM!
CONVERTS
Satan
YOU HAVE ANY IDEA WHAT A LONG, PAINSTAKING PROCESS IT IS TO GROW IT ALL BACK?!

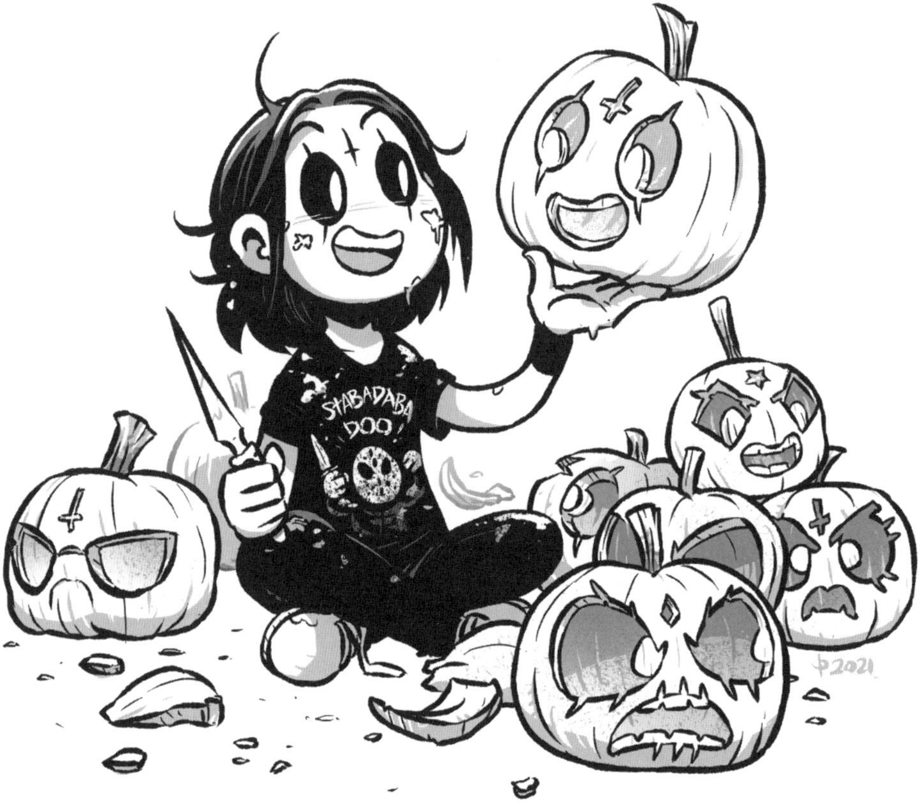

STABADABA
DOO!

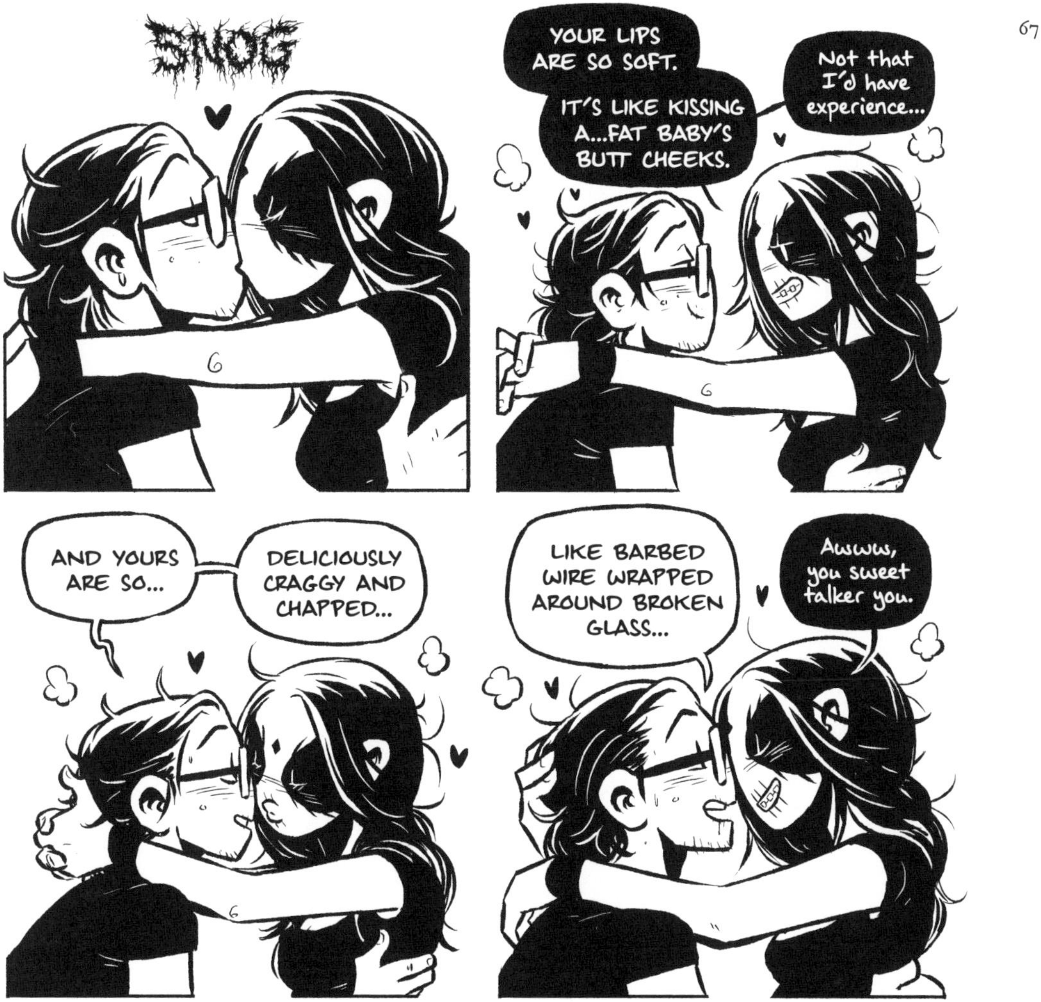
SNOG
YOUR LIPS ARE SO SOFT.
IT'S LIKE KISSING A...FAT BABY'S BUTT CHEEKS.
Not that I'd have experience...
AND YOURS ARE SO...
DELICIOUSLY CRAGGY AND CHAPPED...
LIKE BARBED WIRE WRAPPED AROUND BROKEN GLASS...
Awww, you sweet talker you.

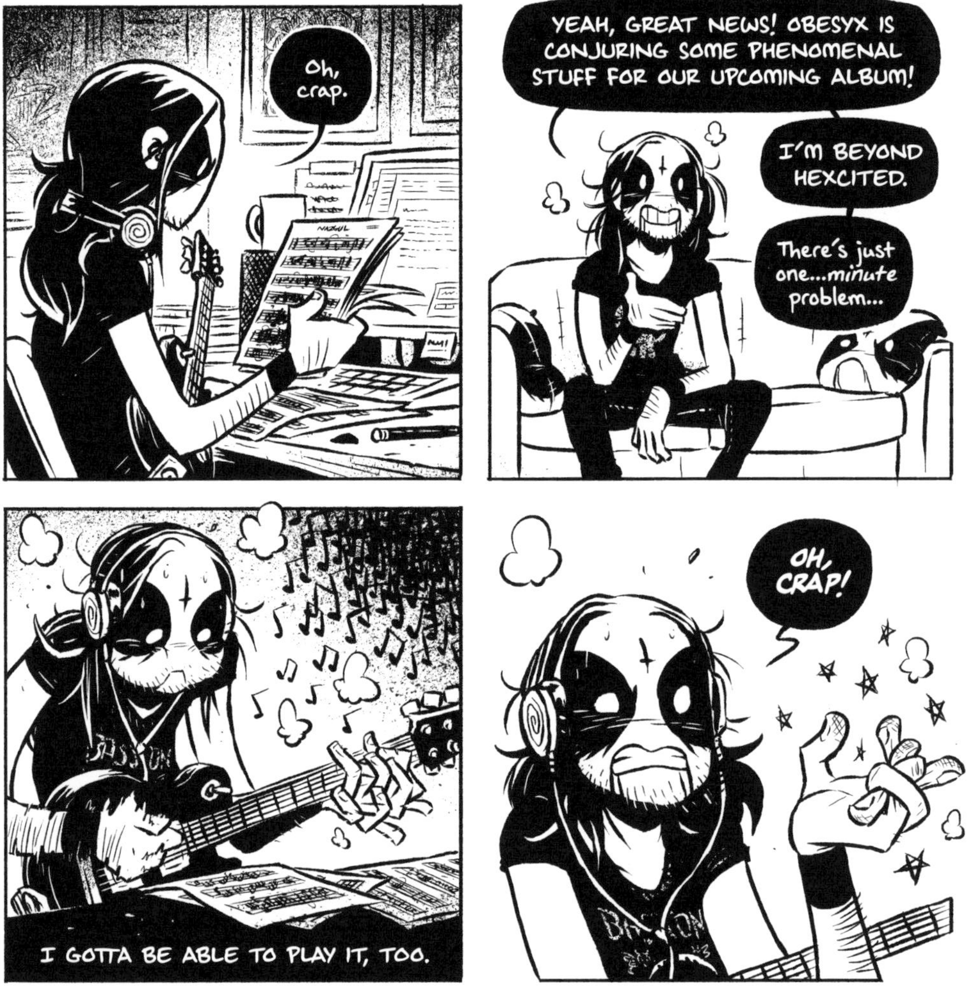
Oh, crap.
YEAH, GREAT NEWS! OBESYX IS CONJURING SOME PHENOMENAL STUFF FOR OUR UPCOMING ALBUM!
I'M BEYOND HEXCITED.
There's just one...minute problem...
I GOTTA BE ABLE TO PLAY IT, TOO.
OH, CRAP!

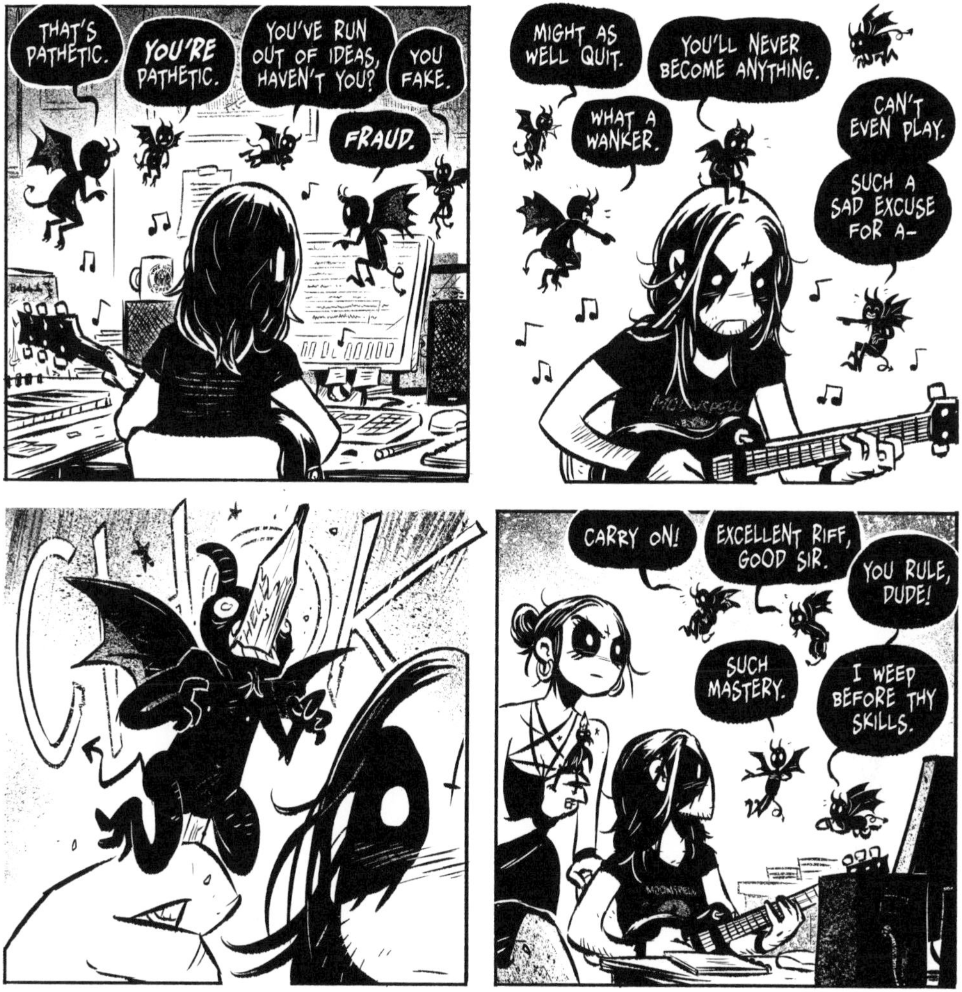
THAT'S PATHETIC.
YOU'RE PATHETIC.
YOU'VE RUN OUT OF IDEAS, HAVEN'T YOU?
YOU FAKE.
FRAUD.
MIGHT AS WELL QUIT.
YOU'LL NEVER BECOME ANYTHING.
WHAT A WANKER.
CAN'T EVEN PLAY.
SUCH A SAD EXCUSE FOR A-
CARRY ON!
EXCELLENT RIFF, GOOD SIR.
YOU RULE, DUDE!
SUCH MASTERY.
I WEEP BEFORE THY SKILLS.

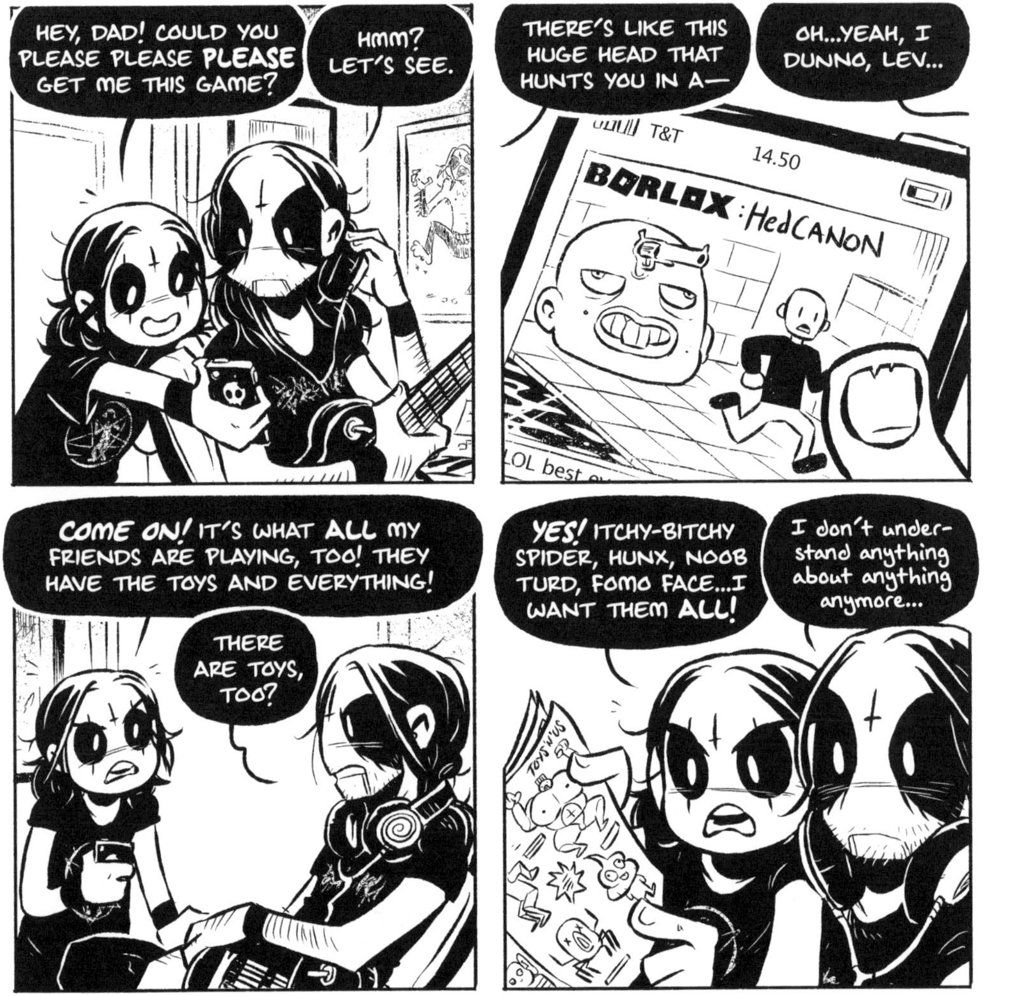
HEY, DAD! COULD YOU PLEASE PLEASE **PLEASE** GET ME THIS GAME?
HMM? LET'S SEE.
THERE'S LIKE THIS HUGE HEAD THAT HUNTS YOU IN A—
OH...YEAH, I DUNNO, LEV...
T&T
14.50
BORLOX :HedCANON
LOL best
COME ON! IT'S WHAT **ALL** MY FRIENDS ARE PLAYING, TOO! THEY HAVE THE TOYS AND EVERYTHING!
THERE ARE TOYS, TOO?
YES! ITCHY-BITCHY SPIDER, HUNX, NOOB TURD, FOMO FACE...I WANT THEM **ALL!**
I don't understand anything about anything anymore...

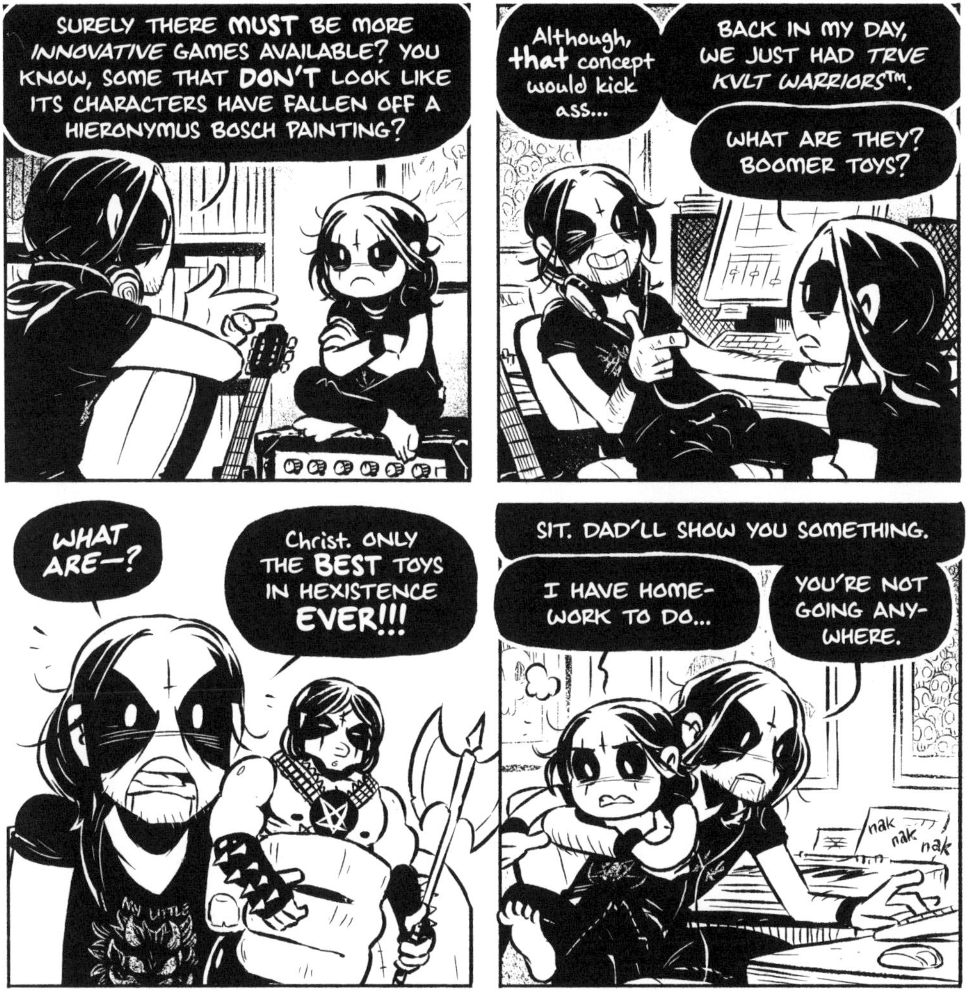
SURELY THERE MUST BE MORE INNOVATIVE GAMES AVAILABLE? YOU KNOW, SOME THAT DON'T LOOK LIKE ITS CHARACTERS HAVE FALLEN OFF A HIERONYMUS BOSCH PAINTING?
Although, that concept would kick ass...
BACK IN MY DAY, WE JUST HAD TRVE KVLT WARRIORS™.
WHAT ARE THEY? BOOMER TOYS?
WHAT ARE—?
Christ. ONLY THE BEST TOYS IN HEXISTENCE EVER!!!
MY LITTLE
SIT. DAD'LL SHOW YOU SOMETHING.
I HAVE HOME-WORK TO DO...
YOU'RE NOT GOING ANY-WHERE.
nak nak nak

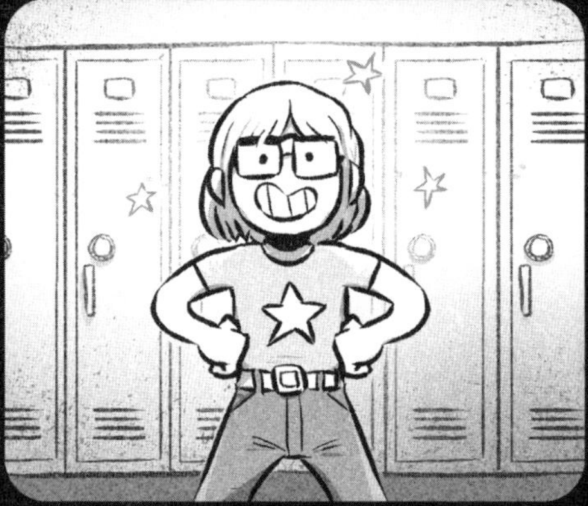

– I am Aaron, the valedictorian
and defender of our grade school!

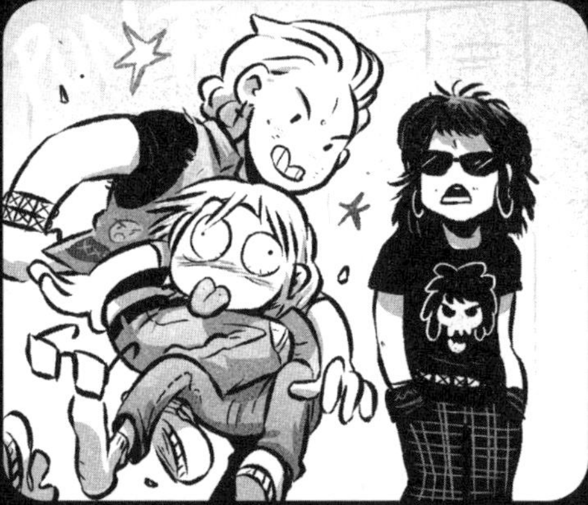

– Who are you talking to, numbskull?
– Yeah, shut up, dork! You're nothing.

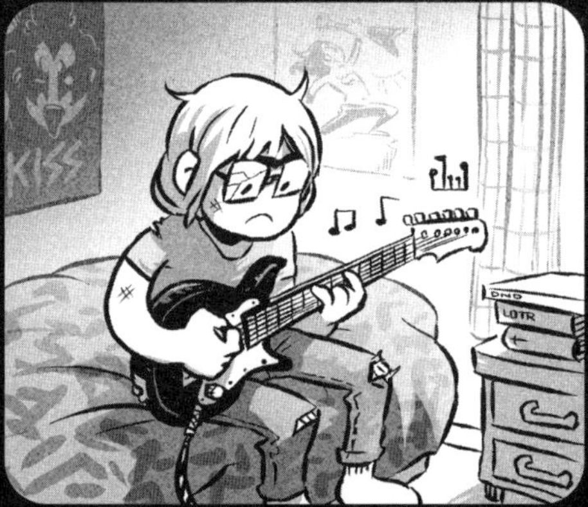
KISS
DND
LOTR

– Secret powers were revealed to me
the day I picked up a guitar and said:

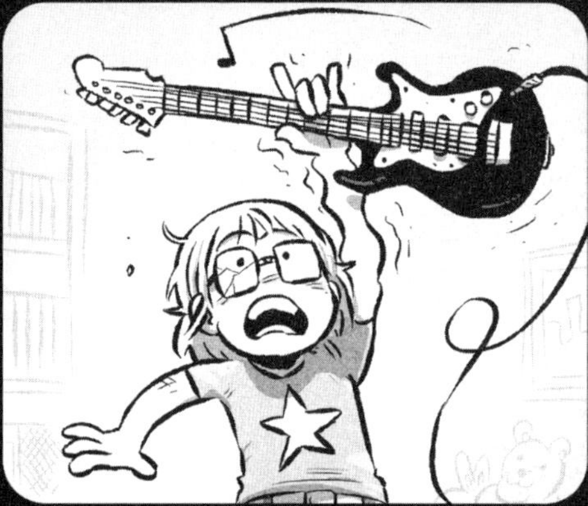

"Oh, boy, this is heavy!
I...have...no...poooweeeerrr!"

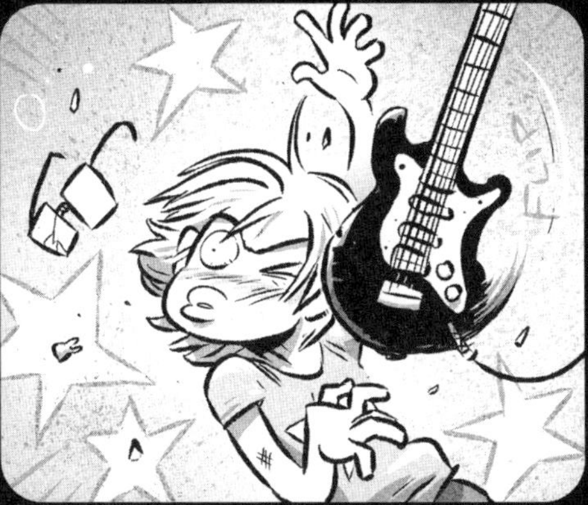

– It was then that I was magically transported into Castle Cracked Skull...

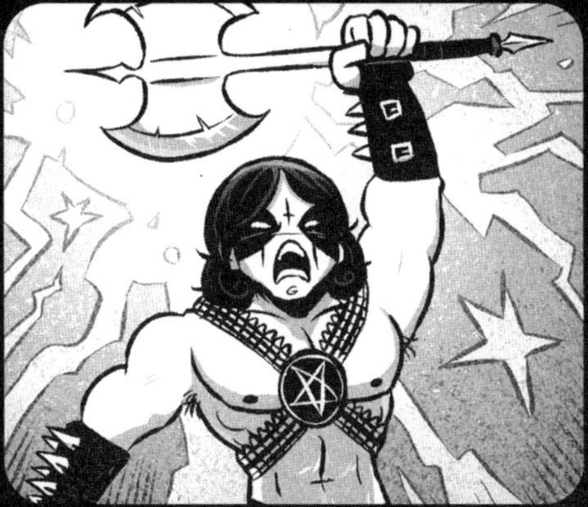

...and became Heathen-Man, the most powerful man in the universe!

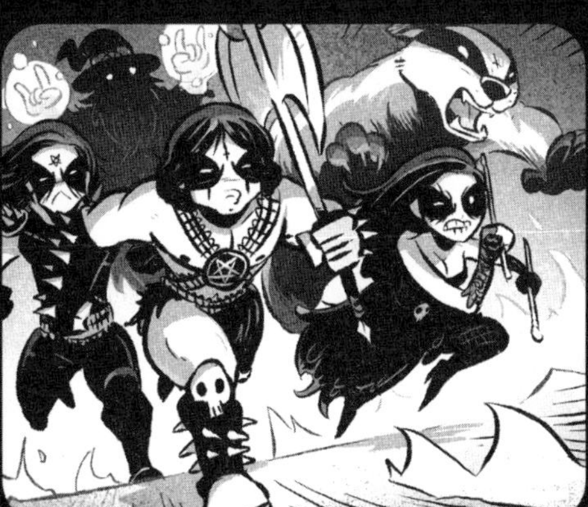

There, in the mystic land of Comatosia, I swore to save the city of Infernia...

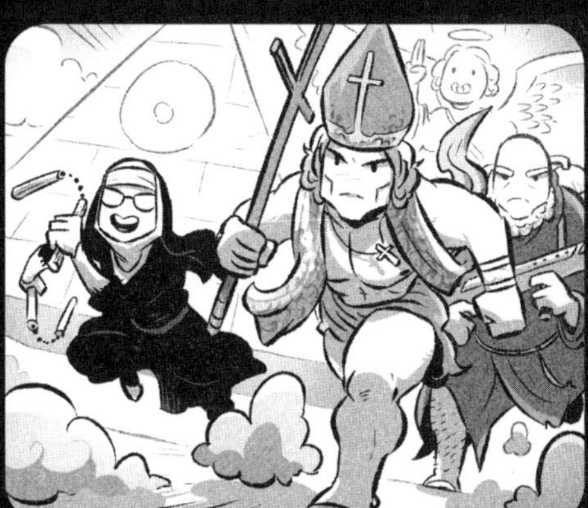

...from the angelic forces of Zealotor and his holy A-MEN!

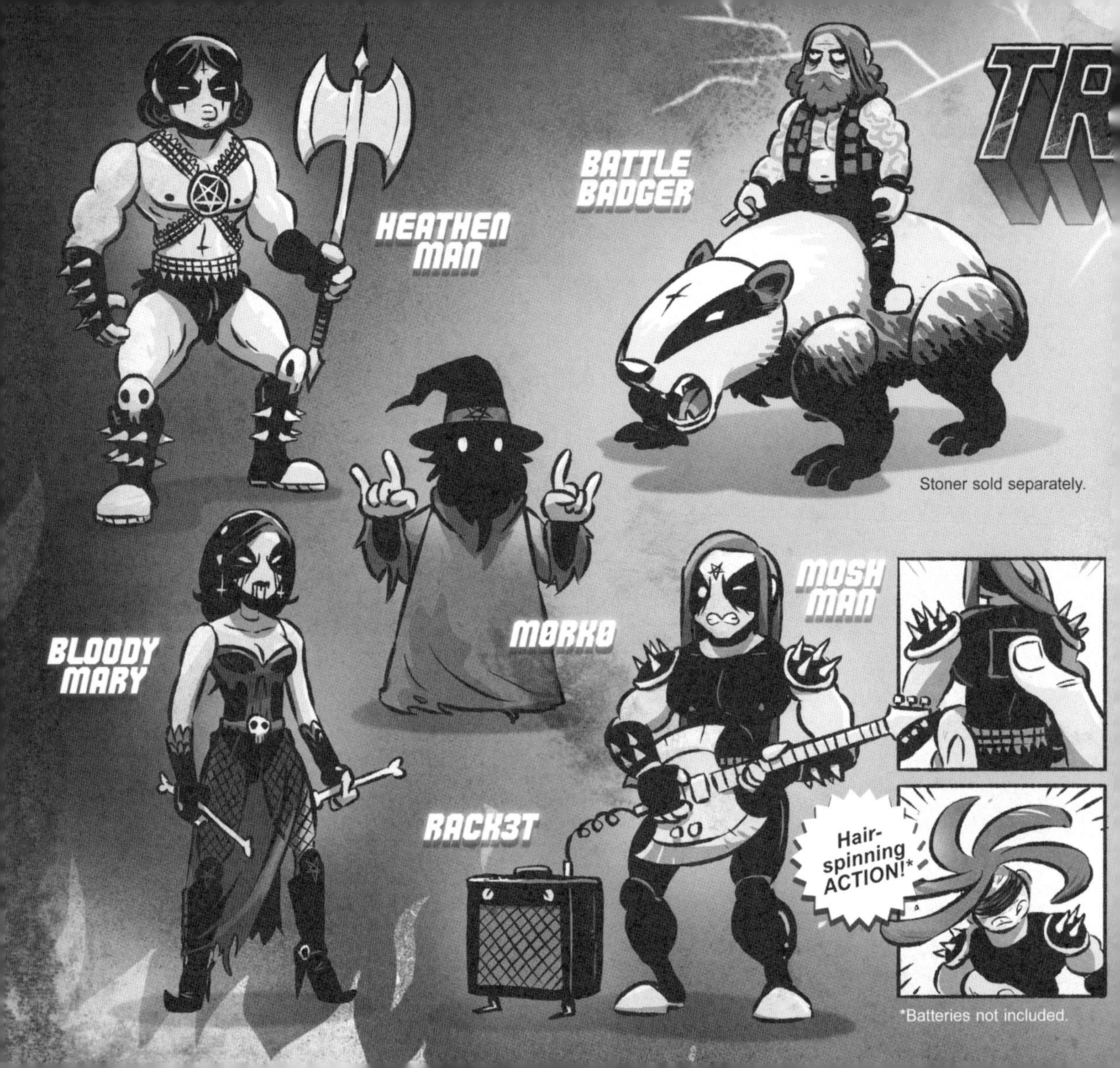
TR
HEATHEN MAN
BATTLE BADGER
Stoner sold separately.
MØRKØ
BLOODY MARY
MOSH MAN
RACK3T
Hair-spinning ACTION!*
*Batteries not included.

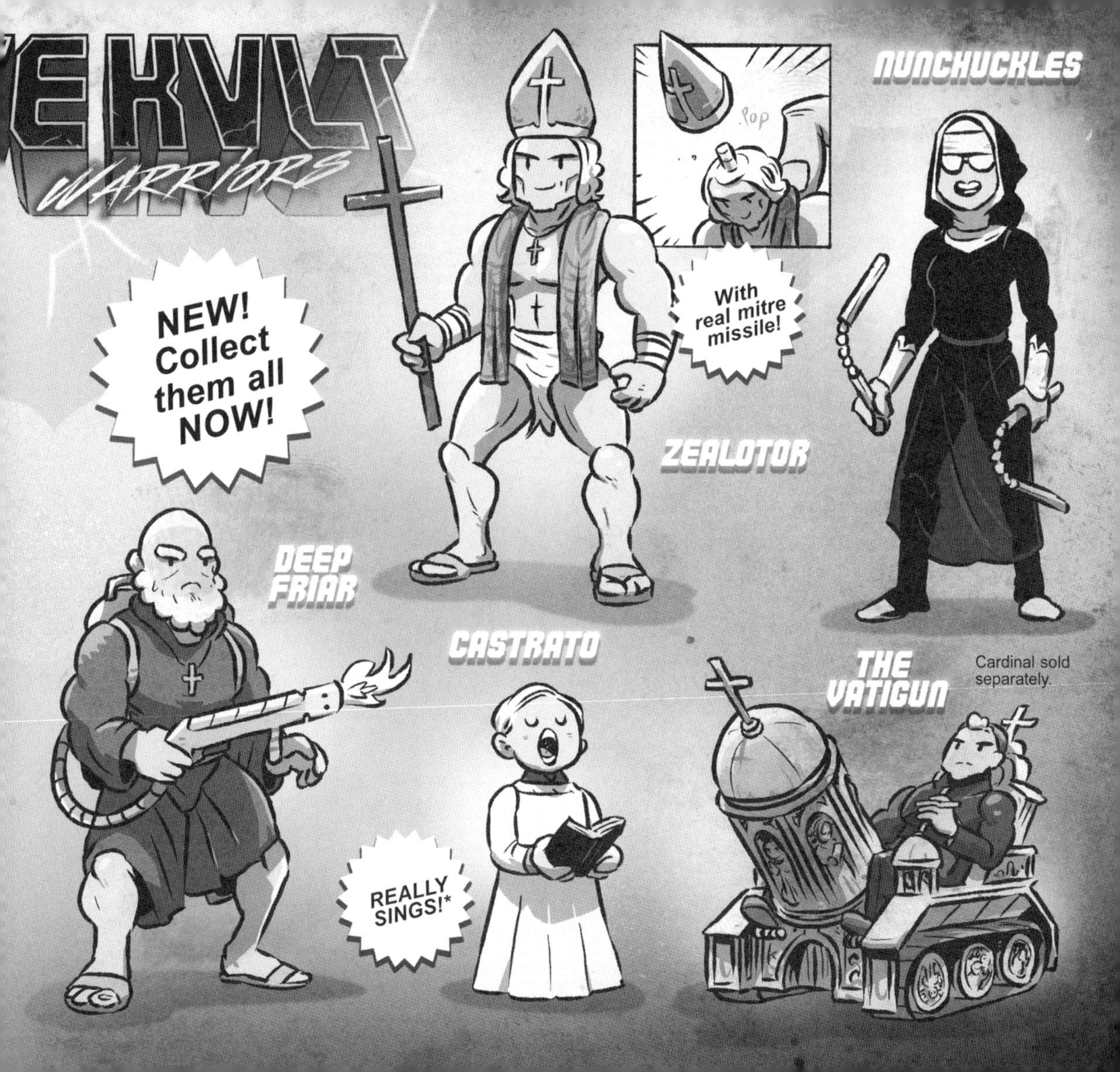

EKVLT
WARRIORS
NEW! Collect them all NOW!
Pop
With real mitre missile!
NUNCHUCKLES
ZEALOTOR
DEEP FRIAR
CASTRATO
THE VATIGUN
Cardinal sold separately.
REALLY SINGS!*

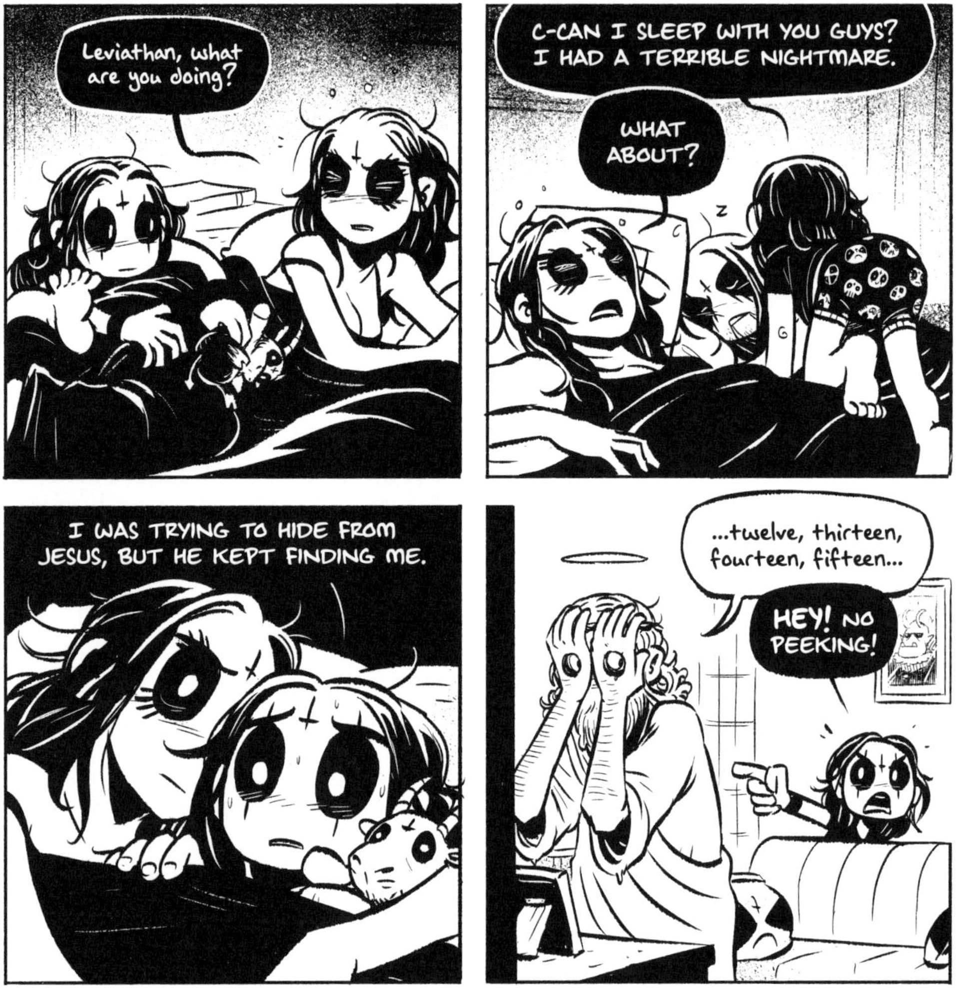
Leviathan, what are you doing?
C-CAN I SLEEP WITH YOU GUYS? I HAD A TERRIBLE NIGHTMARE.
WHAT ABOUT?
Z
I WAS TRYING TO HIDE FROM JESUS, BUT HE KEPT FINDING ME.
...twelve, thirteen, fourteen, fifteen...
HEY! NO PEEKING!

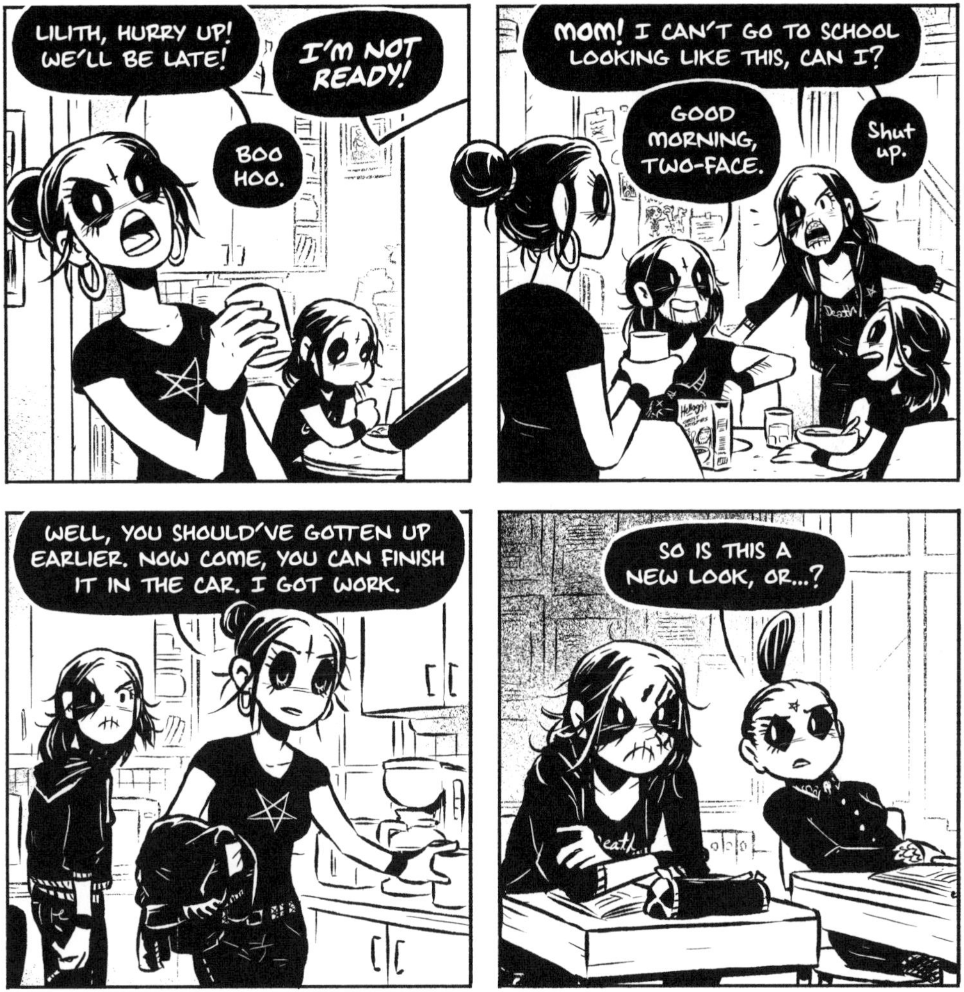
LILITH, HURRY UP! WE'LL BE LATE!
I'M NOT READY!
BOO HOO.
MOM! I CAN'T GO TO SCHOOL LOOKING LIKE THIS, CAN I?
GOOD MORNING, TWO-FACE.
Shut up.
WELL, YOU SHOULD'VE GOTTEN UP EARLIER. NOW COME, YOU CAN FINISH IT IN THE CAR. I GOT WORK.
SO IS THIS A NEW LOOK, OR...?

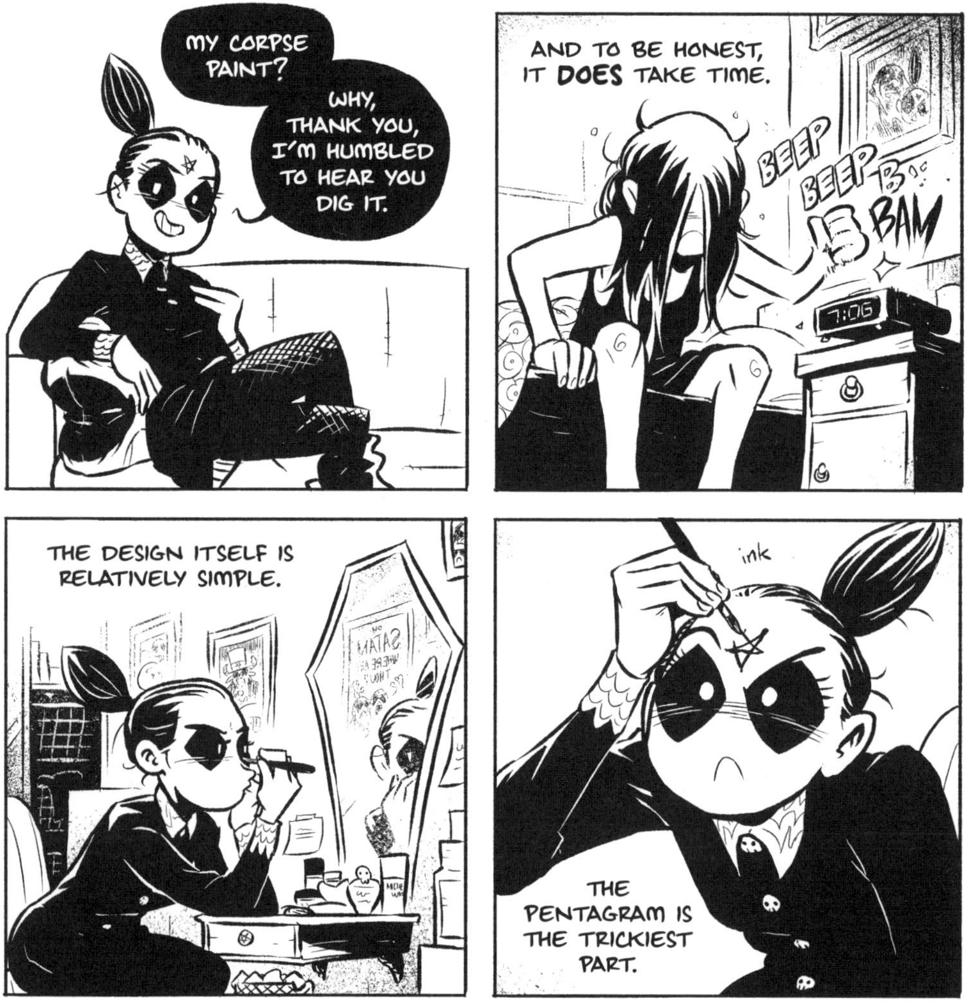
MY CORPSE PAINT?
WHY, THANK YOU, I'M HUMBLED TO HEAR YOU DIG IT.
AND TO BE HONEST, IT DOES TAKE TIME.
BEEP
BEEP
B
BAM
7:06
THE DESIGN ITSELF IS RELATIVELY SIMPLE.
ink
THE PENTAGRAM IS THE TRICKIEST PART.

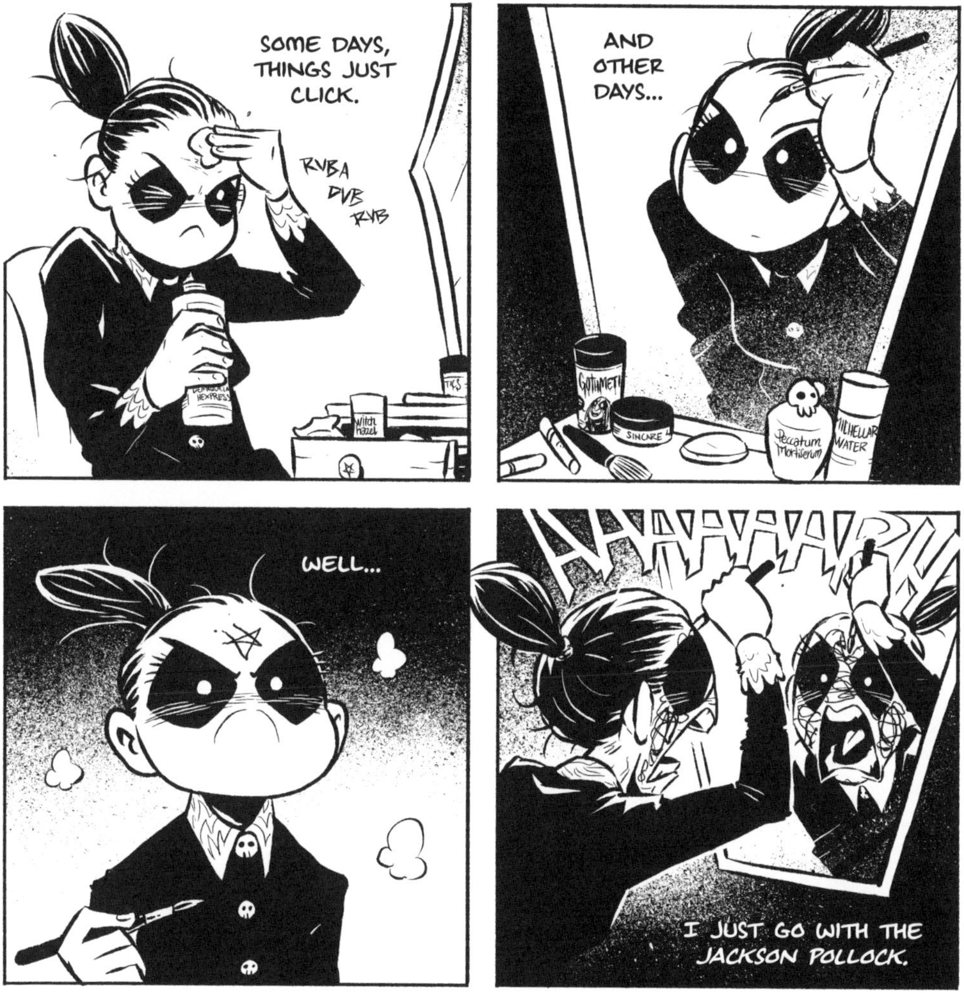
SOME DAYS, THINGS JUST CLICK.
RUBA DUB RUB
DERMASORIA HEXPRESS
Witch hazel
AND OTHER DAYS...
GOTHMETIC
SINCARE
Peccatum Mortiserum
MICHELLAR WATER
WELL...
I JUST GO WITH THE JACKSON POLLOCK.

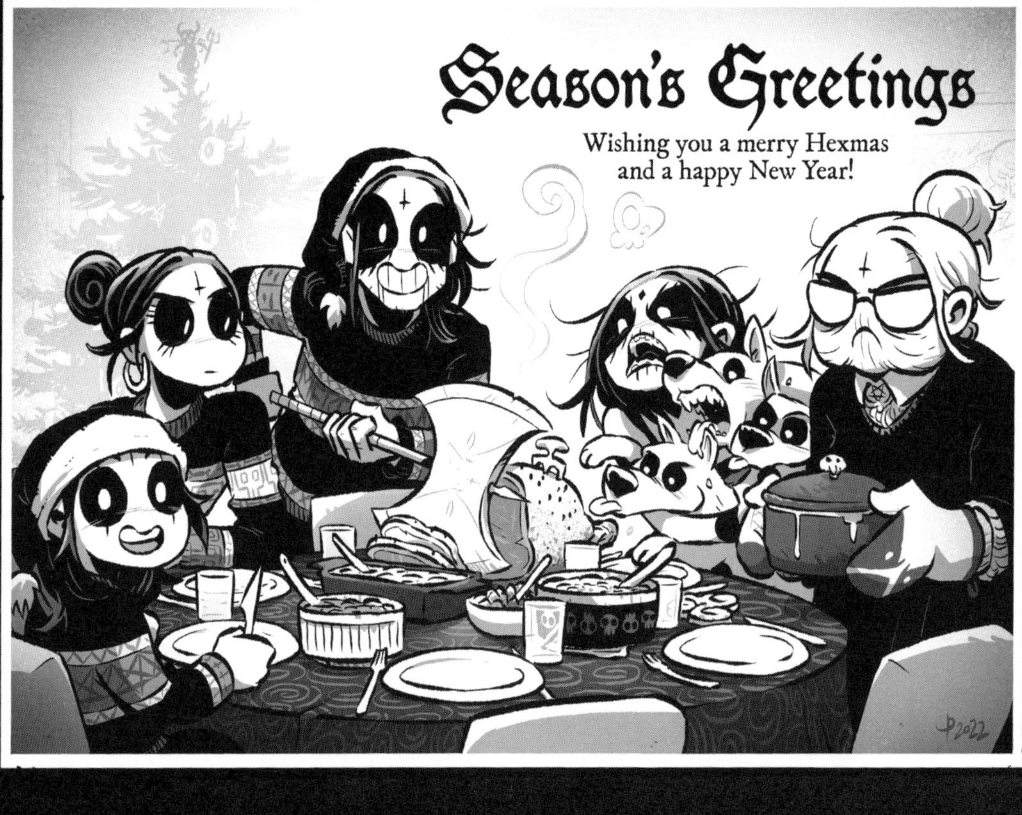
Season's Greetings
Wishing you a merry Hexmas
and a happy New Year!
2022

HEY, YOU HEAR THE NEWS YET, LUCY?

WE GOT TWO NEW **BIG** CLIENTS!

OH YEAH? WHO?

A WHISKY DISTILLERY, SHAKIRA FAUGH, AND—

CHAUGNAR FAUGN?!

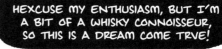

CHAUGNAR FAUGN'S SINGLE MALTS ARE LIKE THE **NECTAR** OF THE GREAT OLD ONES! THEIR SIGNATURE SMOKINESS IS ACHIEVED WITH BURNT CHURCH BEAMS!

THEIR QUARTER CASK ACTUALLY SET OFF OUR FIRE ALARMS!

HEXCUSE MY ENTHUSIASM, BUT I'M A BIT OF A WHISKY CONNOISSEUR, SO THIS IS A DREAM COME TRUE!

I CAN'T WAIT TO GET WORKING WITH THEM!

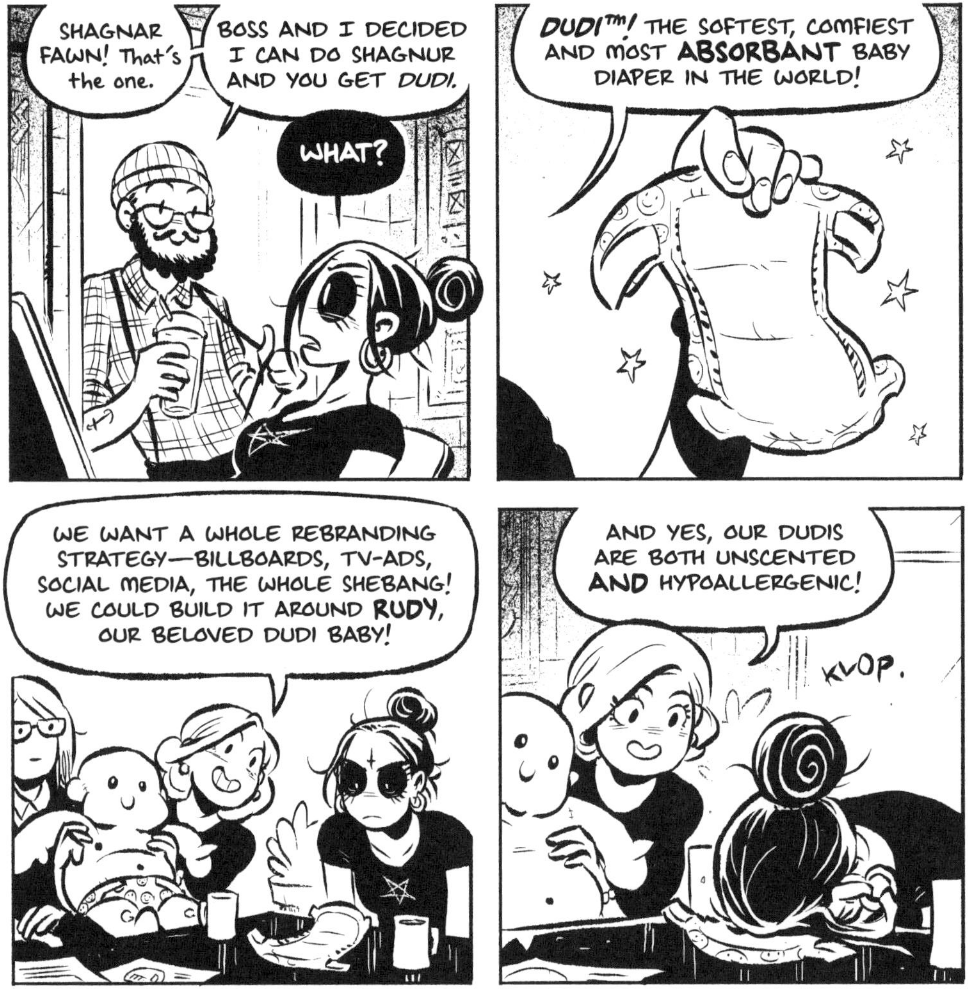
SHAGNAR FAWN! That's the one.
BOSS AND I DECIDED I CAN DO SHAGNUR AND YOU GET DUDI.
WHAT?
DUDI™! THE SOFTEST, COMFIEST AND MOST ABSORBANT BABY DIAPER IN THE WORLD!
WE WANT A WHOLE REBRANDING STRATEGY—BILLBOARDS, TV-ADS, SOCIAL MEDIA, THE WHOLE SHEBANG! WE COULD BUILD IT AROUND RUDY, OUR BELOVED DUDI BABY!
AND YES, OUR DUDIS ARE BOTH UNSCENTED AND HYPOALLERGENIC!
KLOP.

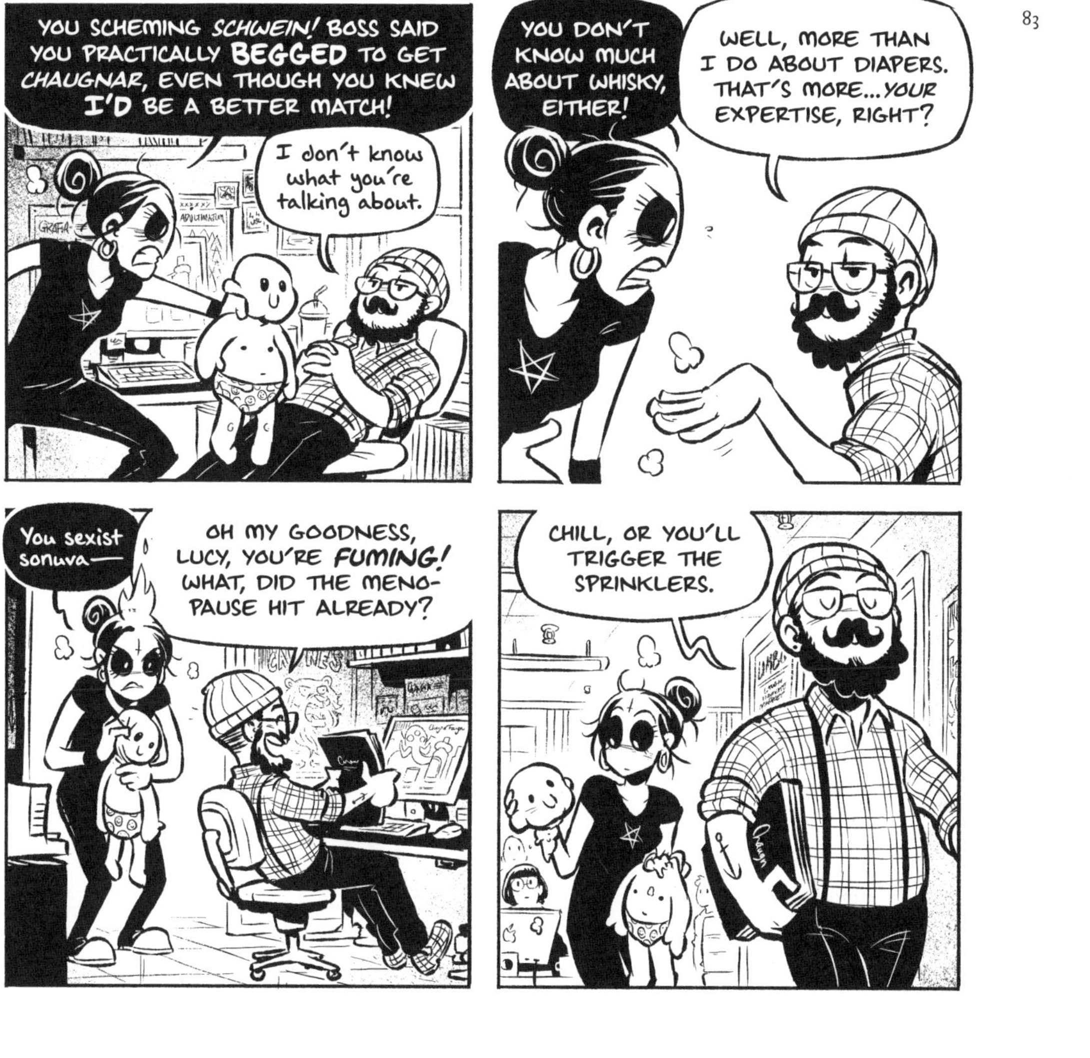
YOU SCHEMING SCHWEIN! BOSS SAID YOU PRACTICALLY BEGGED TO GET CHAUGNAR, EVEN THOUGH YOU KNEW I'D BE A BETTER MATCH!
I don't know what you're talking about.
YOU DON'T KNOW MUCH ABOUT WHISKY, EITHER!
WELL, MORE THAN I DO ABOUT DIAPERS. THAT'S MORE... YOUR EXPERTISE, RIGHT?
You sexist sonuva—
OH MY GOODNESS, LUCY, YOU'RE FUMING! WHAT, DID THE MENO-PAUSE HIT ALREADY?
CHILL, OR YOU'LL TRIGGER THE SPRINKLERS.

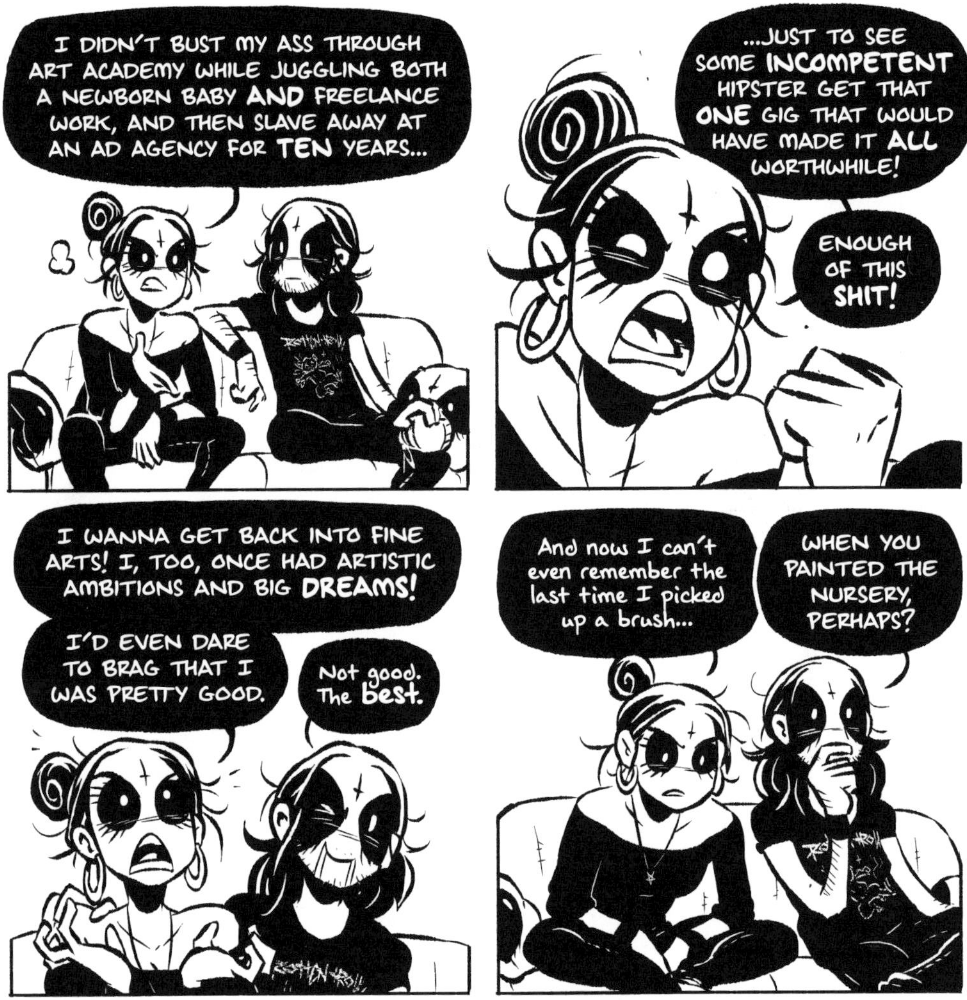
I DIDN'T BUST MY ASS THROUGH ART ACADEMY WHILE JUGGLING BOTH A NEWBORN BABY **AND** FREELANCE WORK, AND THEN SLAVE AWAY AT AN AD AGENCY FOR **TEN** YEARS...
...JUST TO SEE SOME **INCOMPETENT** HIPSTER GET THAT **ONE** GIG THAT WOULD HAVE MADE IT **ALL** WORTHWHILE!
ENOUGH OF THIS **SHIT**!
I WANNA GET BACK INTO FINE ARTS! I, TOO, ONCE HAD ARTISTIC AMBITIONS AND BIG **DREAMS**!
I'D EVEN DARE TO BRAG THAT I WAS PRETTY GOOD.
Not good. The **best**.
And now I can't even remember the last time I picked up a brush...
WHEN YOU PAINTED THE NURSERY, PERHAPS?

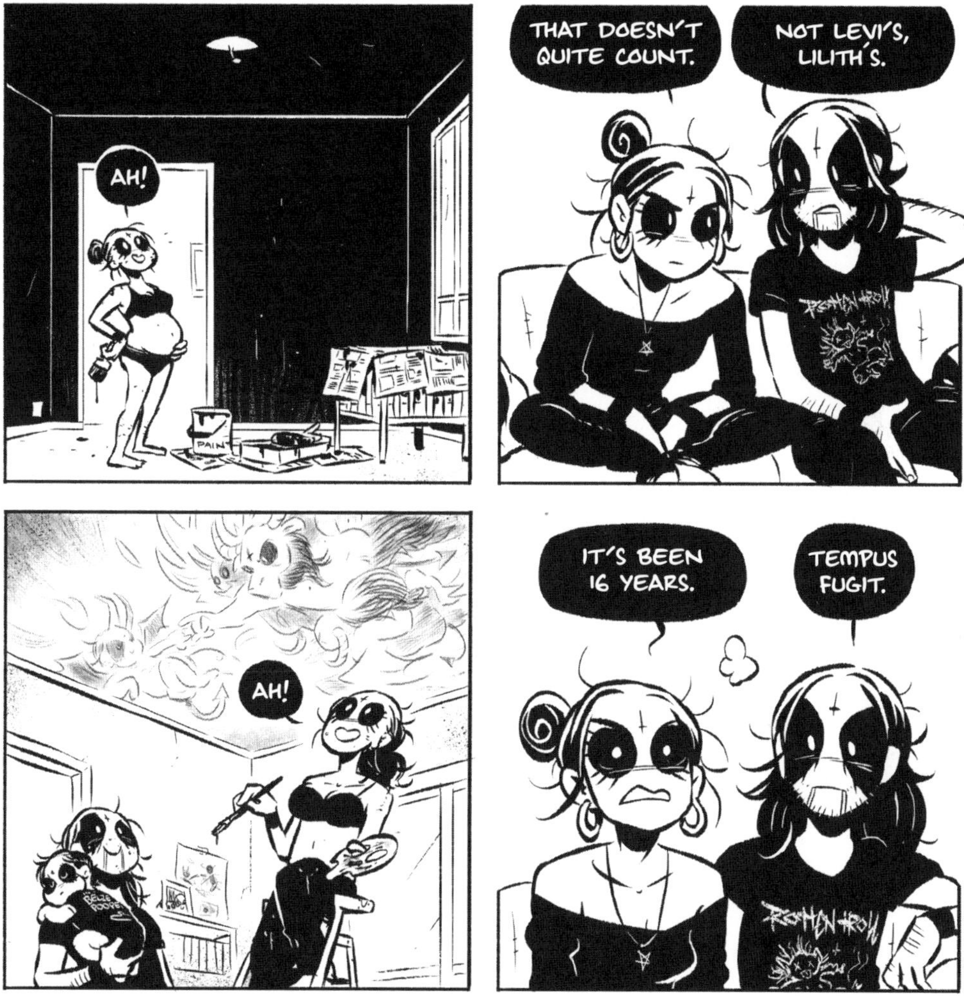
AH!
THAT DOESN'T QUITE COUNT.
NOT LEVI'S, LILITH'S.
AH!
IT'S BEEN 16 YEARS.
TEMPUS FUGIT.

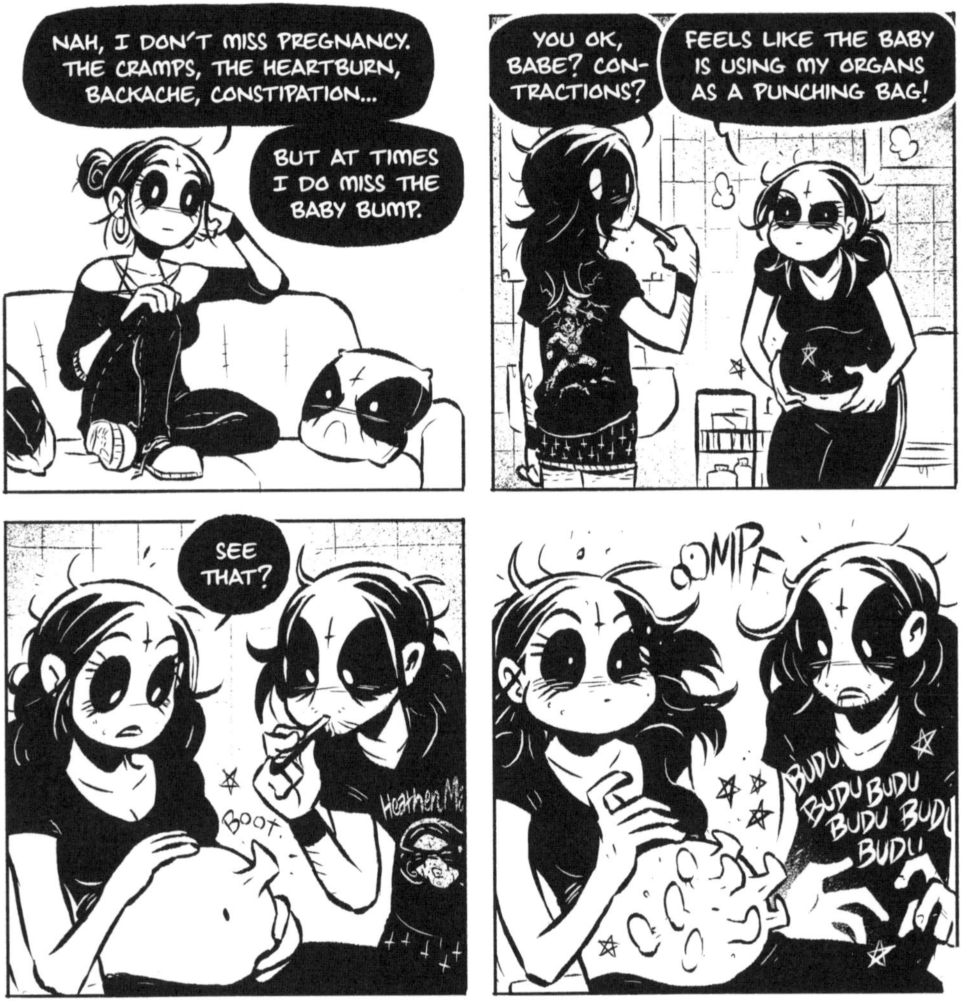
NAH, I DON'T MISS PREGNANCY. THE CRAMPS, THE HEARTBURN, BACKACHE, CONSTIPATION...
BUT AT TIMES I DO MISS THE BABY BUMP.
YOU OK, BABE? CONTRACTIONS?
FEELS LIKE THE BABY IS USING MY ORGANS AS A PUNCHING BAG!
SEE THAT?
BOOT.
OOMPF
BUDU BUDU BUDU BUDU BUDU BUDU

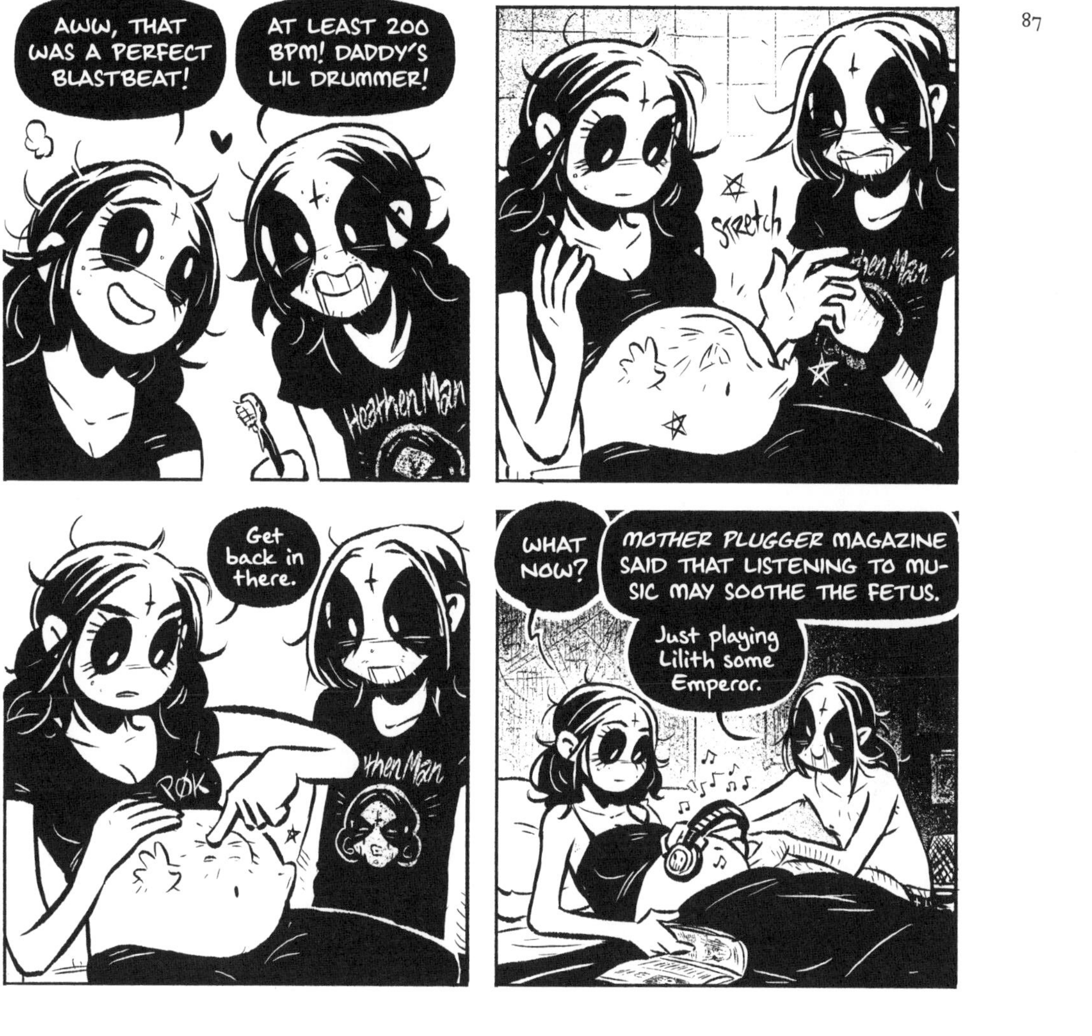
AWW, THAT WAS A PERFECT BLASTBEAT!
AT LEAST 200 BPM! DADDY'S LIL DRUMMER!
Heathen Man
stretch
Get back in there.
PØK
WHAT NOW?
MOTHER PLUGGER MAGAZINE SAID THAT LISTENING TO MU-SIC MAY SOOTHE THE FETUS.
Just playing Lilith some Emperor.

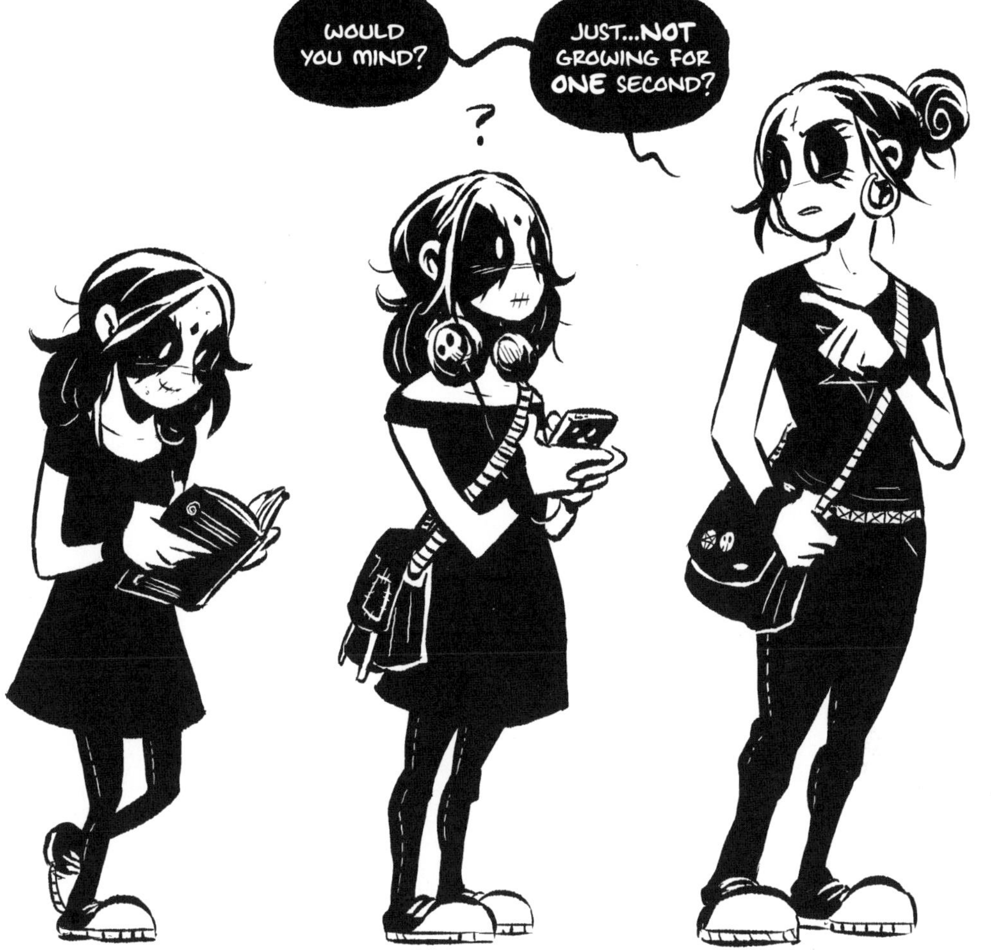
WOULD YOU MIND?
JUST...NOT GROWING FOR ONE SECOND?
?

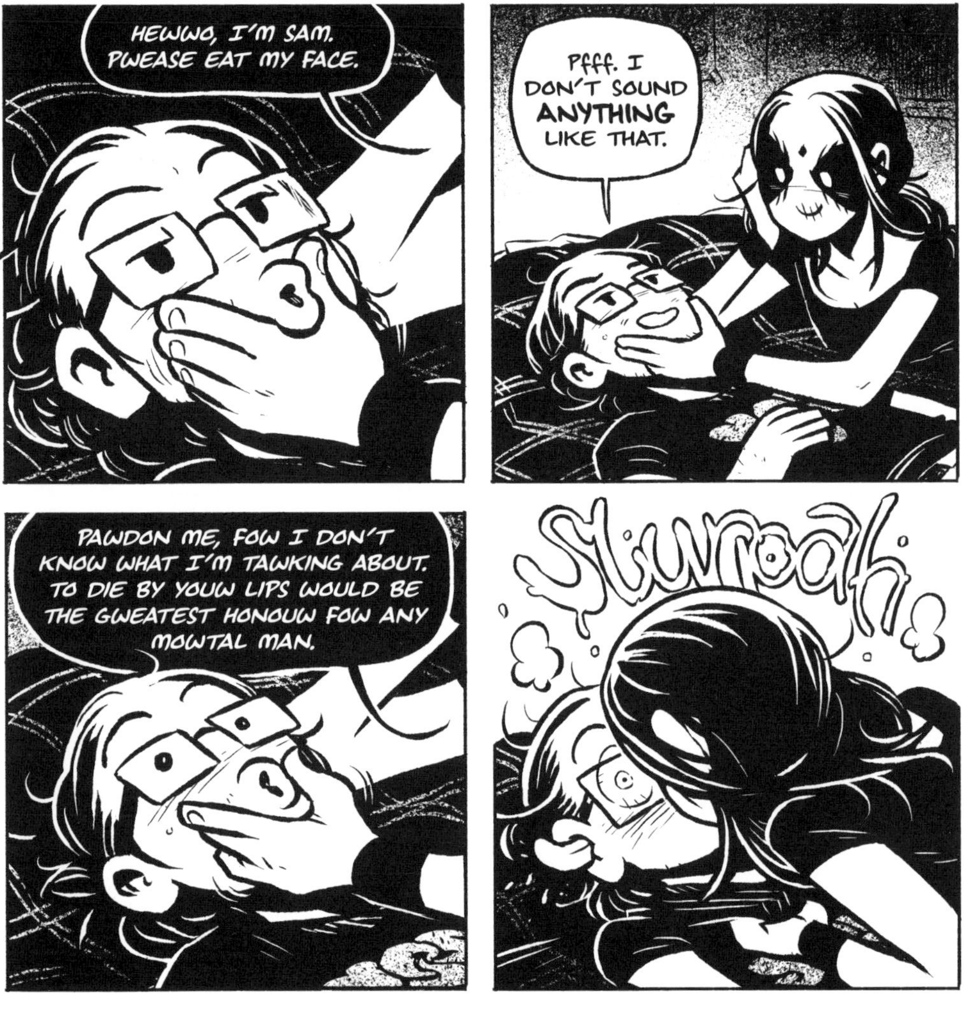
HEWWO, I'M SAM. PWEASE EAT MY FACE.
Pfff. I DON'T SOUND **ANYTHING** LIKE THAT.
PAWDON ME, FOW I DON'T KNOW WHAT I'M TAWKING ABOUT. TO DIE BY YOUW LIPS WOULD BE THE GWEATEST HONOUW FOW ANY MOWTAL MAN.
Sluurpah

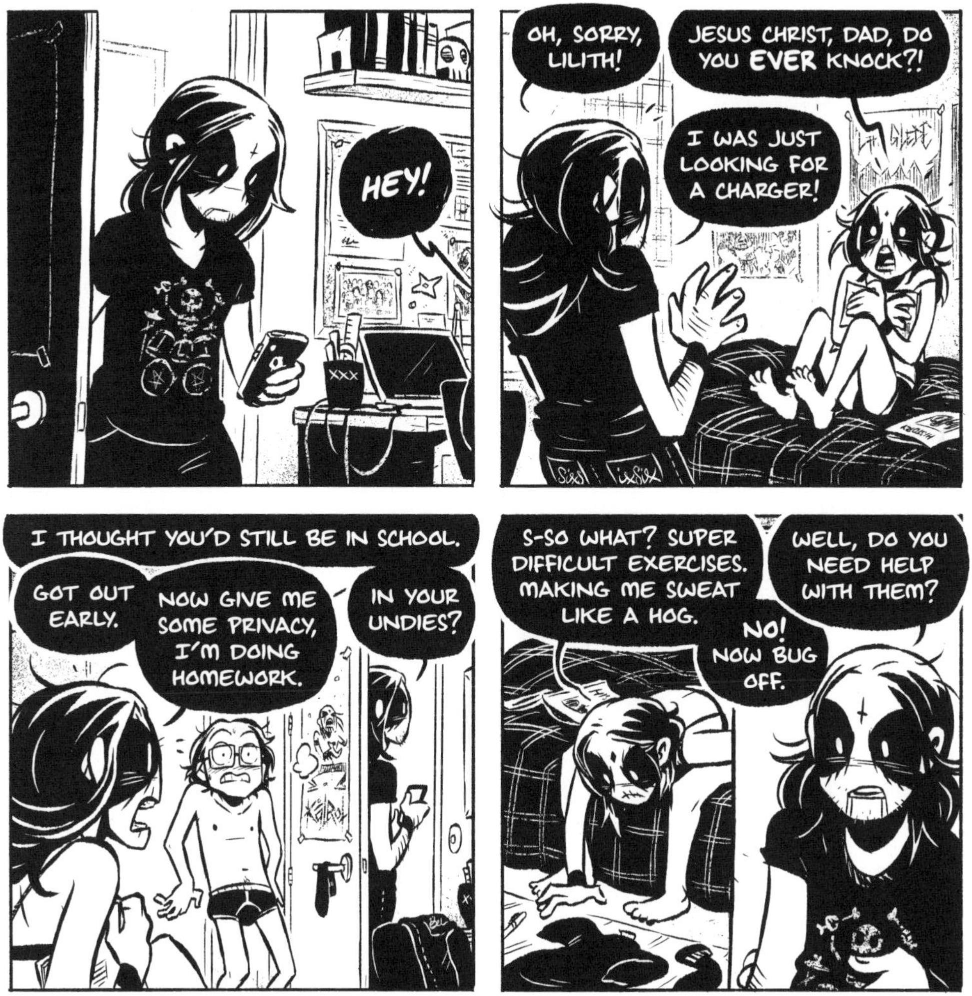
HEY!
OH, SORRY, LILITH!
JESUS CHRIST, DAD, DO YOU **EVER** KNOCK?!
I WAS JUST LOOKING FOR A CHARGER!
I THOUGHT YOU'D STILL BE IN SCHOOL.
GOT OUT EARLY.
NOW GIVE ME SOME PRIVACY, I'M DOING HOMEWORK.
IN YOUR UNDIES?
S-SO WHAT? SUPER DIFFICULT EXERCISES. MAKING ME SWEAT LIKE A HOG.
WELL, DO YOU NEED HELP WITH THEM?
NO! NOW BUG OFF.

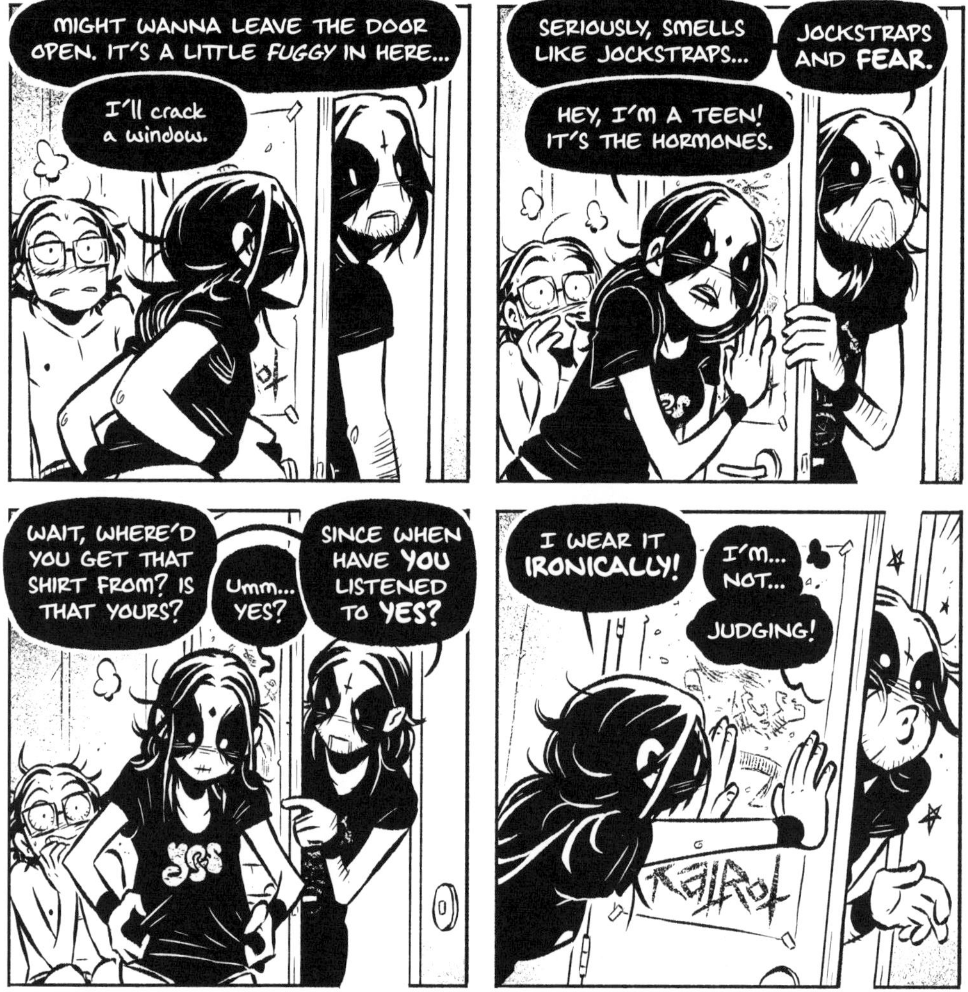
MIGHT WANNA LEAVE THE DOOR OPEN. IT'S A LITTLE *FUGGY* IN HERE...
I'll crack a window.
SERIOUSLY, SMELLS LIKE JOCKSTRAPS...
JOCKSTRAPS AND **FEAR.**
HEY, I'M A TEEN! IT'S THE HORMONES.
WAIT, WHERE'D YOU GET THAT SHIRT FROM? IS THAT YOURS?
Umm... YES?
SINCE WHEN HAVE **YOU** LISTENED TO **YES?**
YES
I WEAR IT **IRONICALLY!**
I'M... NOT... JUDGING!

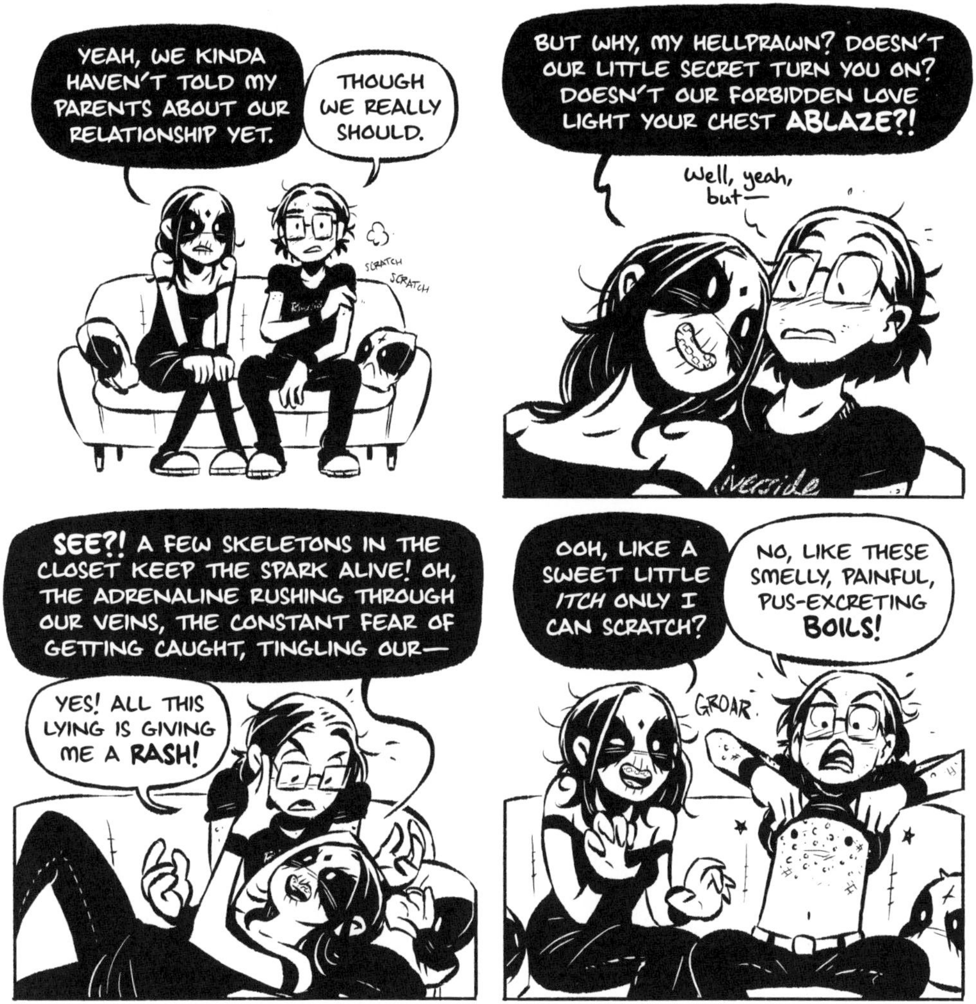
YEAH, WE KINDA HAVEN'T TOLD MY PARENTS ABOUT OUR RELATIONSHIP YET.
THOUGH WE REALLY SHOULD.
SCRATCH SCRATCH
BUT WHY, MY HELLPRAWN? DOESN'T OUR LITTLE SECRET TURN YOU ON? DOESN'T OUR FORBIDDEN LOVE LIGHT YOUR CHEST ABLAZE?!
Well, yeah, but—
SEE?! A FEW SKELETONS IN THE CLOSET KEEP THE SPARK ALIVE! OH, THE ADRENALINE RUSHING THROUGH OUR VEINS, THE CONSTANT FEAR OF GETTING CAUGHT, TINGLING OUR—
YES! ALL THIS LYING IS GIVING ME A RASH!
OOH, LIKE A SWEET LITTLE ITCH ONLY I CAN SCRATCH?
NO, LIKE THESE SMELLY, PAINFUL, PUS-EXCRETING BOILS!
GROAR

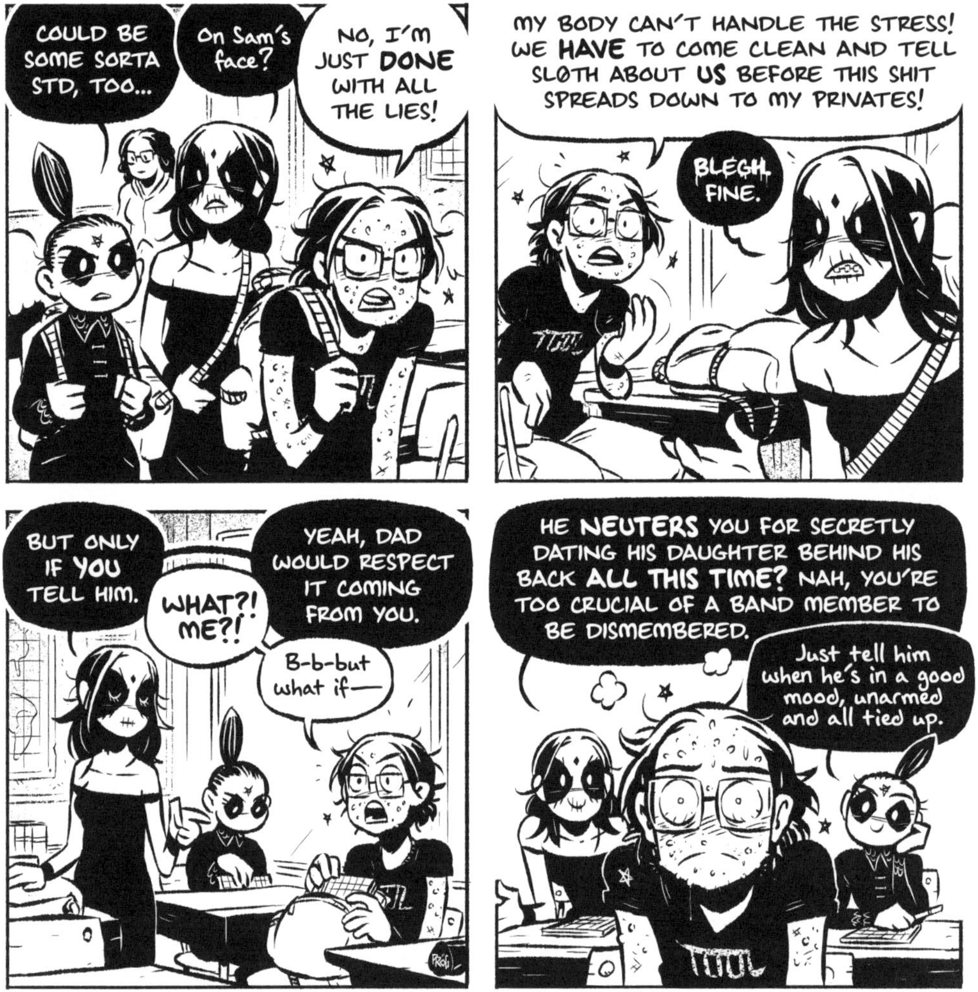
COULD BE SOME SORTA STD, TOO...
On Sam's face?
NO, I'M JUST DONE WITH ALL THE LIES!
MY BODY CAN'T HANDLE THE STRESS! WE HAVE TO COME CLEAN AND TELL SLOTH ABOUT US BEFORE THIS SHIT SPREADS DOWN TO MY PRIVATES!
BLEGH. FINE.
BUT ONLY IF YOU TELL HIM.
WHAT?! ME?!
YEAH, DAD WOULD RESPECT IT COMING FROM YOU.
B-b-but what if—
HE NEUTERS YOU FOR SECRETLY DATING HIS DAUGHTER BEHIND HIS BACK ALL THIS TIME? NAH, YOU'RE TOO CRUCIAL OF A BAND MEMBER TO BE DISMEMBERED.
Just tell him when he's in a good mood, unarmed and all tied up.

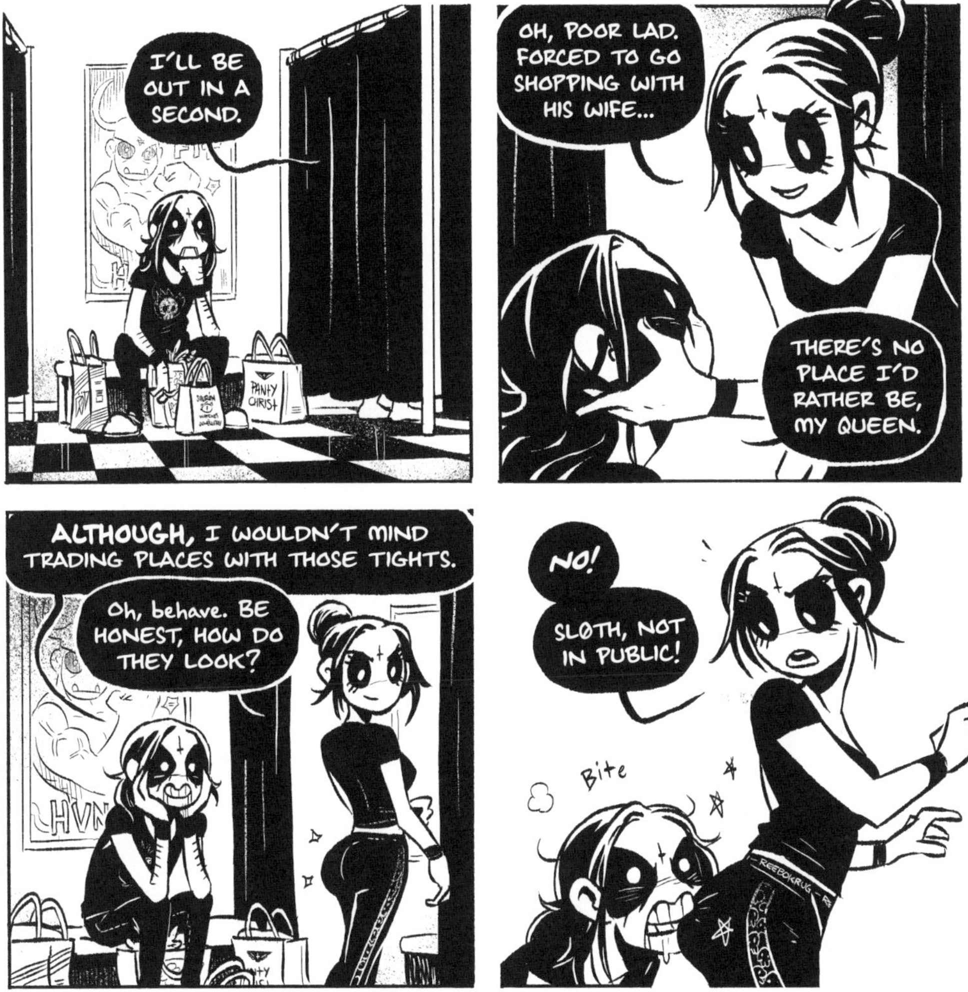
I'LL BE OUT IN A SECOND.
OH, POOR LAD. FORCED TO GO SHOPPING WITH HIS WIFE...
THERE'S NO PLACE I'D RATHER BE, MY QUEEN.
ALTHOUGH, I WOULDN'T MIND TRADING PLACES WITH THOSE TIGHTS.
Oh, behave. BE HONEST, HOW DO THEY LOOK?
NO!
SLØTH, NOT IN PUBLIC!
Bite

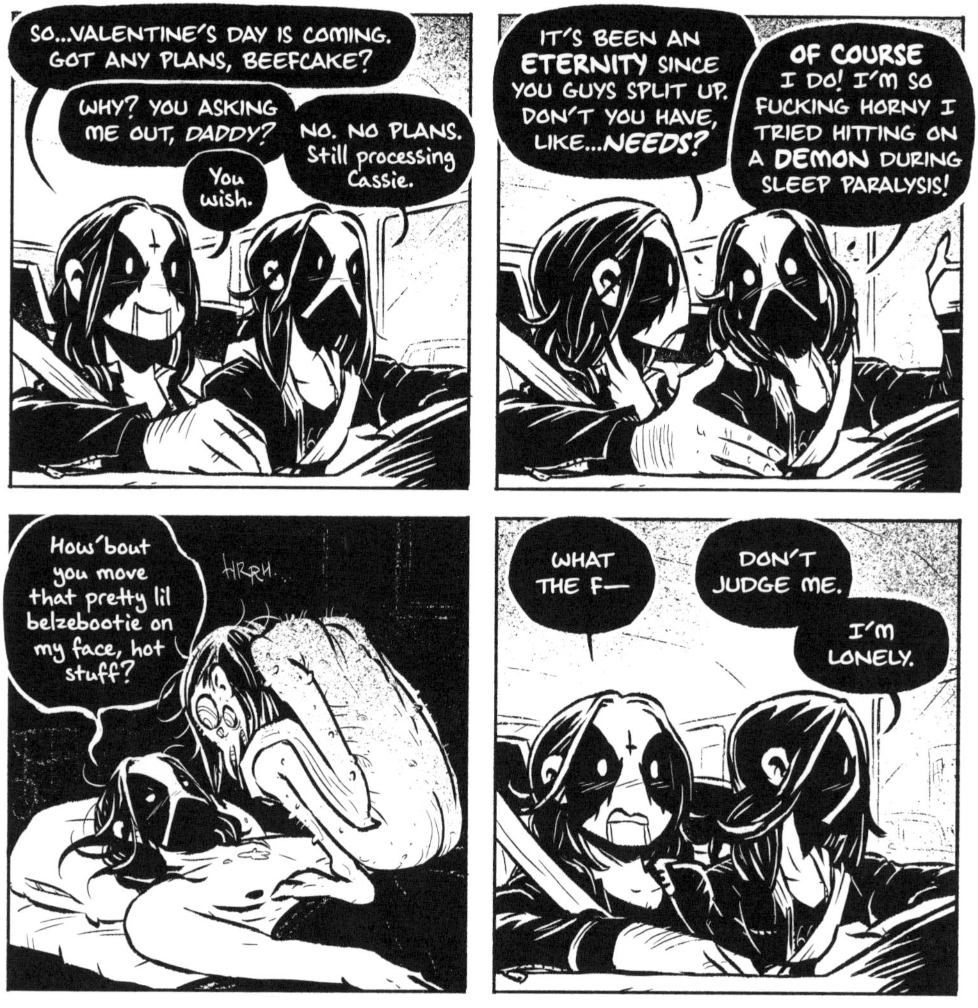
SO...VALENTINE'S DAY IS COMING. GOT ANY PLANS, BEEFCAKE?
WHY? YOU ASKING ME OUT, DADDY?
You wish.
NO. NO PLANS. Still processing Cassie.
IT'S BEEN AN ETERNITY SINCE YOU GUYS SPLIT UP. DON'T YOU HAVE, LIKE...NEEDS?
OF COURSE I DO! I'M SO FUCKING HORNY I TRIED HITTING ON A DEMON DURING SLEEP PARALYSIS!
How'bout you move that pretty lil belzebootie on my face, hot stuff?
HRRH...
WHAT THE F—
DON'T JUDGE ME.
I'M LONELY.

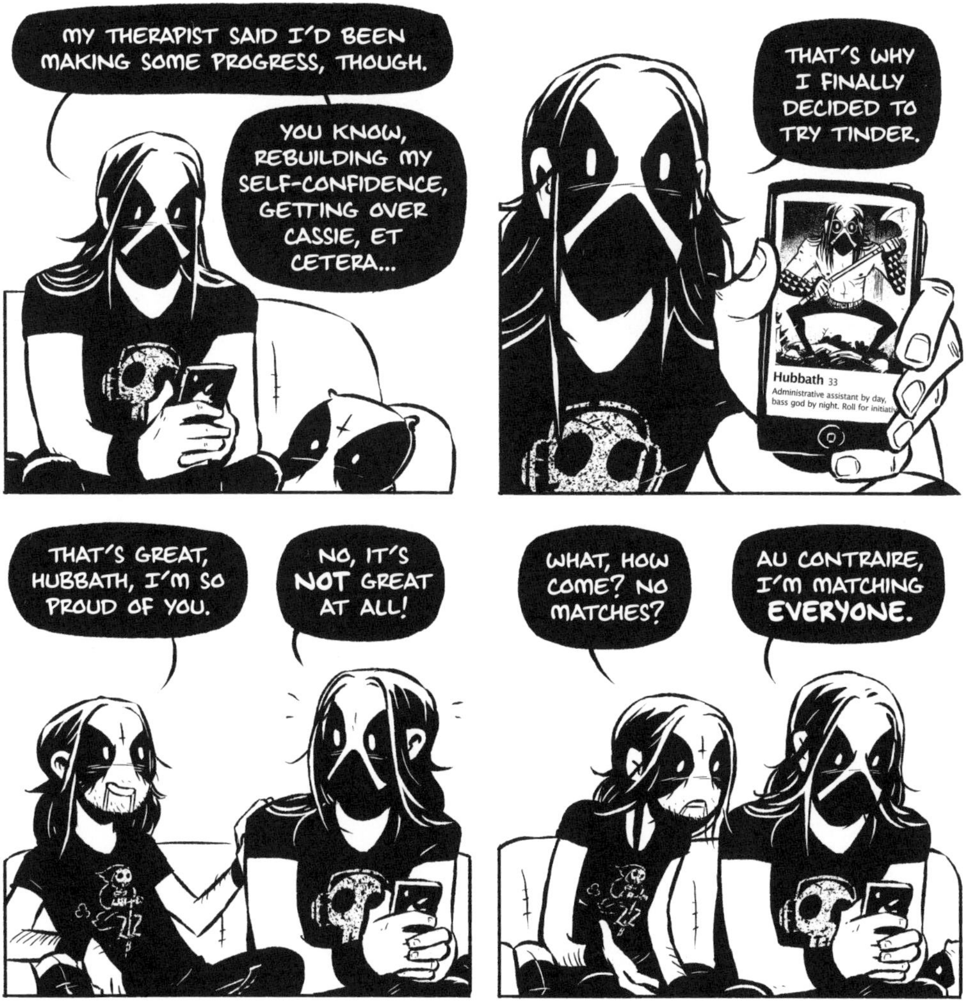
MY THERAPIST SAID I'D BEEN MAKING SOME PROGRESS, THOUGH.
YOU KNOW, REBUILDING MY SELF-CONFIDENCE, GETTING OVER CASSIE, ET CETERA...
THAT'S WHY I FINALLY DECIDED TO TRY TINDER.
Hubbath 33
Administrative assistant by day, bass god by night. Roll for initiativ
THAT'S GREAT, HUBBATH, I'M SO PROUD OF YOU.
NO, IT'S **NOT** GREAT AT ALL!
WHAT, HOW COME? NO MATCHES?
AU CONTRAIRE, I'M MATCHING **EVERYONE.**

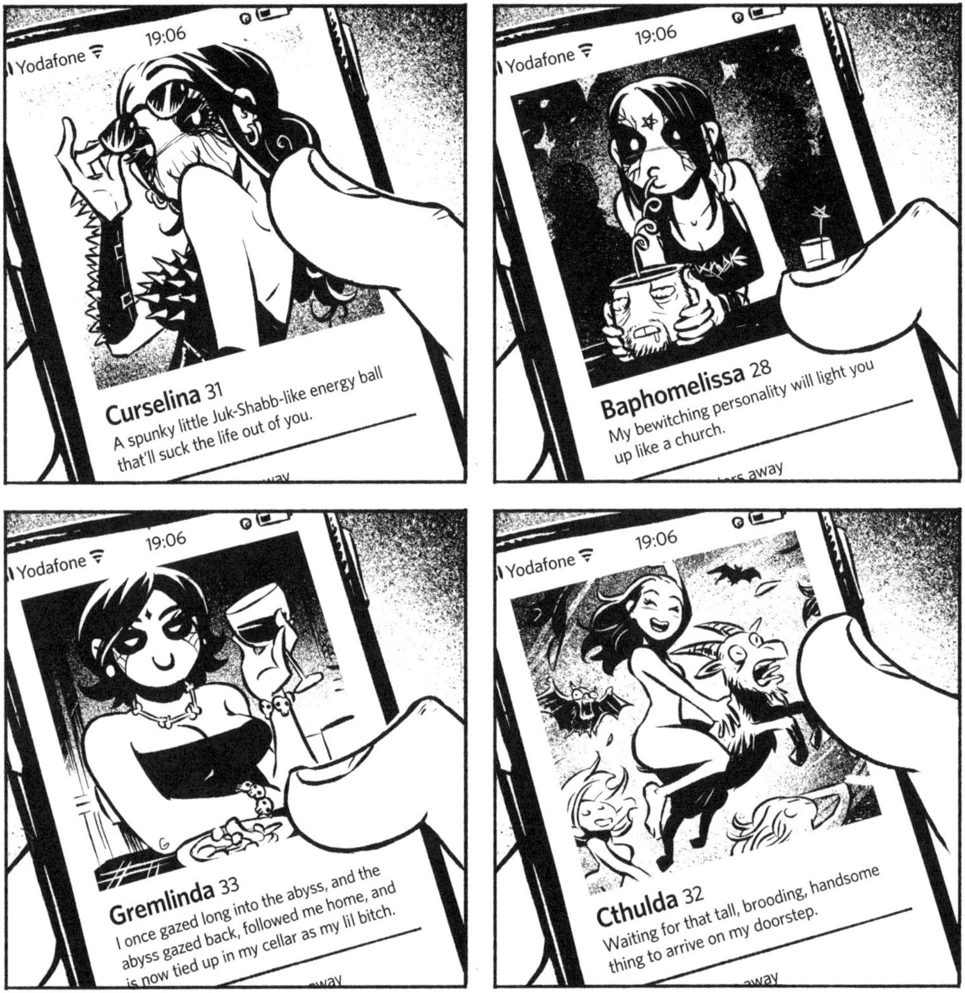

Yodafone
19:06
Curselina 31
A spunky little Juk-Shabb-like energy ball that'll suck the life out of you.
Yodafone
19:06
Baphomelissa 28
My bewitching personality will light you up like a church.
away
Yodafone
19:06
Gremlinda 33
I once gazed long into the abyss, and the abyss gazed back, followed me home, and is now tied up in my cellar as my lil bitch.
away
Yodafone
19:06
Cthulda 32
Waiting for that tall, brooding, handsome thing to arrive on my doorstep.
away

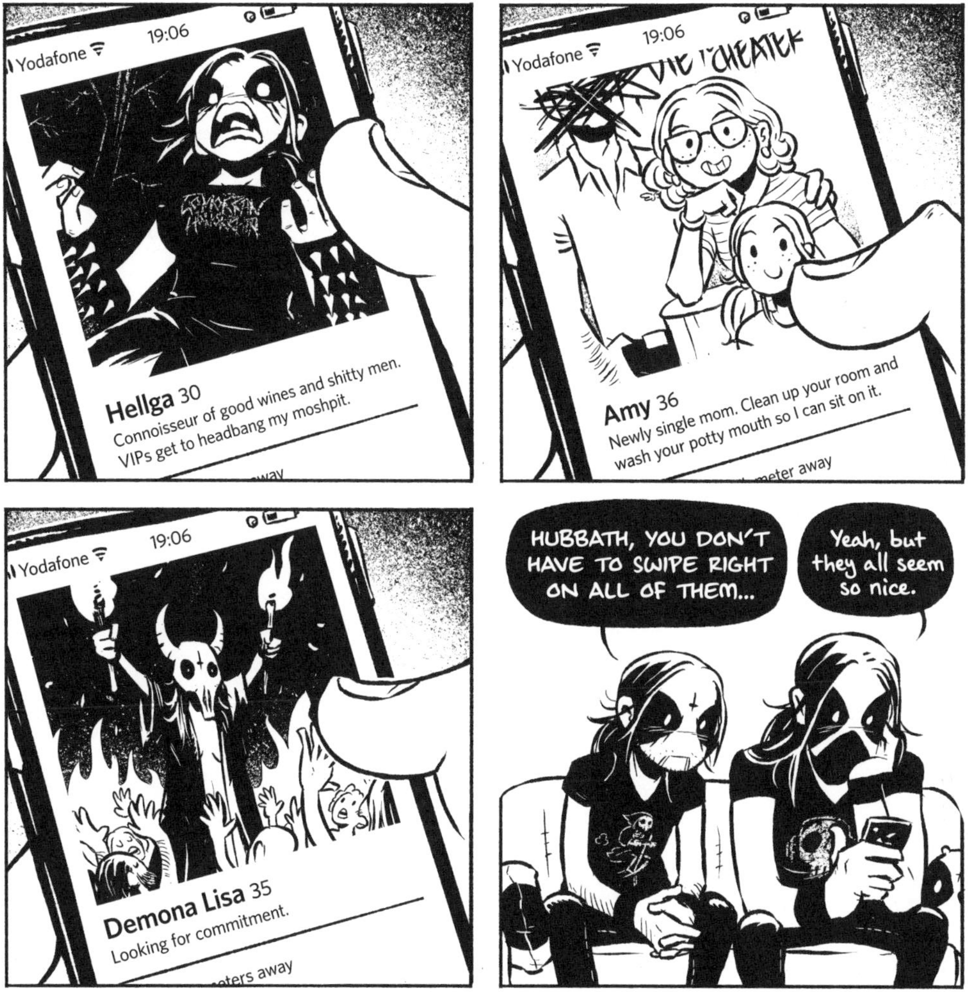
Yodafone
19:06
Hellga 30
Connoisseur of good wines and shitty men.
VIPs get to headbang my moshpit.
Yodafone
19:06
Amy 36
Newly single mom. Clean up your room and
wash your potty mouth so I can sit on it.
Yodafone
19:06
Demona Lisa 35
Looking for commitment.
HUBBATH, YOU DON'T HAVE TO SWIPE RIGHT ON ALL OF THEM...
Yeah, but they all seem so nice.

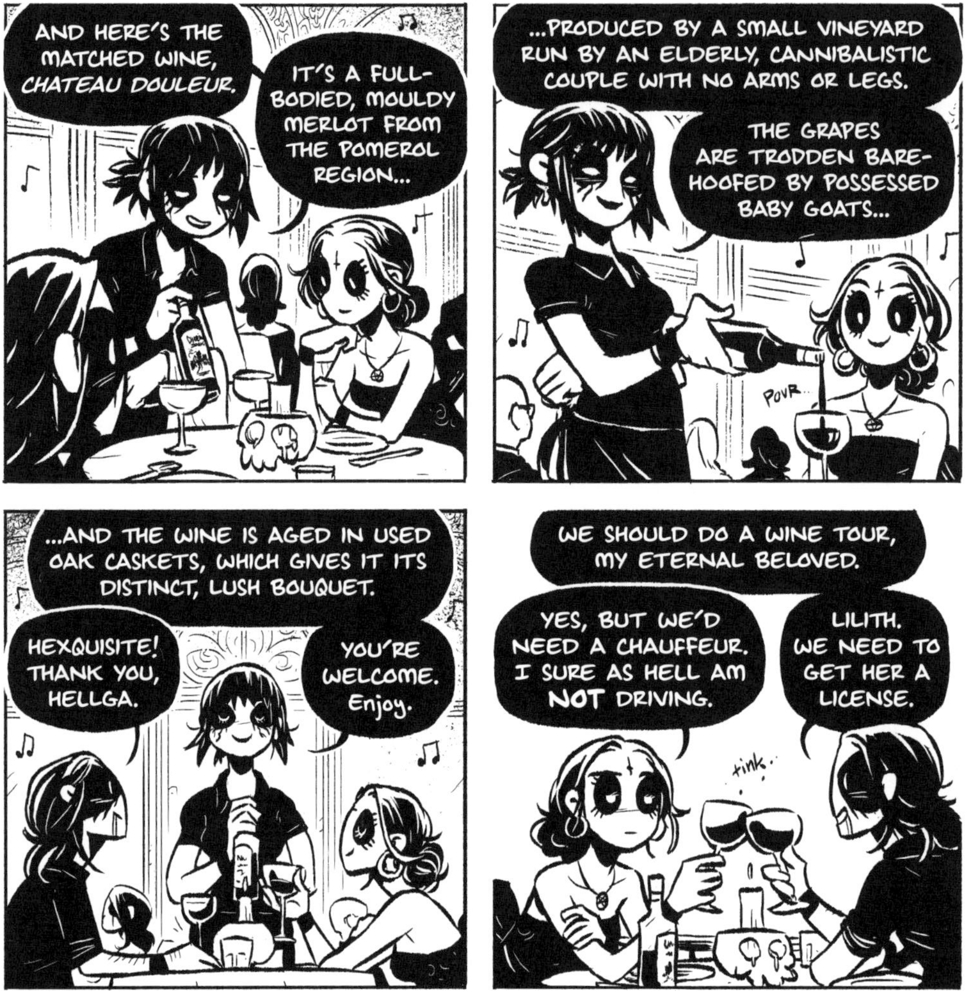
AND HERE'S THE MATCHED WINE, CHATEAU DOULEUR.
IT'S A FULL-BODIED, MOULDY MERLOT FROM THE POMEROL REGION...
...PRODUCED BY A SMALL VINEYARD RUN BY AN ELDERLY, CANNIBALISTIC COUPLE WITH NO ARMS OR LEGS.
THE GRAPES ARE TRODDEN BARE-HOOFED BY POSSESSED BABY GOATS...
POUR..
...AND THE WINE IS AGED IN USED OAK CASKETS, WHICH GIVES IT ITS DISTINCT, LUSH BOUQUET.
HEXQUISITE! THANK YOU, HELLGA.
YOU'RE WELCOME. Enjoy.
WE SHOULD DO A WINE TOUR, MY ETERNAL BELOVED.
YES, BUT WE'D NEED A CHAUFFEUR. I SURE AS HELL AM NOT DRIVING.
LILITH. WE NEED TO GET HER A LICENSE.
tink..

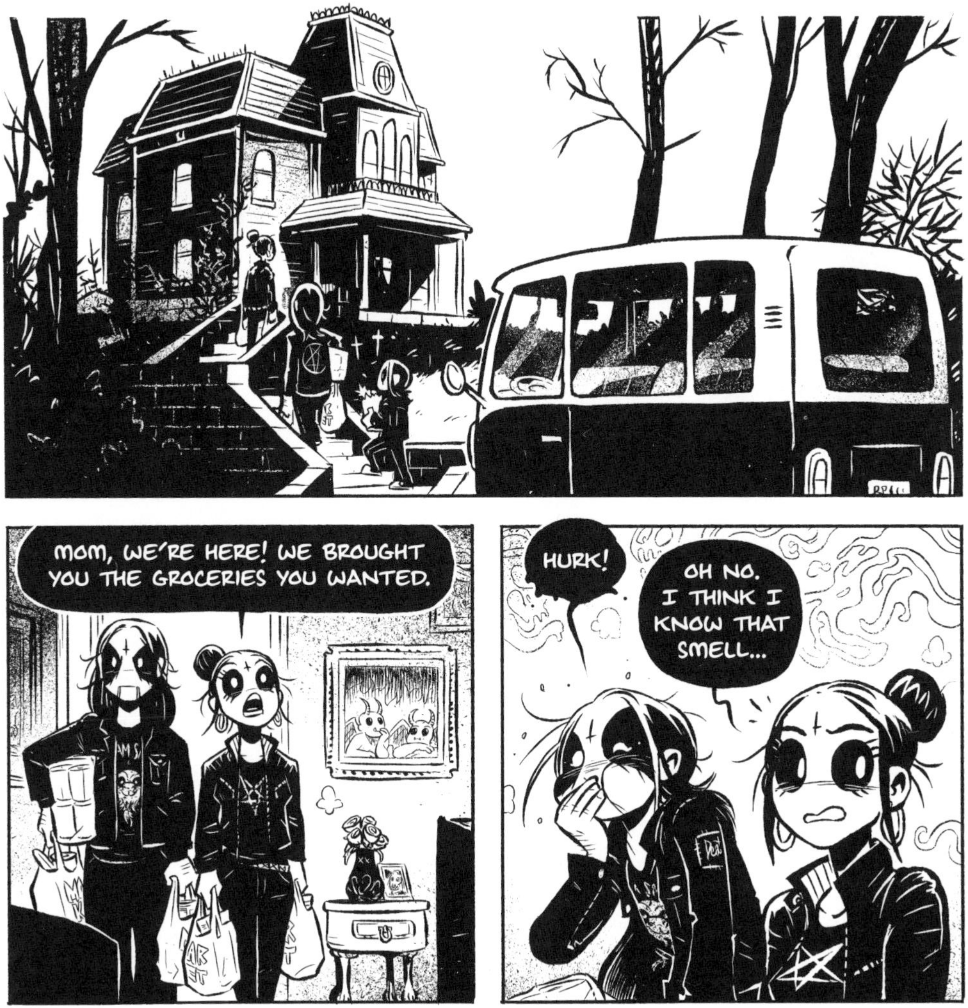
MOM, WE'RE HERE! WE BROUGHT YOU THE GROCERIES YOU WANTED.
HURK!
OH NO. I THINK I KNOW THAT SMELL...

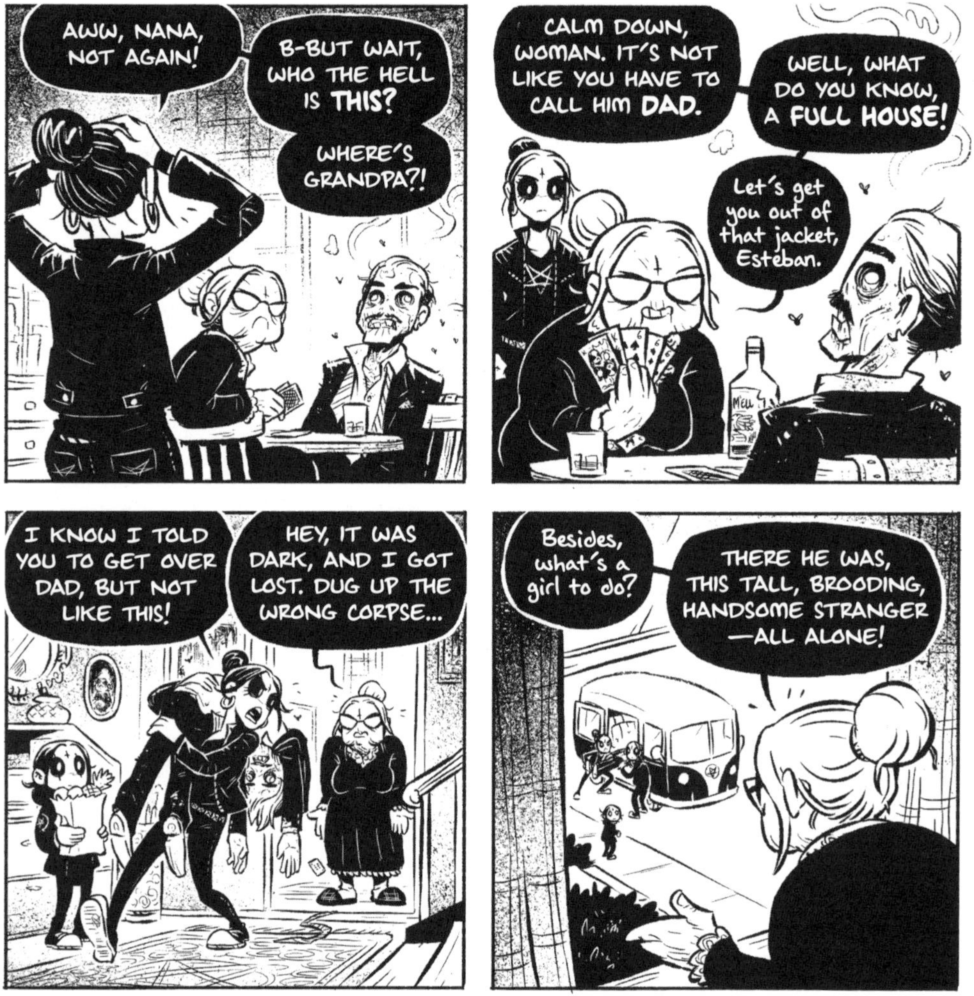
AWW, NANA, NOT AGAIN!
B-BUT WAIT, WHO THE HELL IS THIS?
WHERE'S GRANDPA?!
CALM DOWN, WOMAN. IT'S NOT LIKE YOU HAVE TO CALL HIM DAD.
WELL, WHAT DO YOU KNOW, A FULL HOUSE!
Let's get you out of that jacket, Esteban.
I KNOW I TOLD YOU TO GET OVER DAD, BUT NOT LIKE THIS!
HEY, IT WAS DARK, AND I GOT LOST. DUG UP THE WRONG CORPSE...
Besides, what's a girl to do?
THERE HE WAS, THIS TALL, BROODING, HANDSOME STRANGER—ALL ALONE!

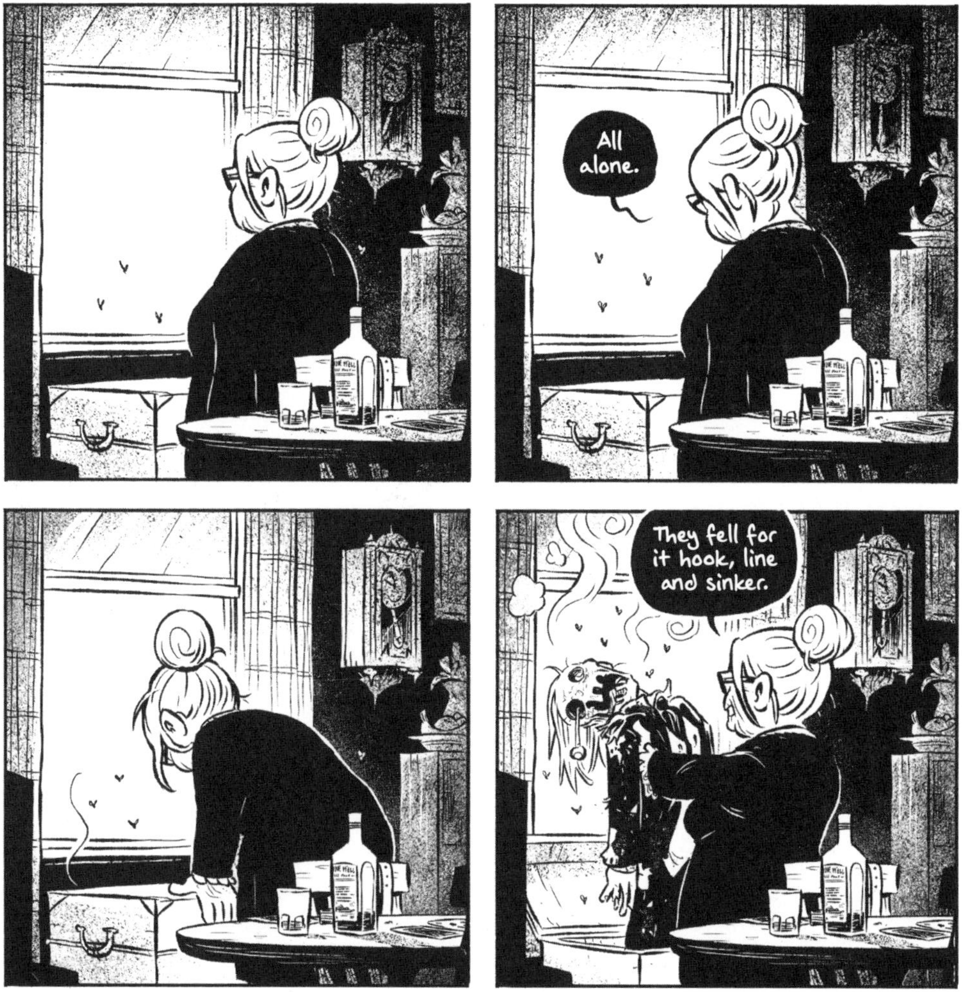
All alone.
They fell for it hook, line and sinker.

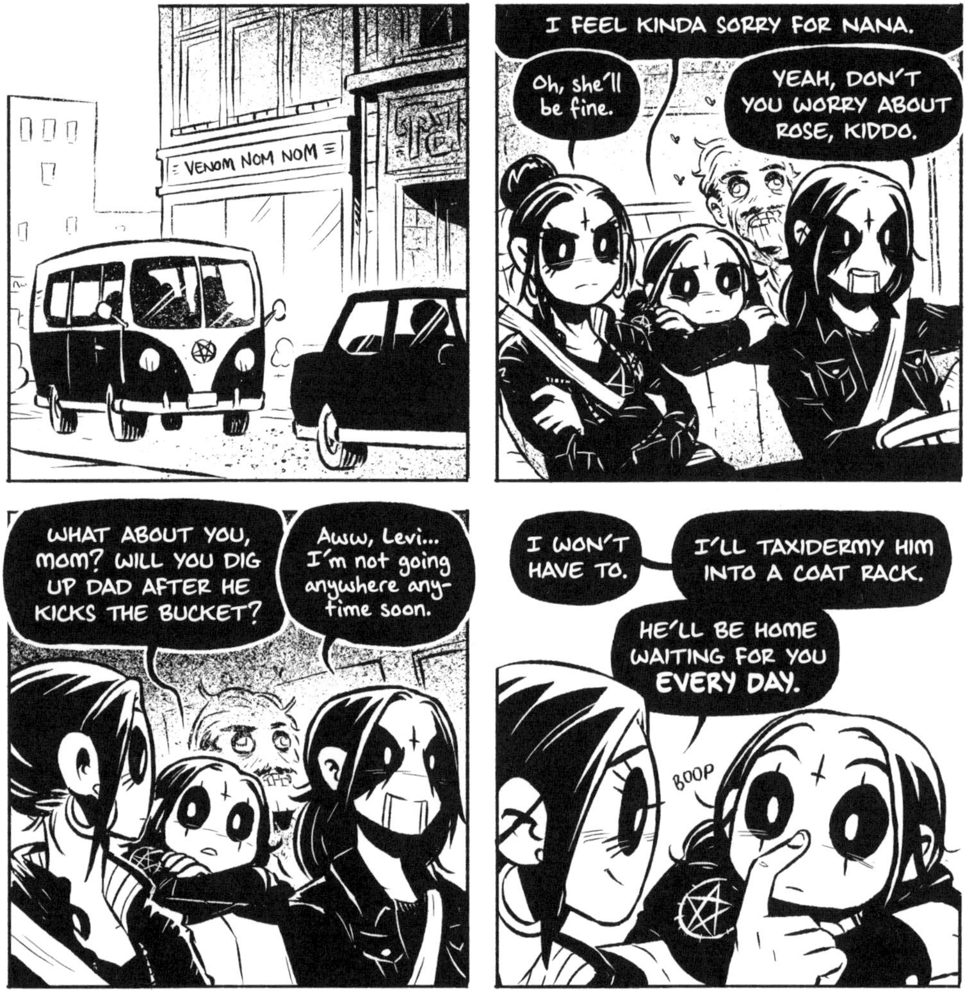

VENOM NOM NOM
I FEEL KINDA SORRY FOR NANA.
Oh, she'll be fine.
YEAH, DON'T YOU WORRY ABOUT ROSE, KIDDO.
WHAT ABOUT YOU, MOM? WILL YOU DIG UP DAD AFTER HE KICKS THE BUCKET?
Aww, Levi... I'm not going anywhere any-time soon.
I WON'T HAVE TO.
I'LL TAXIDERMY HIM INTO A COAT RACK.
HE'LL BE HOME WAITING FOR YOU EVERY DAY.
BOOP

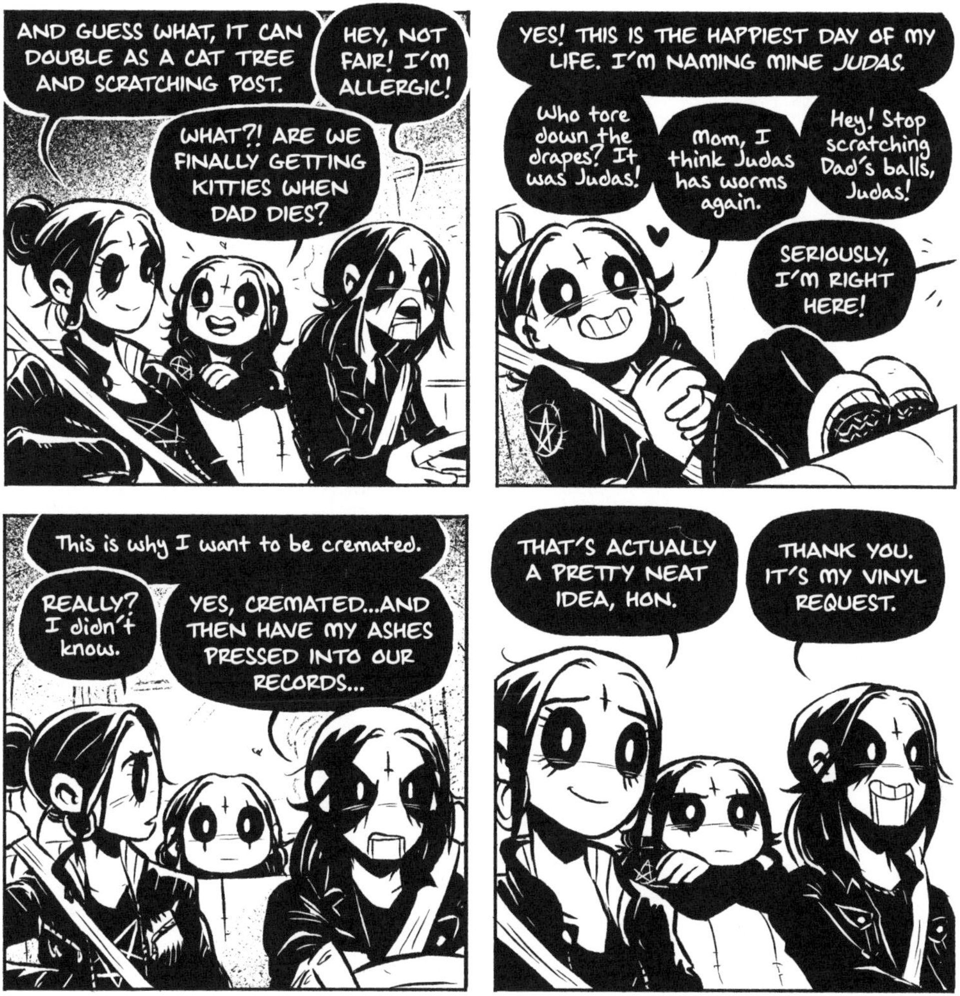
AND GUESS WHAT, IT CAN DOUBLE AS A CAT TREE AND SCRATCHING POST.
HEY, NOT FAIR! I'M ALLERGIC!
WHAT?! ARE WE FINALLY GETTING KITTIES WHEN DAD DIES?
YES! THIS IS THE HAPPIEST DAY OF MY LIFE. I'M NAMING MINE JUDAS.
Who tore down the drapes? It was Judas!
Mom, I think Judas has worms again.
Hey! Stop scratching Dad's balls, Judas!
SERIOUSLY, I'M RIGHT HERE!
This is why I want to be cremated.
REALLY? I didn't know.
YES, CREMATED...AND THEN HAVE MY ASHES PRESSED INTO OUR RECORDS...
THAT'S ACTUALLY A PRETTY NEAT IDEA, HON.
THANK YOU. IT'S MY VINYL REQUEST.

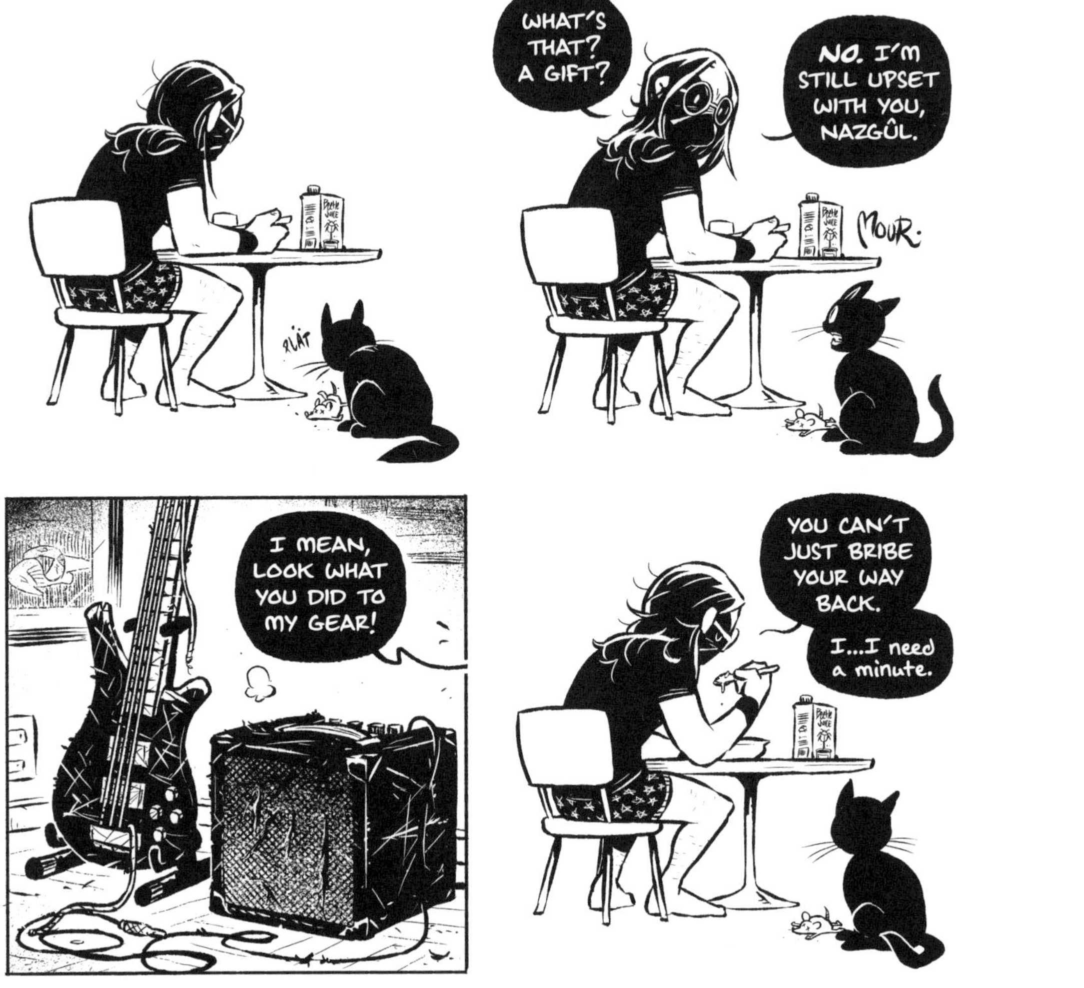
WHAT'S THAT? A GIFT?
NO. I'M STILL UPSET WITH YOU, NAZGÛL.
MOUR.
I MEAN, LOOK WHAT YOU DID TO MY GEAR!
YOU CAN'T JUST BRIBE YOUR WAY BACK.
I...I need a minute.

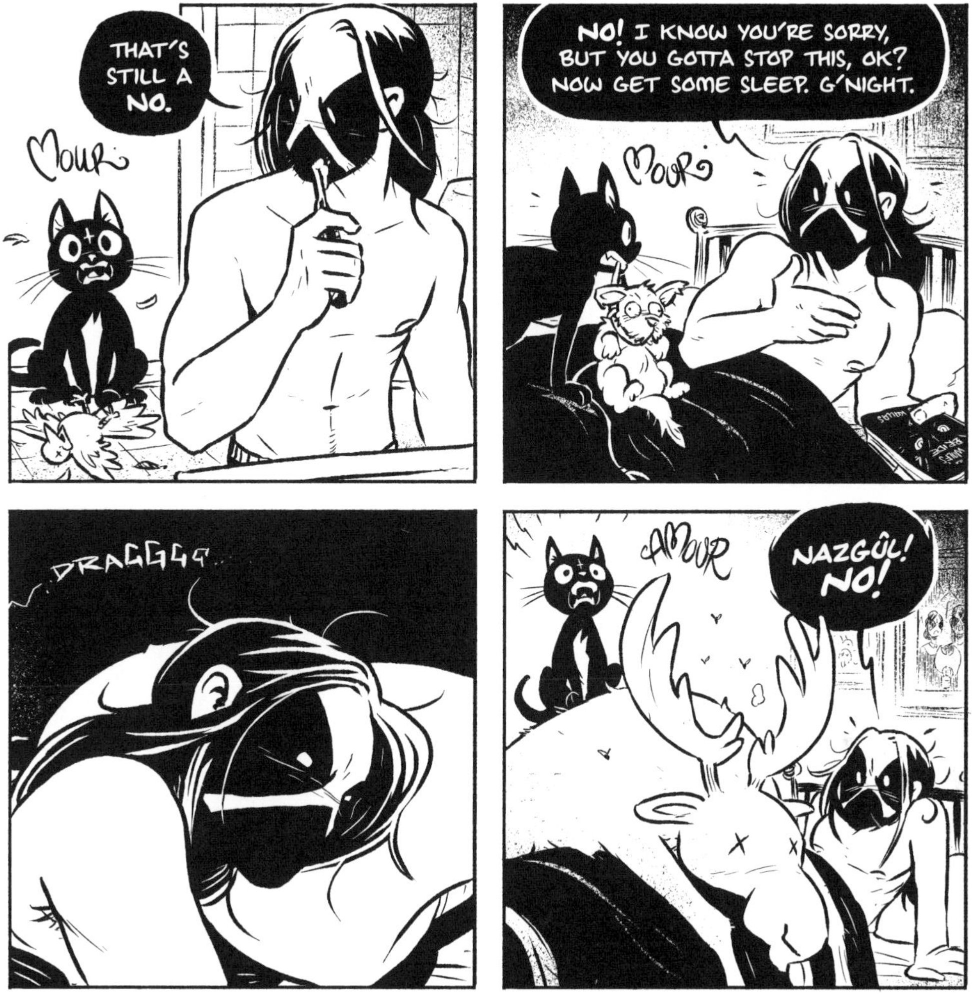
THAT'S STILL A NO.
MOUR
NO! I KNOW YOU'RE SORRY, BUT YOU GOTTA STOP THIS, OK? NOW GET SOME SLEEP. G'NIGHT.
MOUR
DRAGGGG...
AMOUR
NAZGÛL! NO!

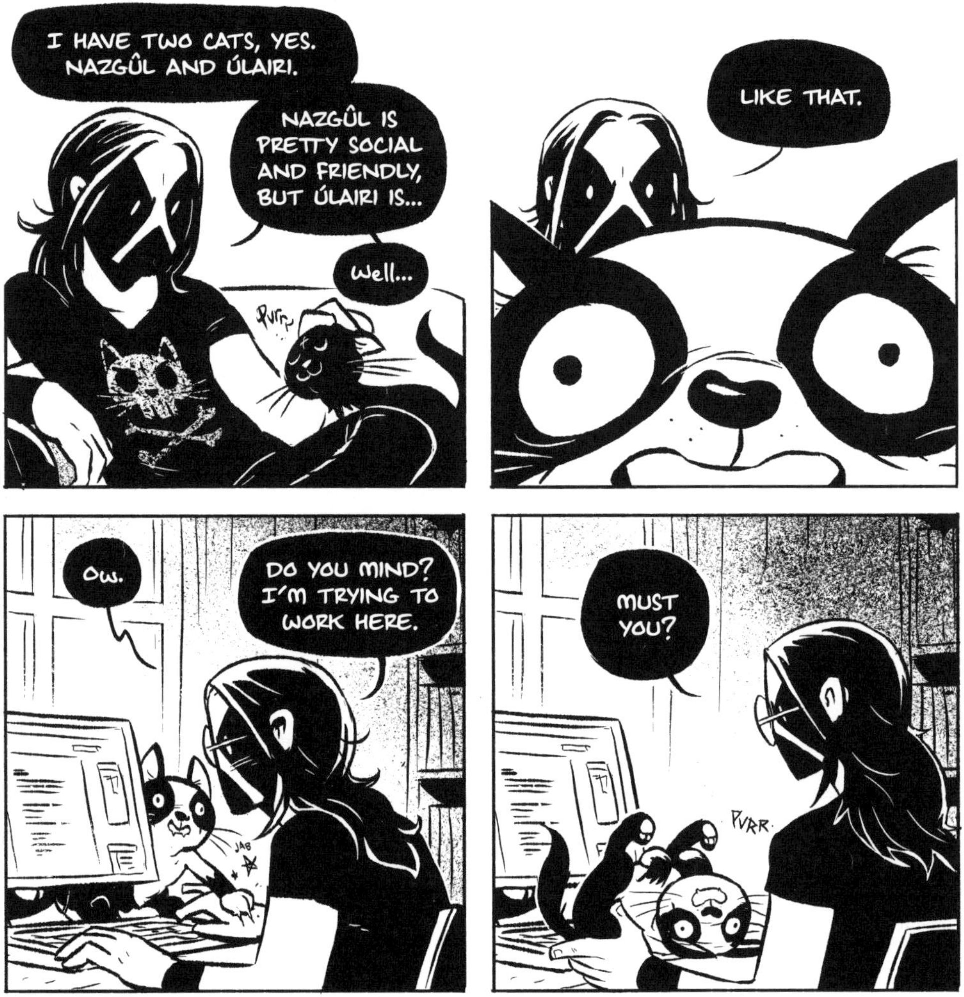
I HAVE TWO CATS, YES. NAZGÛL AND ÚLAIRI.
NAZGÛL IS PRETTY SOCIAL AND FRIENDLY, BUT ÚLAIRI IS...
Well...
PVRR
LIKE THAT.
OW.
DO YOU MIND? I'M TRYING TO WORK HERE.
JAB
MUST YOU?
PVRR

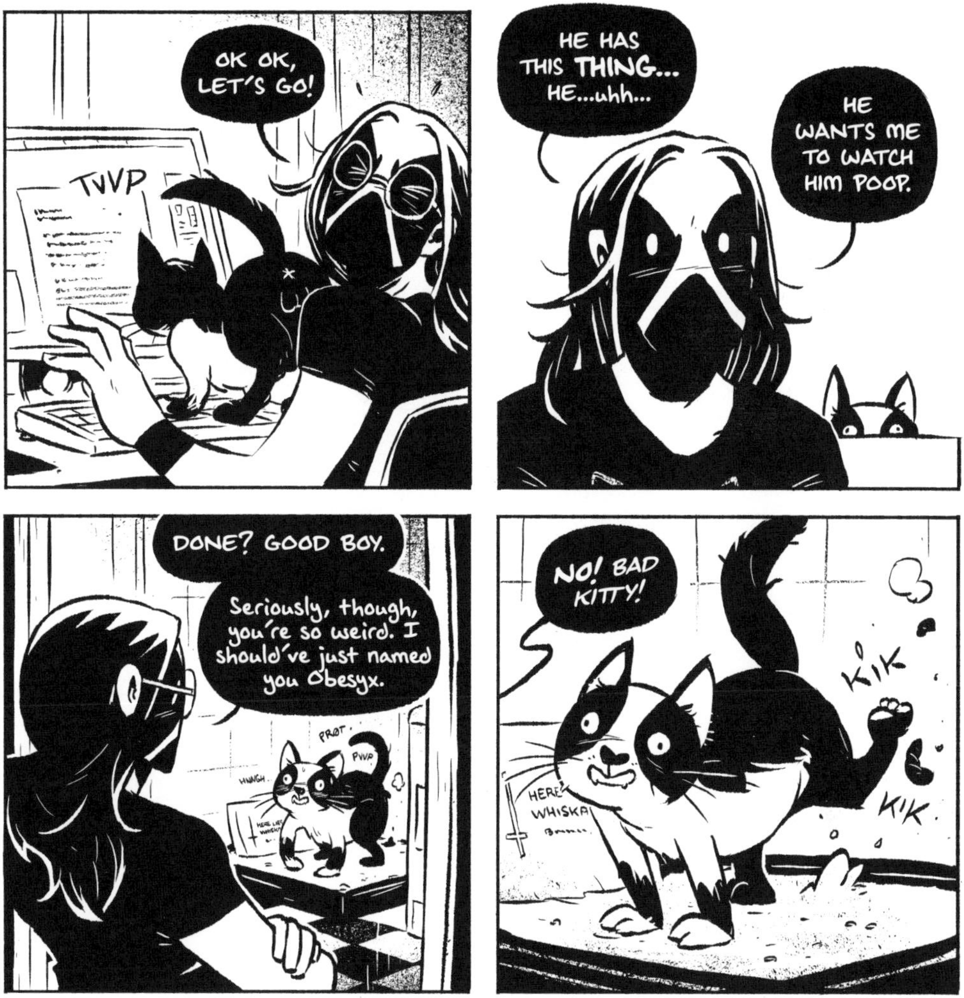
OK OK, LET'S GO!
TVVP
HE HAS THIS THING... HE...uhh...
HE WANTS ME TO WATCH HIM POOP.
DONE? GOOD BOY.
Seriously, though, you're so weird. I should've just named you Obesyx.
PVVP
NO! BAD KITTY!
KIK
KIK
HERE WHISKA

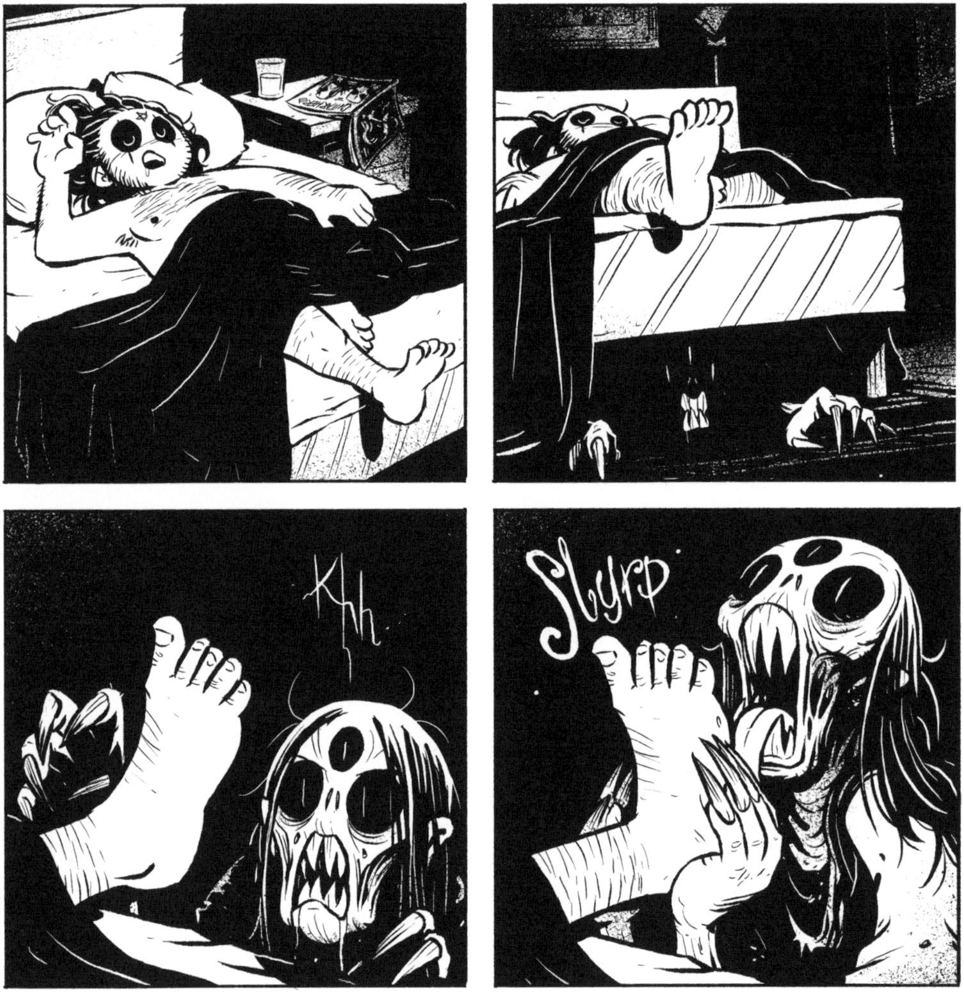
Khh.
Slurp

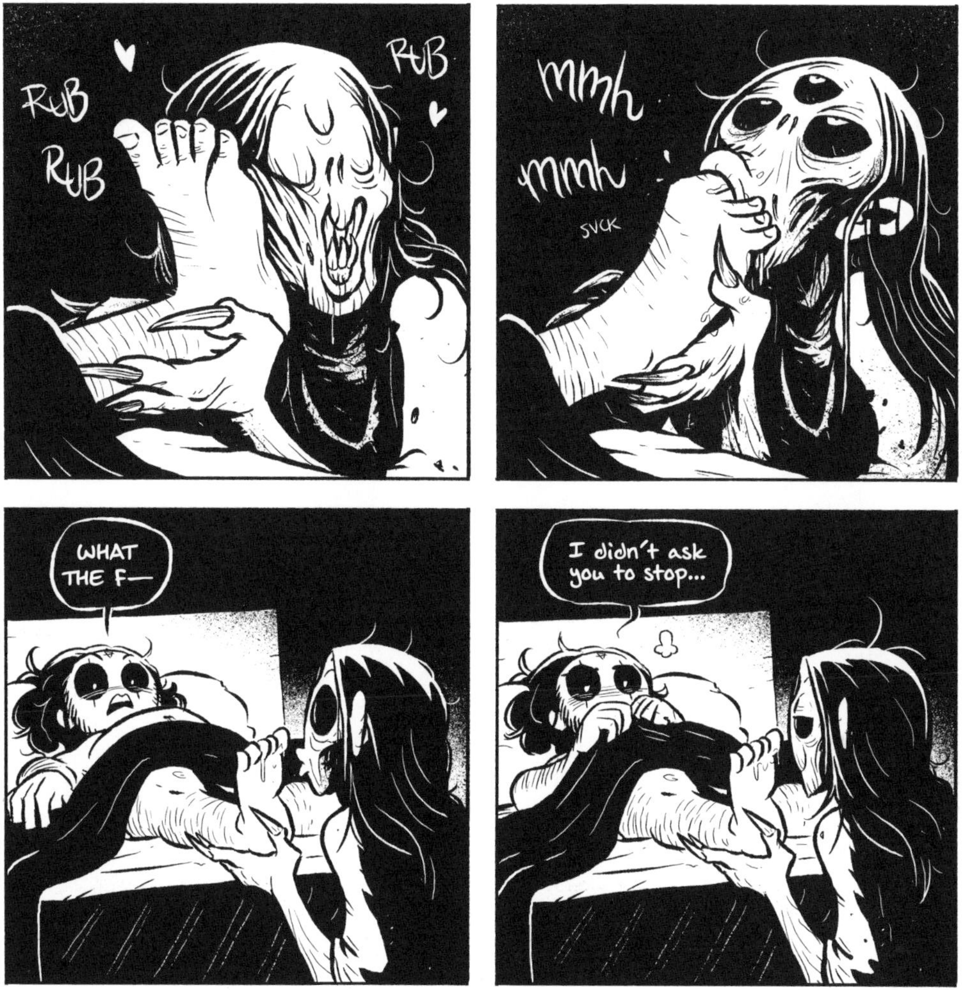
RUB
RUB
RUB
mmh
mmh
SUCK
WHAT THE F—
I didn't ask you to stop...

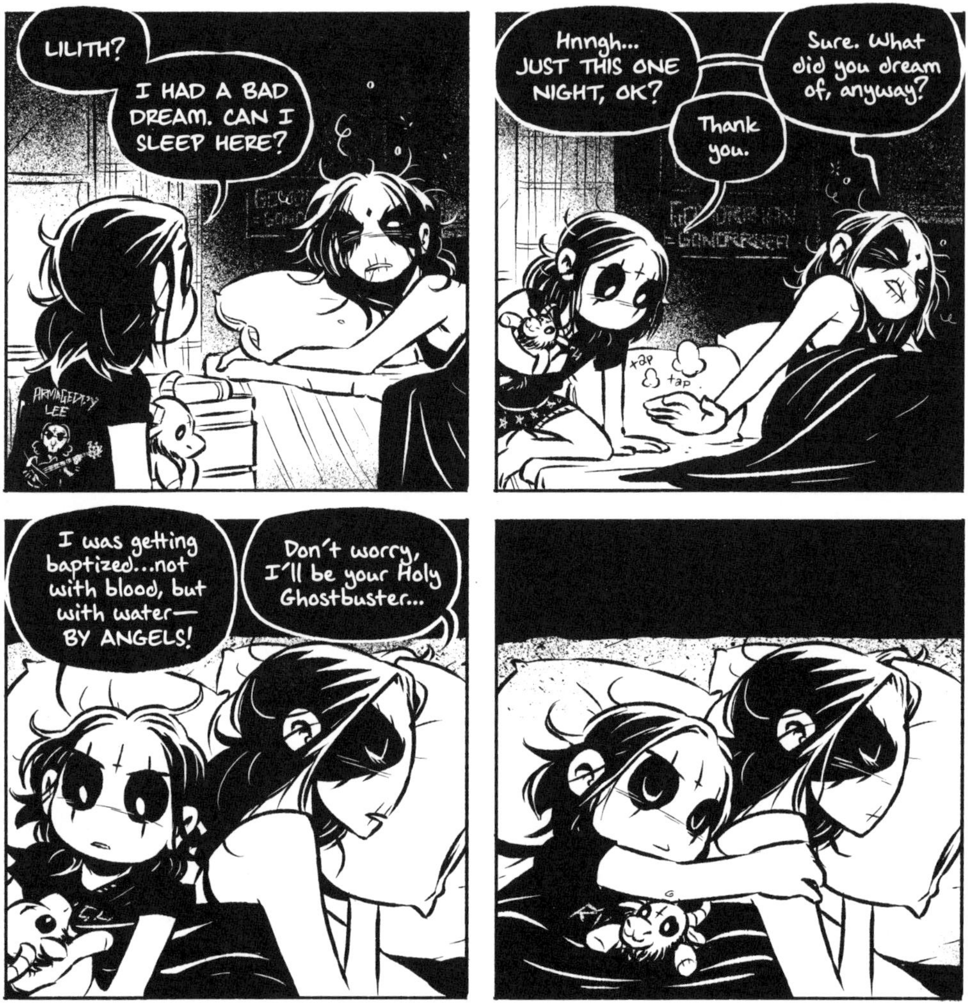
LILITH?
I HAD A BAD DREAM. CAN I SLEEP HERE?
ARMAGEDDON LEE
Hnngh... JUST THIS ONE NIGHT, OK?
Thank you.
Sure. What did you dream of, anyway?
tap tap
I was getting baptized...not with blood, but with water—BY ANGELS!
Don't worry, I'll be your Holy Ghostbuster...

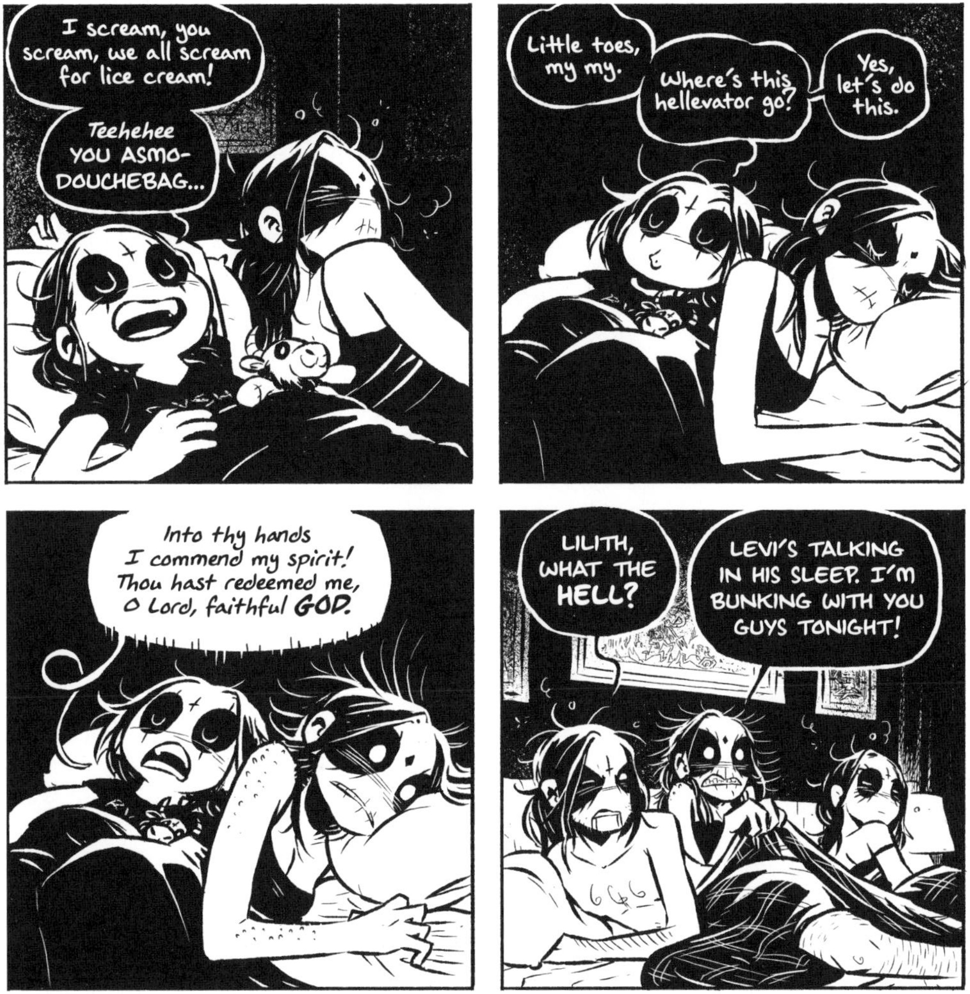
I scream, you scream, we all scream for lice cream!
Teehehee YOU ASMO-DOUCHEBAG...
Little toes, my my.
Where's this hellevator go?
Yes, let's do this.
Into thy hands I commend my spirit! Thou hast redeemed me, O Lord, faithful GOD.
LILITH, WHAT THE HELL?
LEVI'S TALKING IN HIS SLEEP. I'M BUNKING WITH YOU GUYS TONIGHT!

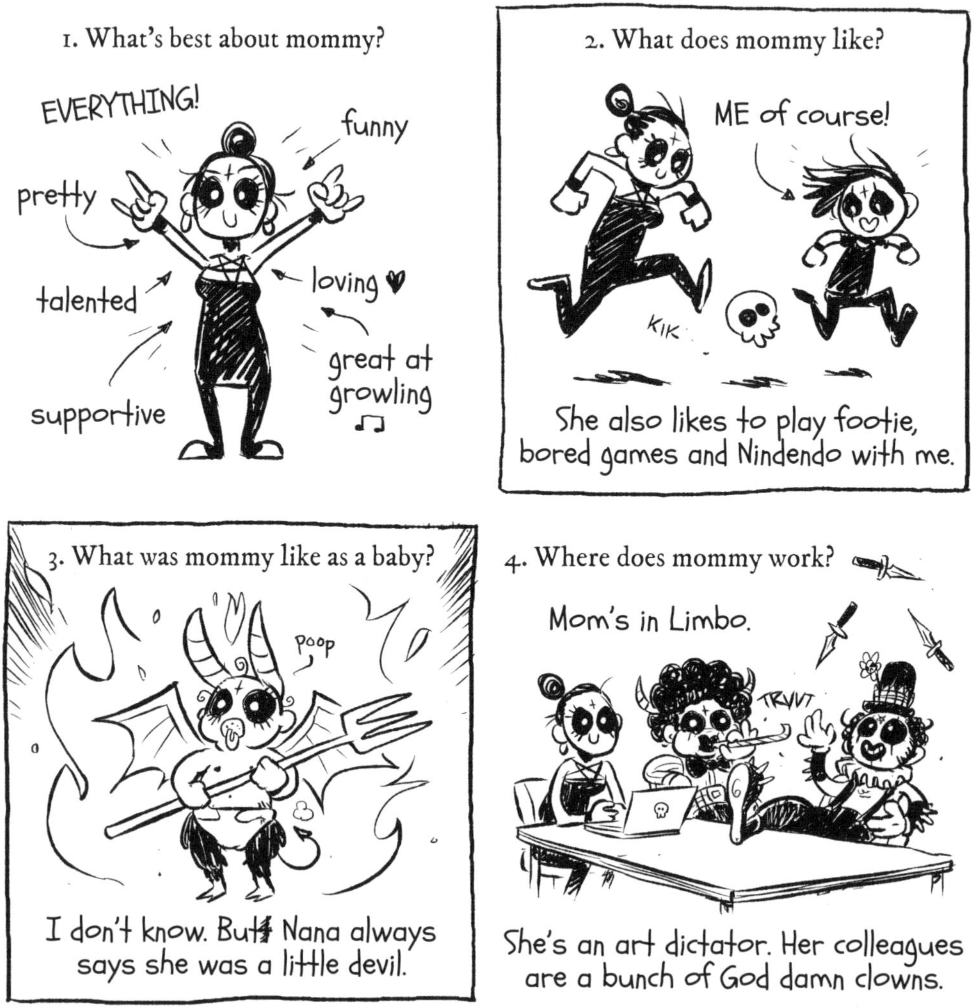
1. What's best about mommy?
EVERYTHING!
funny
pretty
talented
loving
supportive
great at growling
2. What does mommy like?
ME of course!
KIK
She also likes to play footie, bored games and Nindendo with me.
3. What was mommy like as a baby?
poop
I don't know. But~~t~~ Nana always says she was a little devil.
4. Where does mommy work?
Mom's in Limbo.
TRVVT
She's an art dictator. Her colleagues are a bunch of God damn clowns.

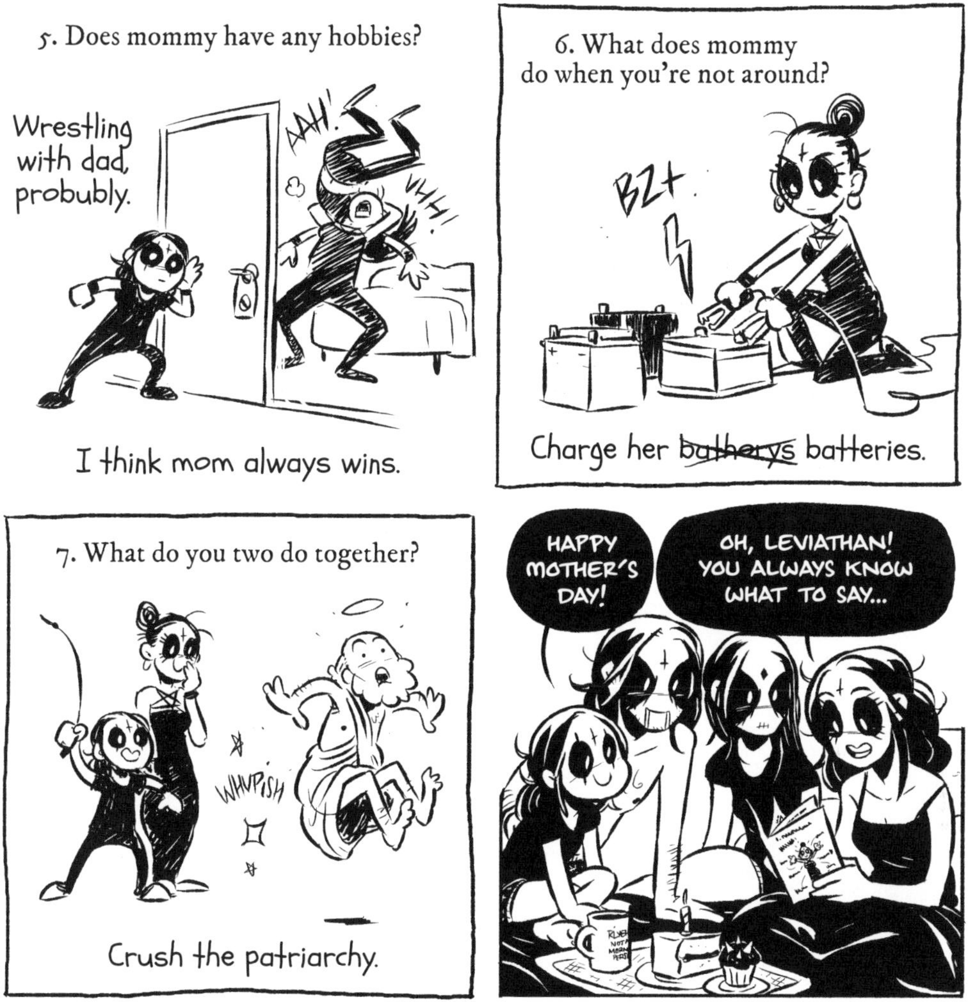
5. Does mommy have any hobbies?
Wrestling with dad, probubly.
AAH!
WHH!
I think mom always wins.
6. What does mommy do when you're not around?
BZT
Charge her ~~batherys~~ batteries.
7. What do you two do together?
WHUPISH
Crush the patriarchy.
HAPPY MOTHER'S DAY!
OH, LEVIATHAN! YOU ALWAYS KNOW WHAT TO SAY...

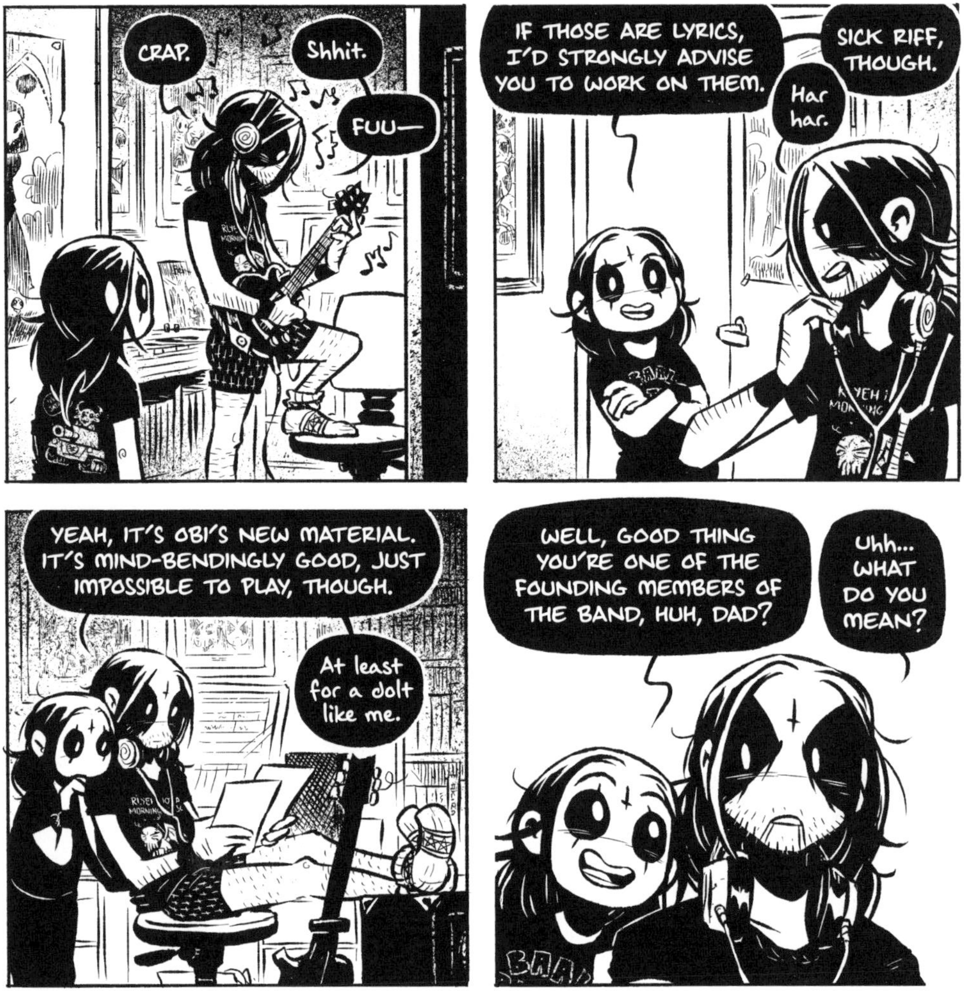
CRAP.
Shhit.
FUU—
IF THOSE ARE LYRICS, I'D STRONGLY ADVISE YOU TO WORK ON THEM.
Har har.
SICK RIFF, THOUGH.
YEAH, IT'S OBI'S NEW MATERIAL. IT'S MIND-BENDINGLY GOOD, JUST IMPOSSIBLE TO PLAY, THOUGH.
At least for a dolt like me.
WELL, GOOD THING YOU'RE ONE OF THE FOUNDING MEMBERS OF THE BAND, HUH, DAD?
Uhh... WHAT DO YOU MEAN?

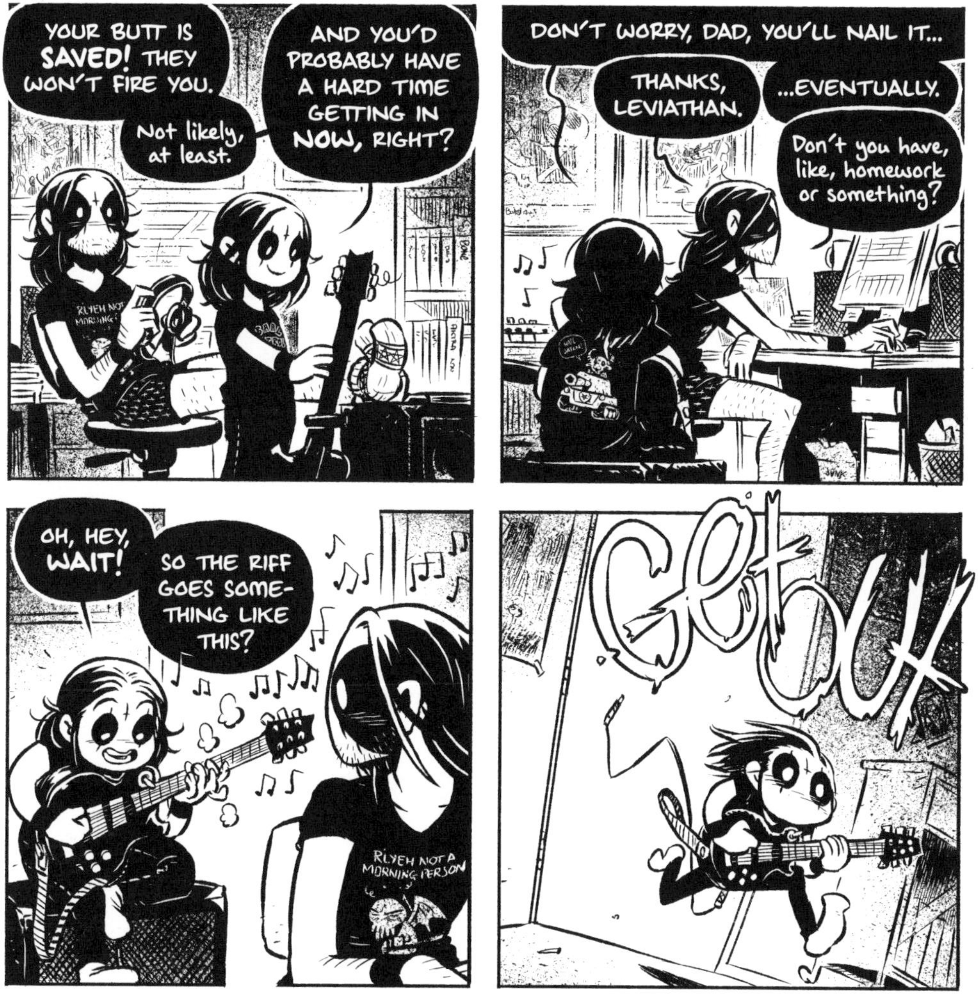
YOUR BUTT IS SAVED! THEY WON'T FIRE YOU.
Not likely, at least.
AND YOU'D PROBABLY HAVE A HARD TIME GETTING IN NOW, RIGHT?
DON'T WORRY, DAD, YOU'LL NAIL IT...
THANKS, LEVIATHAN.
...EVENTUALLY.
Don't you have, like, homework or something?
OH, HEY, WAIT!
SO THE RIFF GOES SOMETHING LIKE THIS?
RLYEH NOT A MORNING PERSON

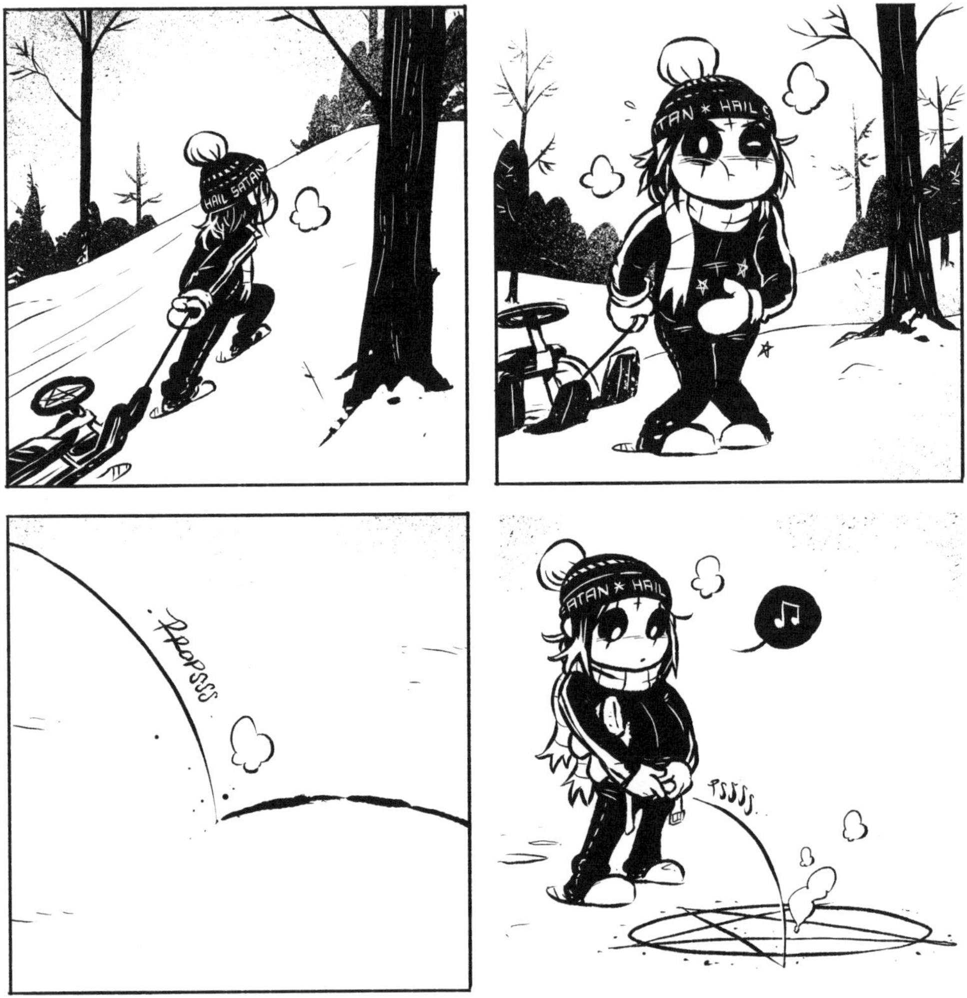
HAIL SATAN
PSSSS.

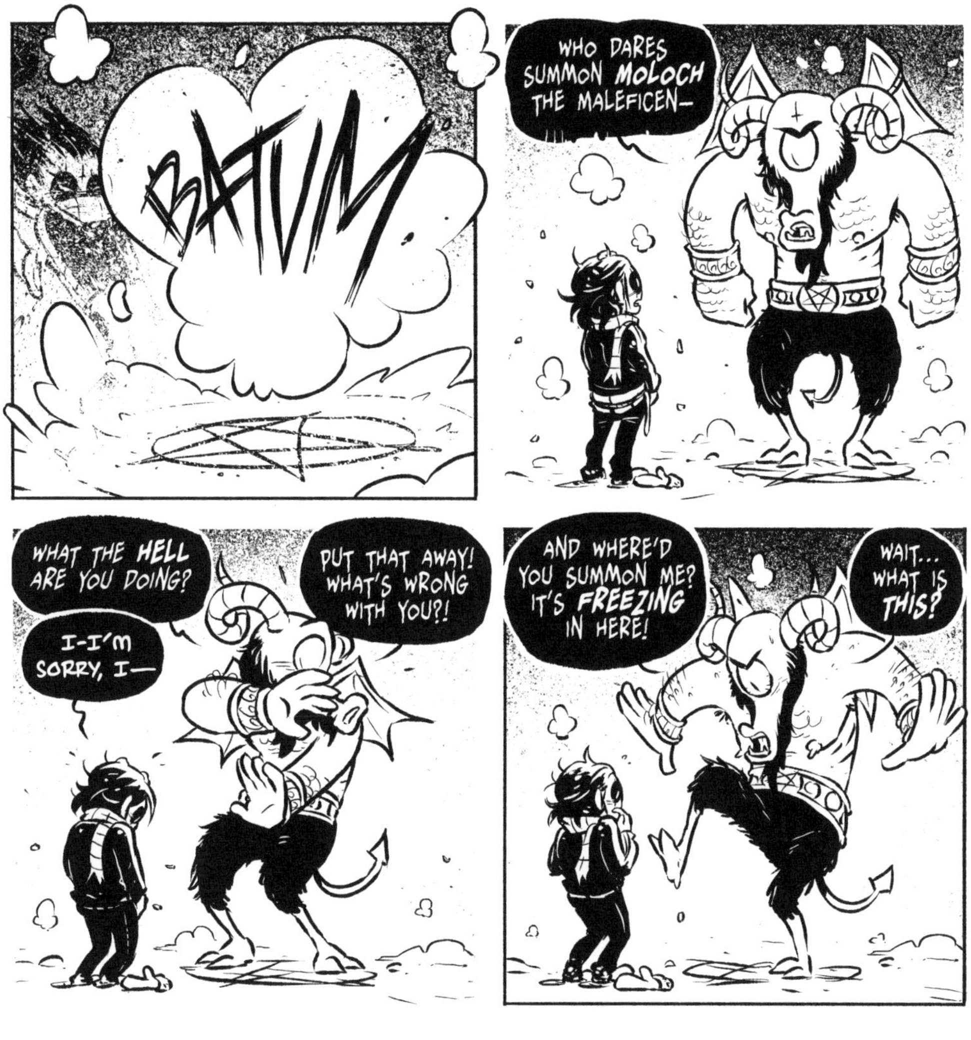
BATUM
WHO DARES SUMMON MOLOCH THE MALEFICEN—
WHAT THE HELL ARE YOU DOING?
PUT THAT AWAY! WHAT'S WRONG WITH YOU?!
I-I'M SORRY, I—
AND WHERE'D YOU SUMMON ME? IT'S FREEZING IN HERE!
WAIT... WHAT IS THIS?

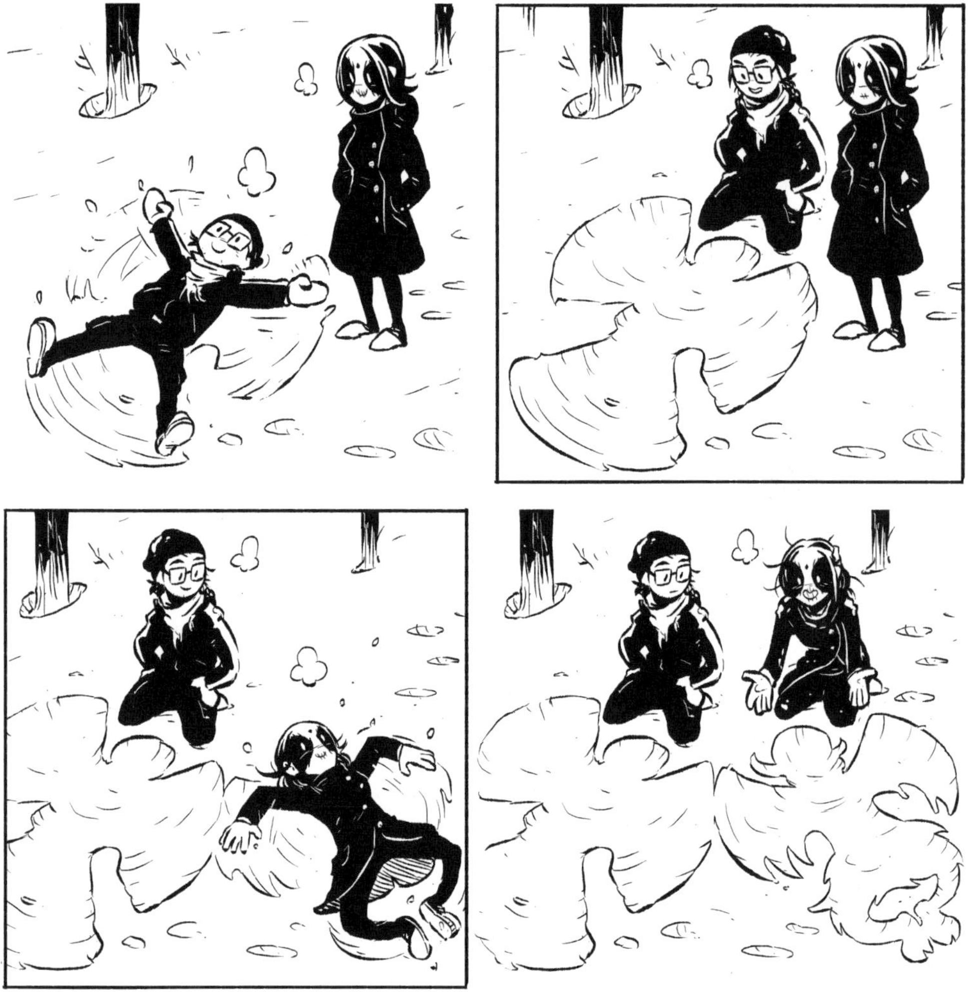

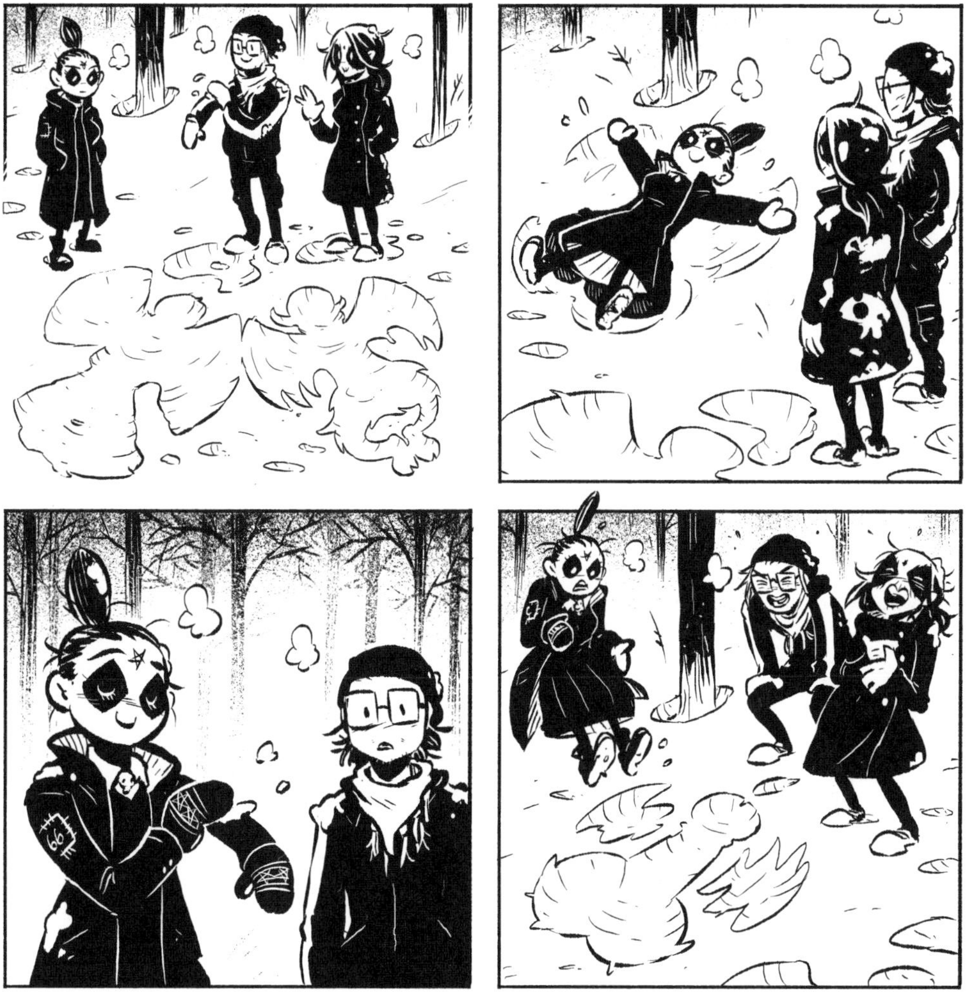

Umm...I THINK YOU SHOULD COME TO BED, HON...
I CAN'T! I HAVE A DIAPER CAMPAIGN TO POOP OUT!
IT'S LIKE I'M TRYING TO SQUEEZE A DEUCE THROUGH MY CEREBRUM! I'M DIZZY AND ABOUT TO POP A VEIN...
Yeah... you need sleep.
I ALSO NEED THIS JOB!
WELL, umm...CAN I HELP?
THE OCEAN. RUDY SWIMMING WITH HIS MOM. OMINOUS MUSIC CREEPS IN, AS IN JAWS! THEN, SCREAMS FROM THE BEACH! THE WATER TURNS BROWN!
IT'S A SHART ATTACK! THE MEGALODUNG STRIKES FROM BEHIND!
Ok ok, keep it coming.

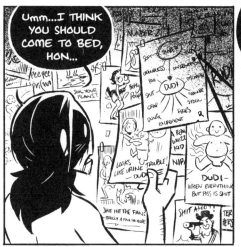

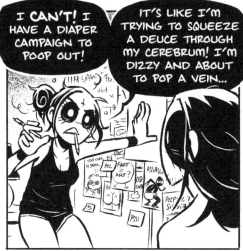

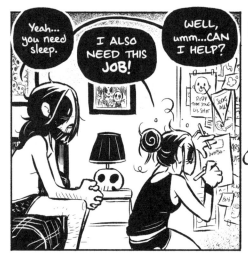

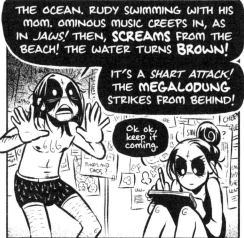

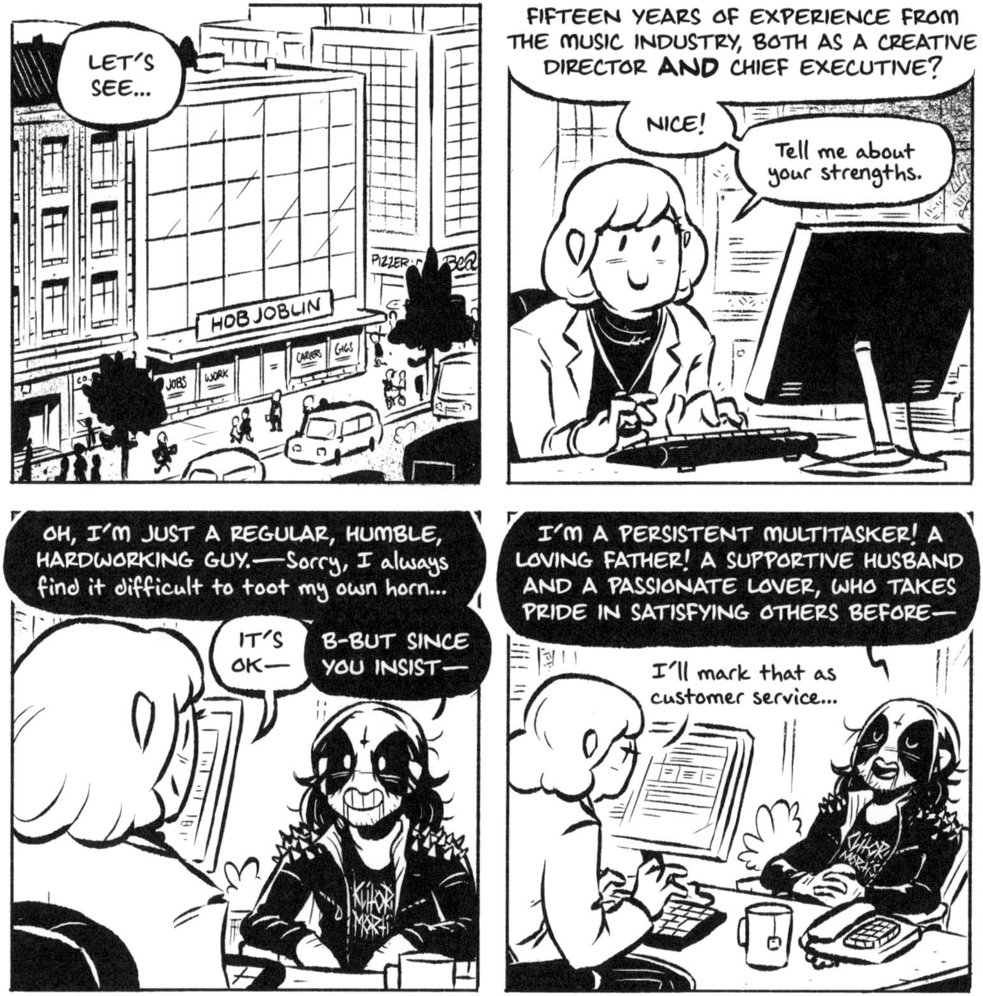
LET'S SEE...
HOBJOBLIN
PIZZER
JOBS
WORK
CAREERS
GIGS
FIFTEEN YEARS OF EXPERIENCE FROM THE MUSIC INDUSTRY, BOTH AS A CREATIVE DIRECTOR AND CHIEF EXECUTIVE?
NICE!
Tell me about your strengths.
OH, I'M JUST A REGULAR, HUMBLE, HARDWORKING GUY.—Sorry, I always find it difficult to toot my own horn...
IT'S OK—
B-BUT SINCE YOU INSIST—
I'M A PERSISTENT MULTITASKER! A LOVING FATHER! A SUPPORTIVE HUSBAND AND A PASSIONATE LOVER, WHO TAKES PRIDE IN SATISFYING OTHERS BEFORE—
I'll mark that as customer service...

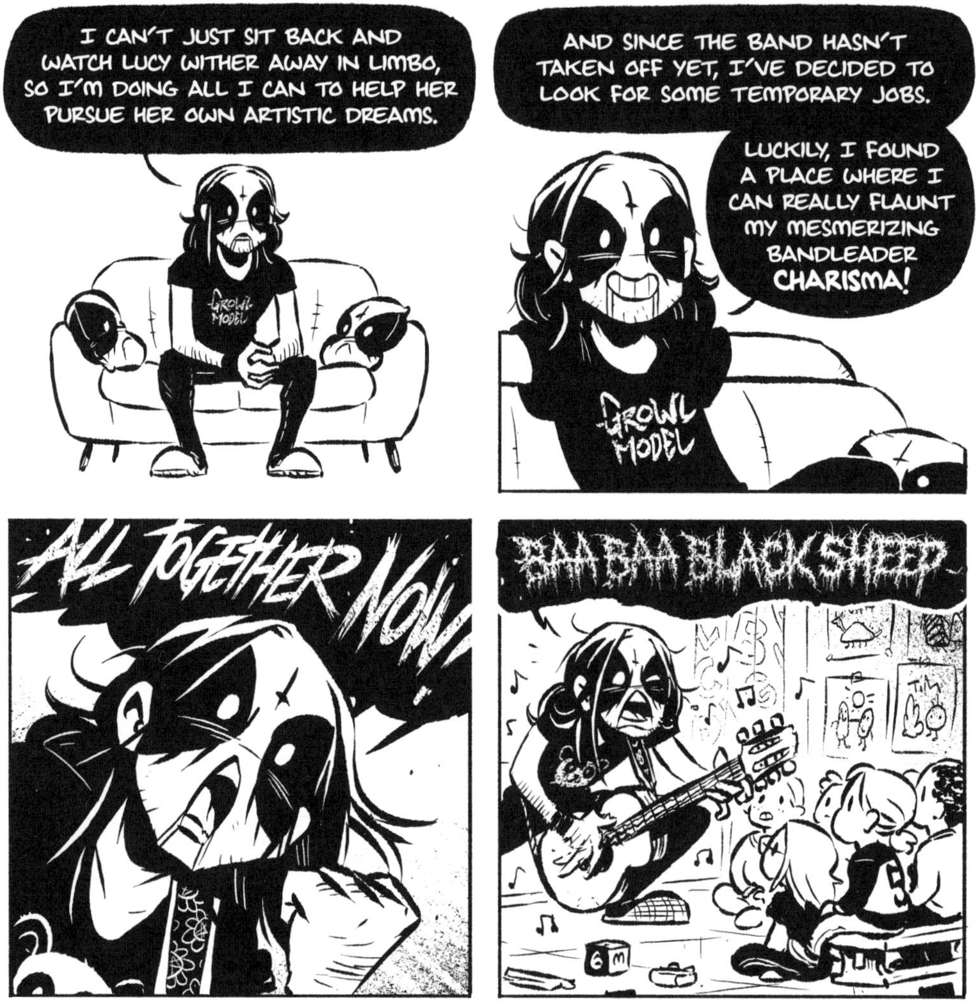
I CAN'T JUST SIT BACK AND WATCH LUCY WITHER AWAY IN LIMBO, SO I'M DOING ALL I CAN TO HELP HER PURSUE HER OWN ARTISTIC DREAMS.
GROWL MODEL
AND SINCE THE BAND HASN'T TAKEN OFF YET, I'VE DECIDED TO LOOK FOR SOME TEMPORARY JOBS.
LUCKILY, I FOUND A PLACE WHERE I CAN REALLY FLAUNT MY MESMERIZING BANDLEADER CHARISMA!
GROWL MODEL
ALL TOGETHER NOW!
BAA BAA BLACK SHEEP
TIM
6 M

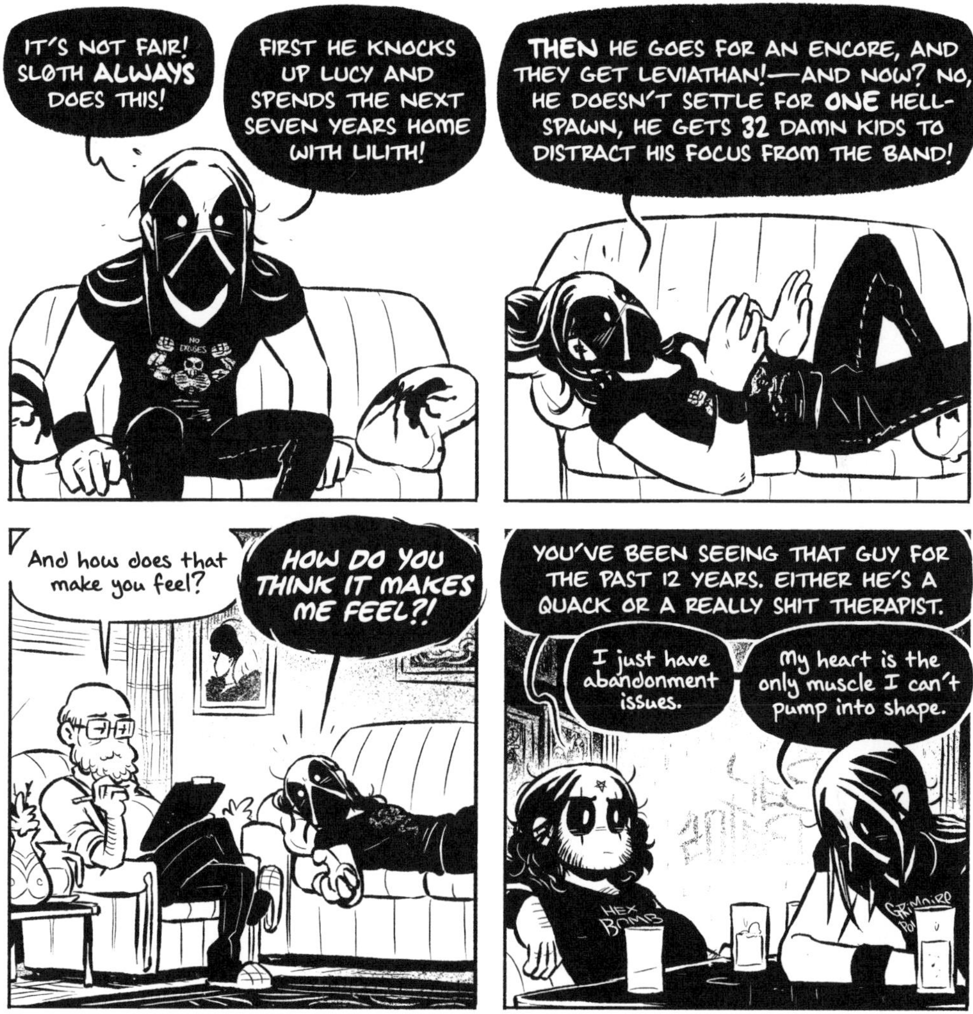
IT'S NOT FAIR! SLOTH **ALWAYS** DOES THIS!
FIRST HE KNOCKS UP LUCY AND SPENDS THE NEXT SEVEN YEARS HOME WITH LILITH!
THEN HE GOES FOR AN ENCORE, AND THEY GET LEVIATHAN!—AND NOW? NO, HE DOESN'T SETTLE FOR **ONE** HELL-SPAWN, HE GETS **32** DAMN KIDS TO DISTRACT HIS FOCUS FROM THE BAND!
NO EXCUSES
And how does that make you feel?
HOW DO YOU THINK IT MAKES ME FEEL?!
YOU'VE BEEN SEEING THAT GUY FOR THE PAST 12 YEARS. EITHER HE'S A QUACK OR A REALLY SHIT THERAPIST.
I just have abandonment issues.
My heart is the only muscle I can't pump into shape.
HEX BOMB

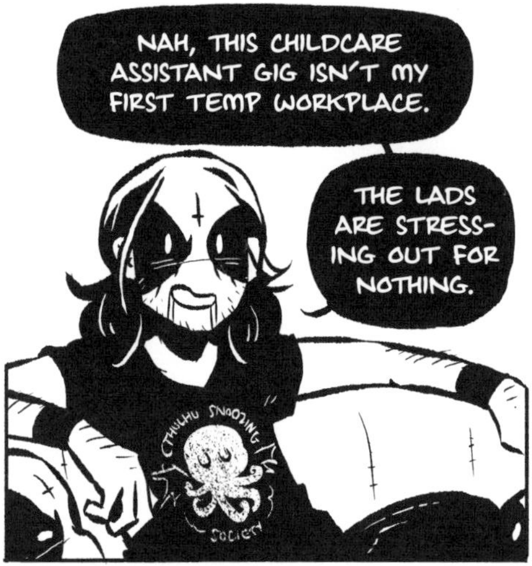
NAH, THIS CHILDCARE ASSISTANT GIG ISN'T MY FIRST TEMP WORKPLACE.
THE LADS ARE STRESSING OUT FOR NOTHING.
CTHULHU SNOOZING UNICORNS SOCIETY

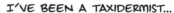

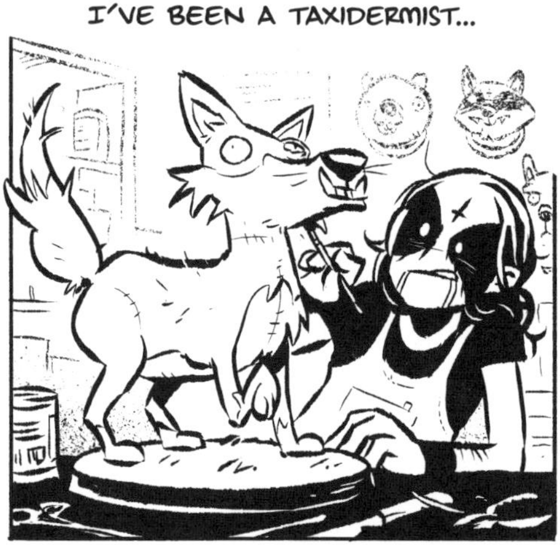
I'VE BEEN A TAXIDERMIST...

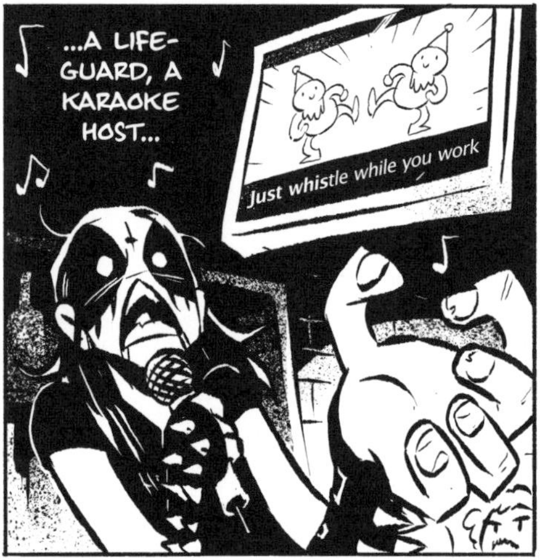
...A LIFEGUARD, A KARAOKE HOST...
Just whistle while you work

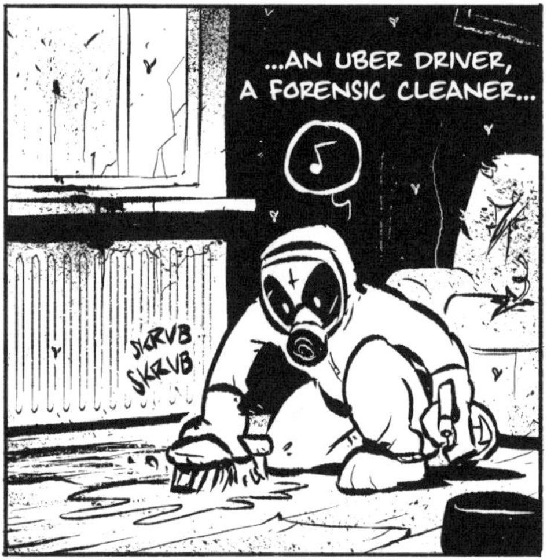
...AN UBER DRIVER, A FORENSIC CLEANER...
SKRUB SKRUB

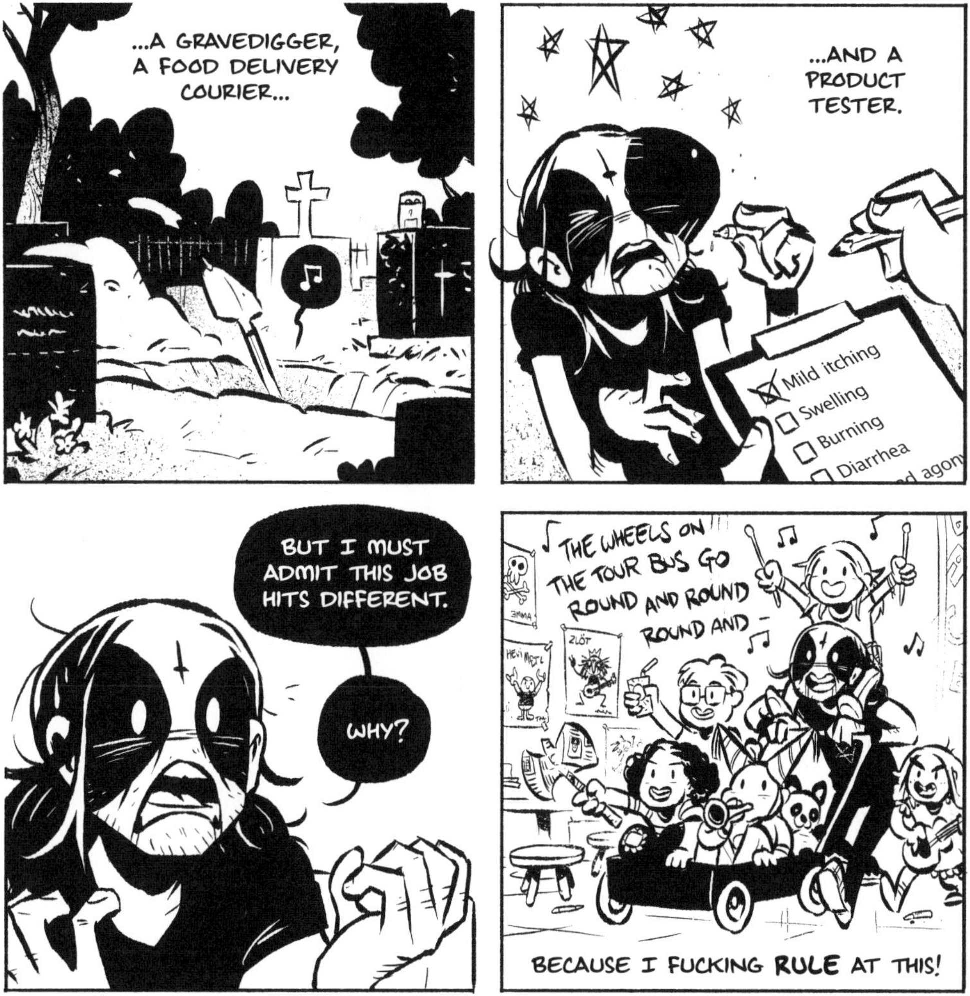
...A GRAVEDIGGER, A FOOD DELIVERY COURIER...
...AND A PRODUCT TESTER.
Mild itching
Swelling
Burning
Diarrhea
BUT I MUST ADMIT THIS JOB HITS DIFFERENT.
WHY?
THE WHEELS ON THE TOUR BUS GO ROUND AND ROUND ROUND AND –
ZLÖT
BECAUSE I FUCKING **RULE** AT THIS!

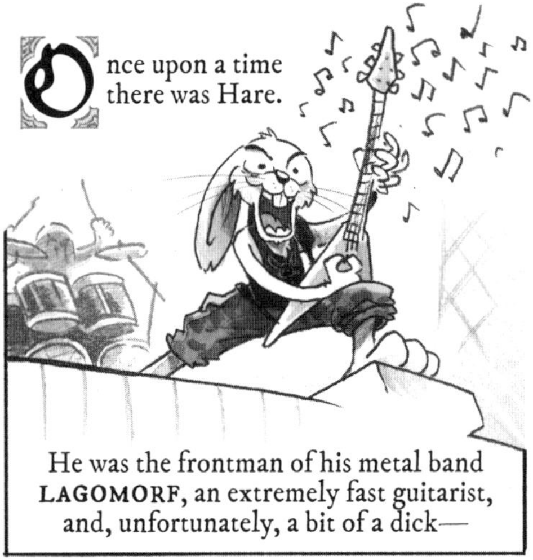
Once upon a time there was Hare.
He was the frontman of his metal band **LAGOMORF**, an extremely fast guitarist, and, unfortunately, a bit of a dick—

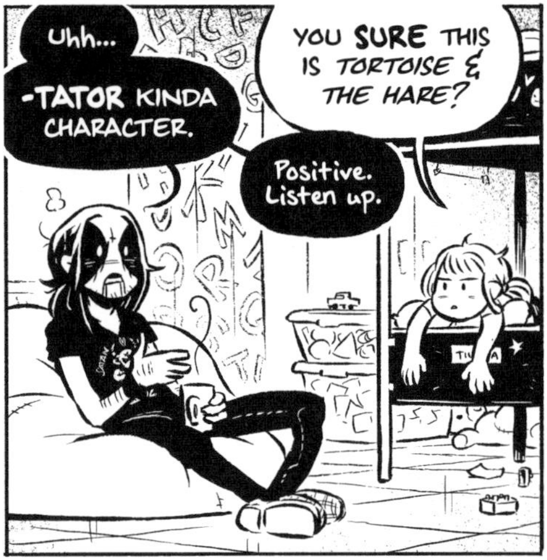
Uhh...
-TATOR KINDA CHARACTER.
YOU SURE THIS IS TORTOISE & THE HARE?
Positive. Listen up.

You see, just like many other lead guitarists, Hare had an ego problem.

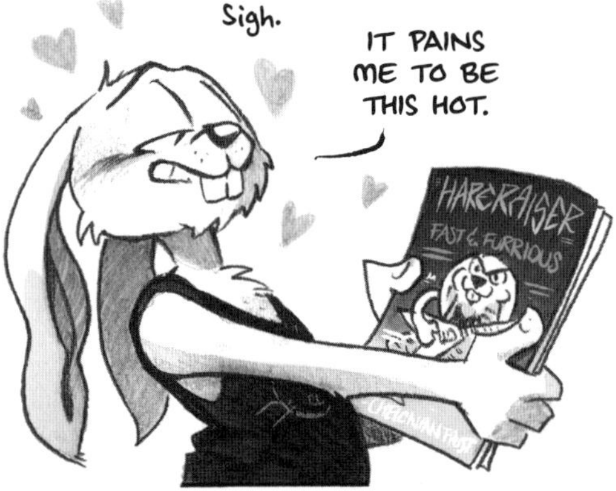
Sigh.
IT PAINS ME TO BE THIS HOT.

So when **CHELONIAN FROST**'s new LP came out, receiving rave reviews and topping **LAGOMORF**'s *Rabid Season* album...

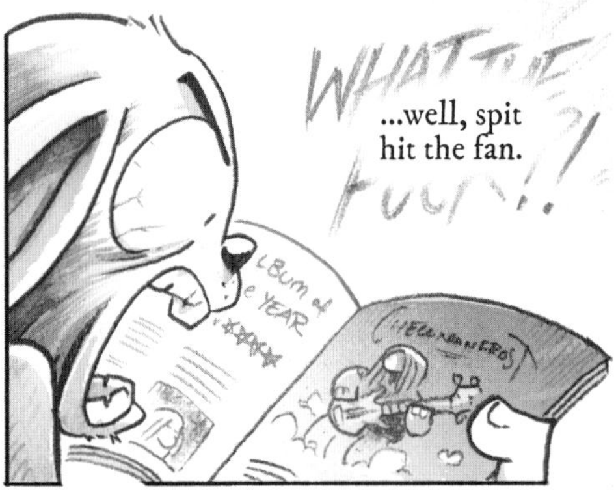
...well, spit hit the fan.

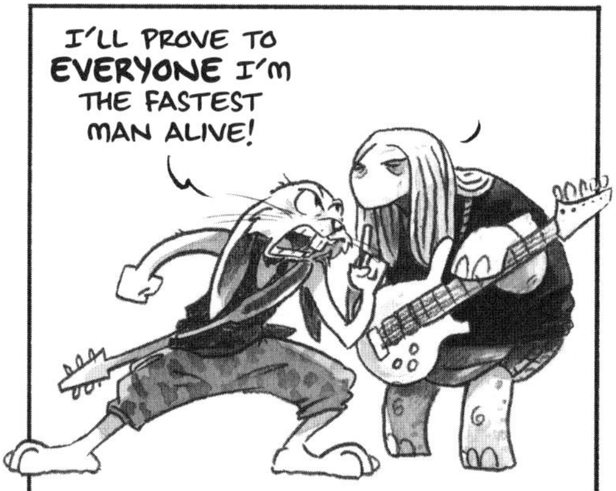
I'LL PROVE TO EVERYONE I'M THE FASTEST MAN ALIVE!

Hare challenged Tortoise, CHELONIAN FROST'S frontman, to a guitar duel.

But the reptilian slow-poke wasn't into that sort of stuff.

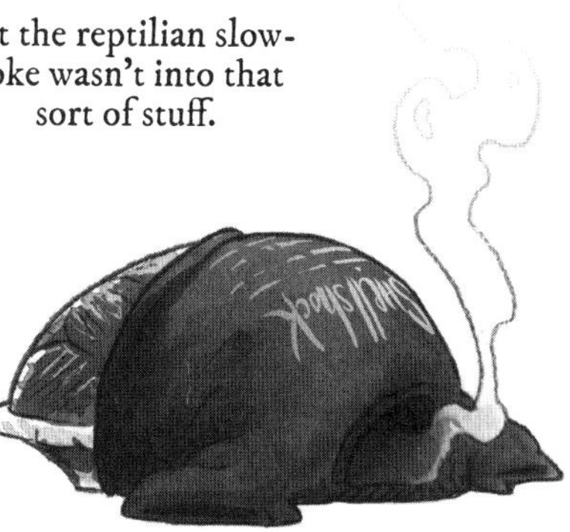

All he wanted was to do his own thing, focus on his own art, at his own pace.

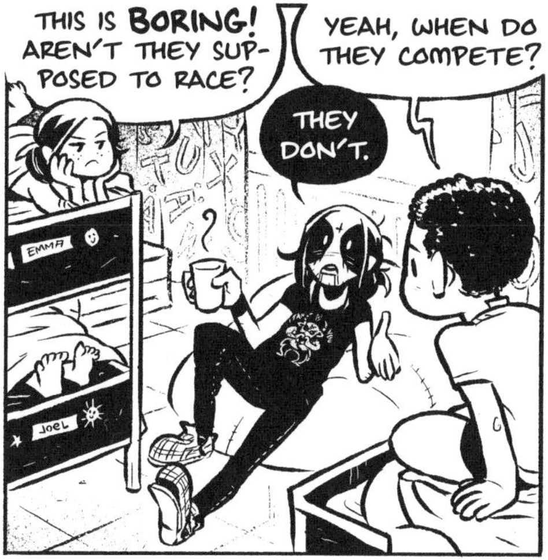
THIS IS BORING! AREN'T THEY SUPPOSED TO RACE?
YEAH, WHEN DO THEY COMPETE?
THEY DON'T.
EMMA
JOEL

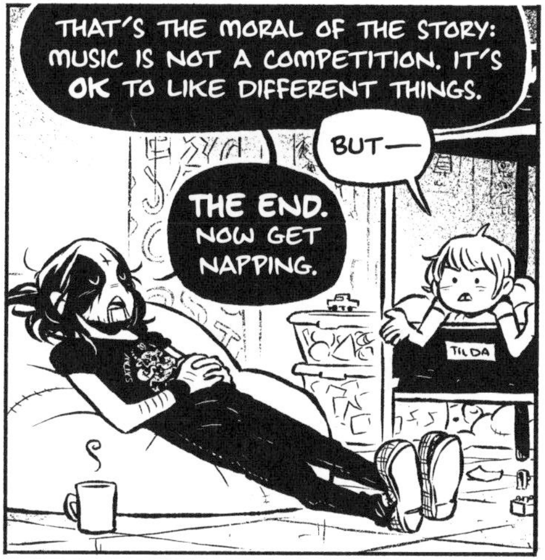
THAT'S THE MORAL OF THE STORY: MUSIC IS NOT A COMPETITION. IT'S OK TO LIKE DIFFERENT THINGS.
BUT—
THE END. NOW GET NAPPING.
TILDA

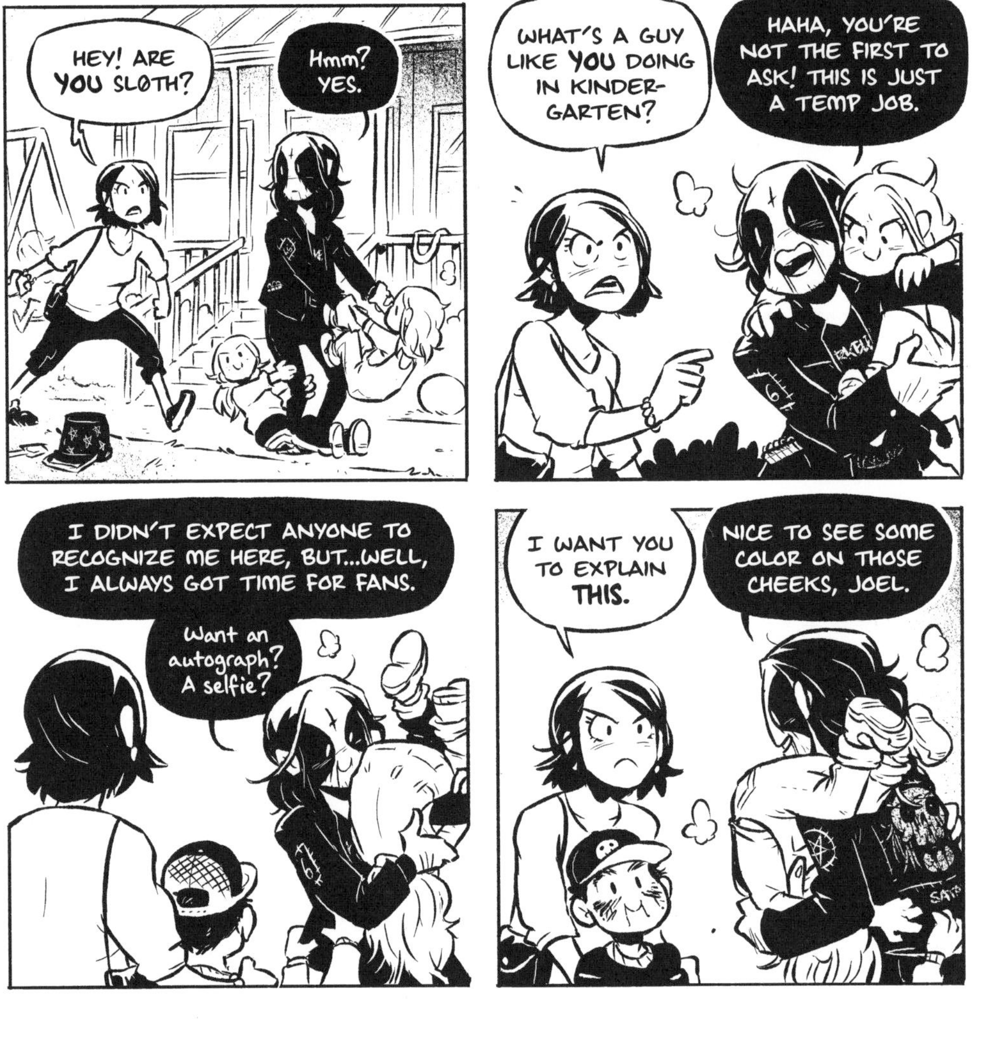
HEY! ARE YOU SLOTH?
Hmm? YES.
WHAT'S A GUY LIKE YOU DOING IN KINDER-GARTEN?
HAHA, YOU'RE NOT THE FIRST TO ASK! THIS IS JUST A TEMP JOB.
I DIDN'T EXPECT ANYONE TO RECOGNIZE ME HERE, BUT...WELL, I ALWAYS GOT TIME FOR FANS.
Want an autograph? A selfie?
I WANT YOU TO EXPLAIN THIS.
NICE TO SEE SOME COLOR ON THOSE CHEEKS, JOEL.

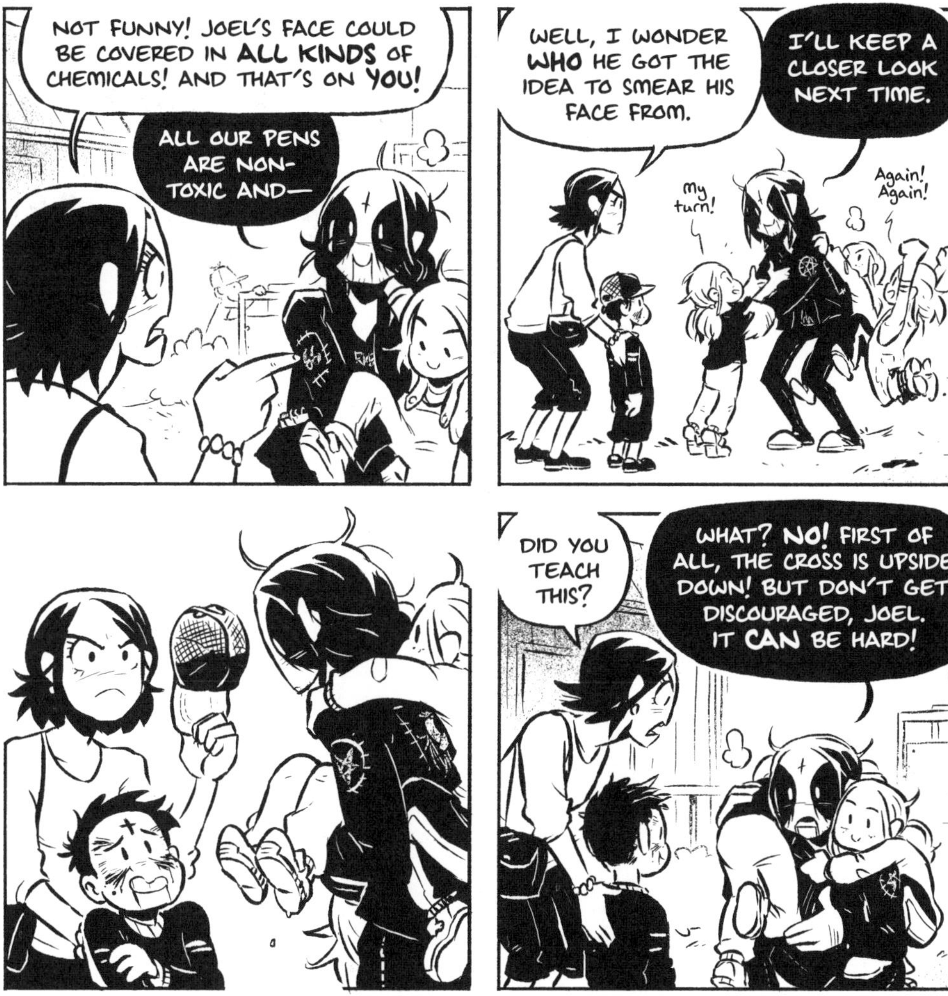
NOT FUNNY! JOEL'S FACE COULD BE COVERED IN ALL KINDS OF CHEMICALS! AND THAT'S ON YOU!
ALL OUR PENS ARE NON-TOXIC AND—
WELL, I WONDER WHO HE GOT THE IDEA TO SMEAR HIS FACE FROM.
I'LL KEEP A CLOSER LOOK NEXT TIME.
my turn!
Again! Again!
DID YOU TEACH THIS?
WHAT? NO! FIRST OF ALL, THE CROSS IS UPSIDE DOWN! BUT DON'T GET DISCOURAGED, JOEL. IT CAN BE HARD!

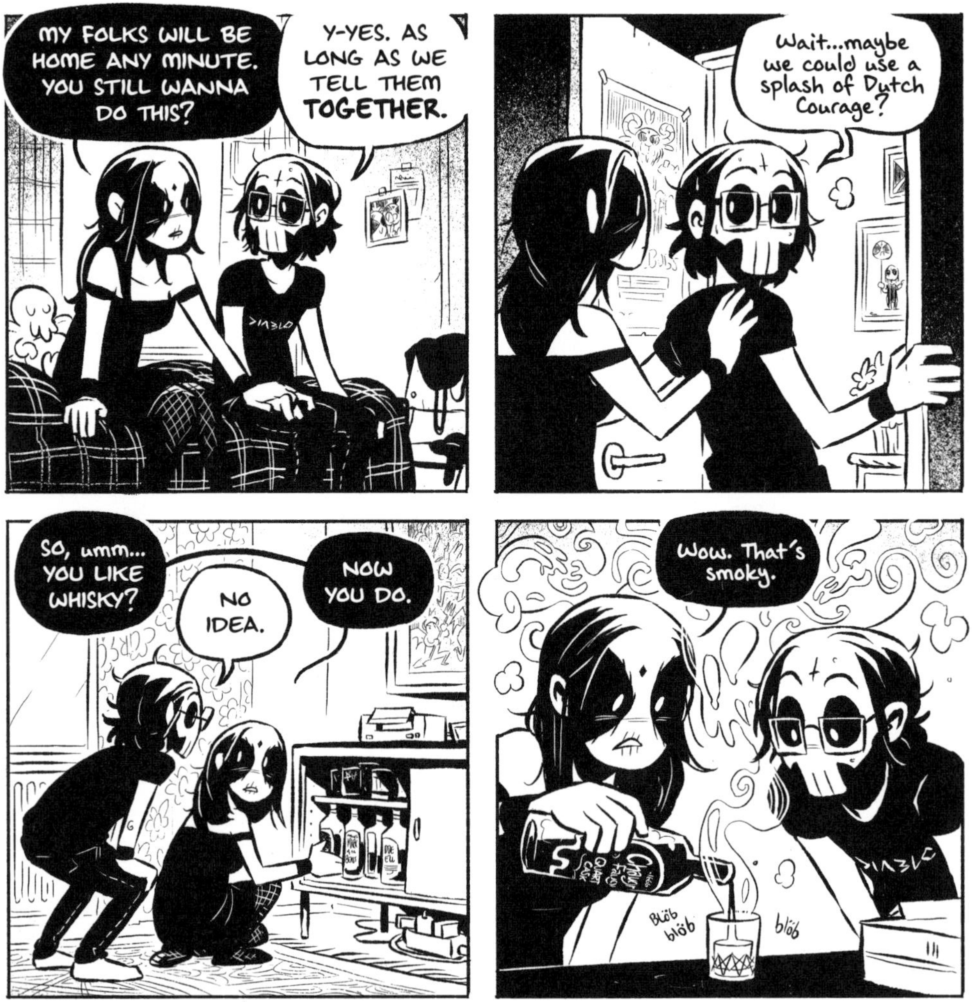
MY FOLKS WILL BE HOME ANY MINUTE. YOU STILL WANNA DO THIS?
Y-YES. AS LONG AS WE TELL THEM TOGETHER.
DIABLO
Wait...maybe we could use a splash of Dutch Courage?
SO, umm... YOU LIKE WHISKY?
NO IDEA.
NOW YOU DO.
Wow. That's smoky.
QUART CASK
Blöb blöb
blöb
DIABLO

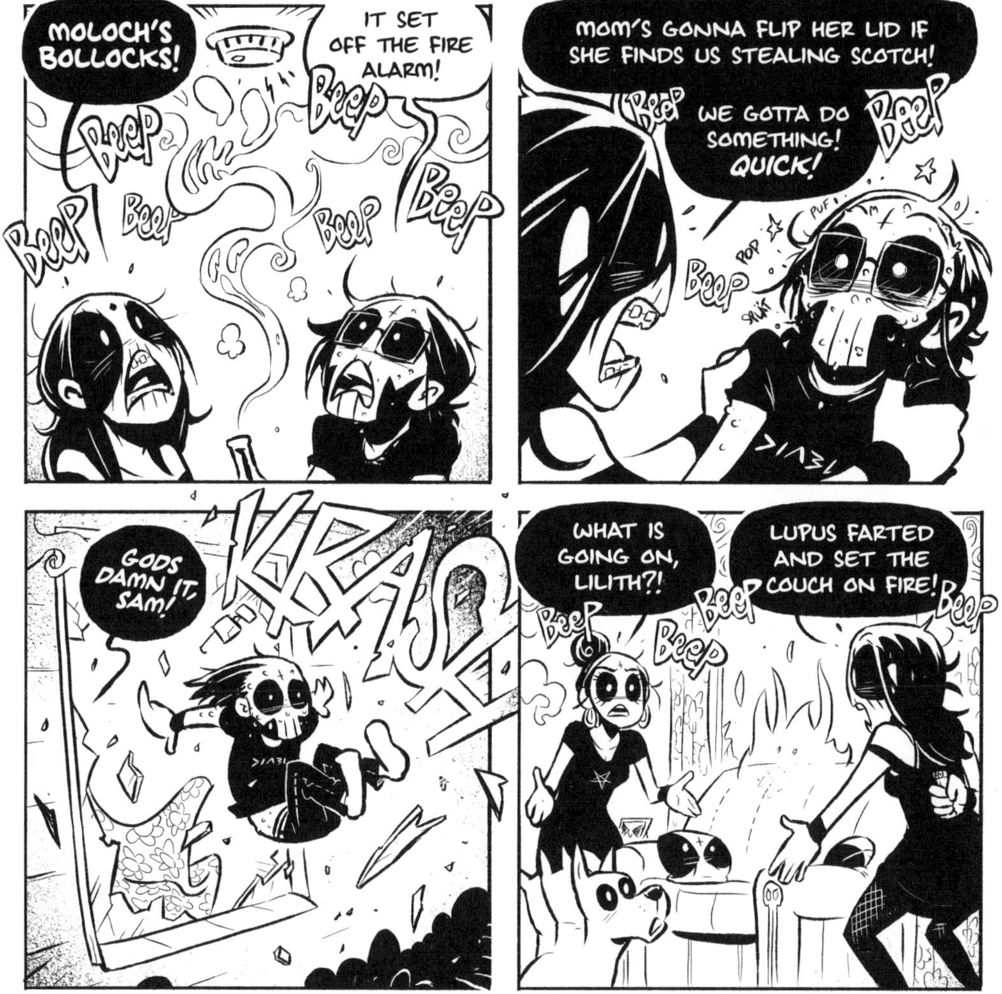
MOLOCH'S BOLLOCKS!
IT SET OFF THE FIRE ALARM!
BEEP BEEP BEEP BEEP BEEP BEEP
MOM'S GONNA FLIP HER LID IF SHE FINDS US STEALING SCOTCH!
BEEP
WE GOTTA DO SOMETHING! QUICK!
BEEP
PUF
POP
BEEP
GODS DAMN IT, SAM!
KRASH
WHAT IS GOING ON, LILITH?!
LUPUS FARTED AND SET THE COUCH ON FIRE!
BEEP BEEP BEEP BEEP

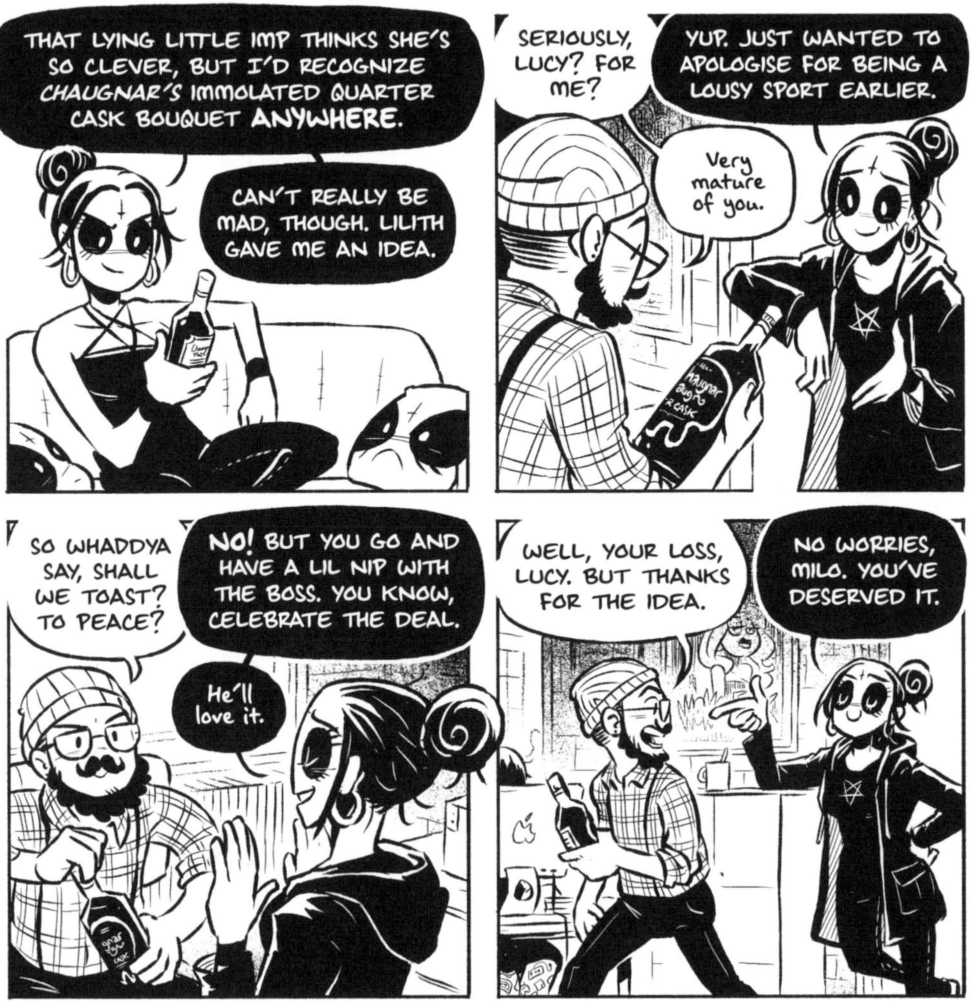
THAT LYING LITTLE IMP THINKS SHE'S SO CLEVER, BUT I'D RECOGNIZE CHAUGNAR'S IMMOLATED QUARTER CASK BOUQUET ANYWHERE.
CAN'T REALLY BE MAD, THOUGH. LILITH GAVE ME AN IDEA.
SERIOUSLY, LUCY? FOR ME?
YUP. JUST WANTED TO APOLOGISE FOR BEING A LOUSY SPORT EARLIER.
Very mature of you.
SO WHADDYA SAY, SHALL WE TOAST? TO PEACE?
NO! BUT YOU GO AND HAVE A LIL NIP WITH THE BOSS. YOU KNOW, CELEBRATE THE DEAL.
He'll love it.
WELL, YOUR LOSS, LUCY. BUT THANKS FOR THE IDEA.
NO WORRIES, MILO. YOU'VE DESERVED IT.

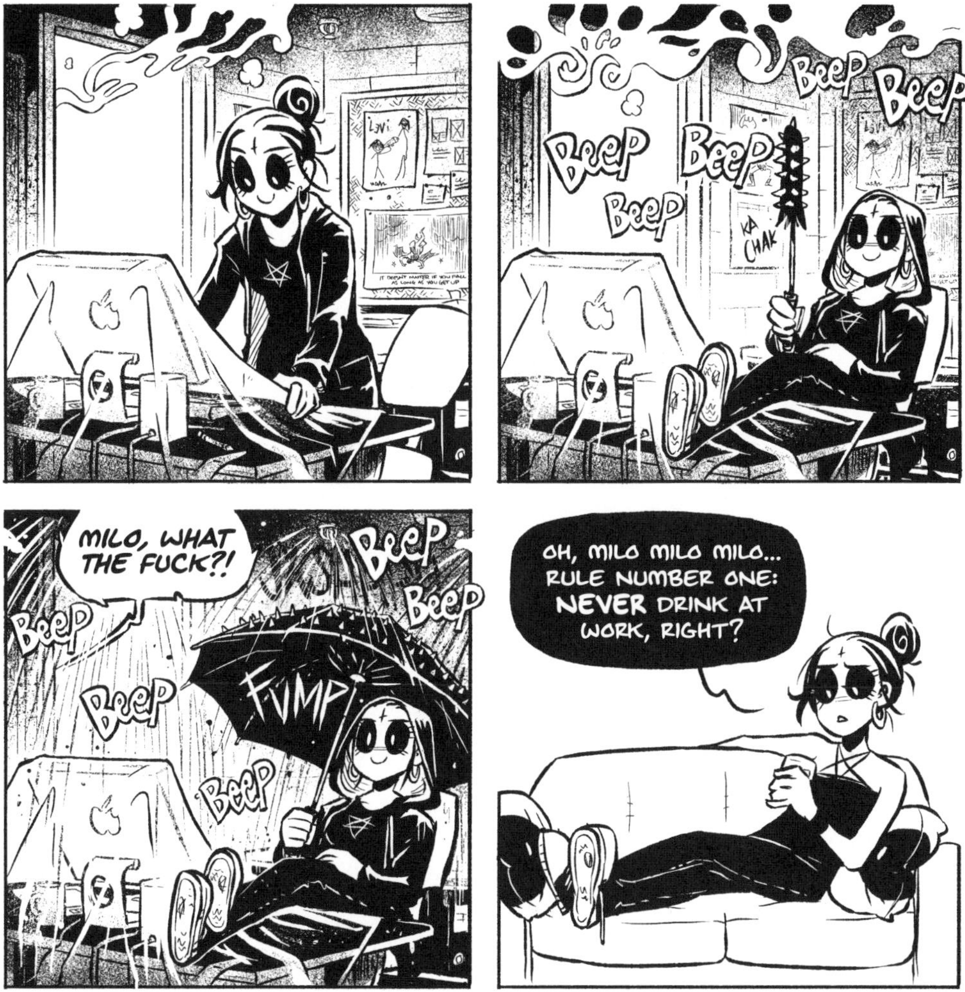
IT DOESN'T MATTER IF YOU FALL AS LONG AS YOU GET UP
BEEP BEEP
BEEP BEEP
BEEP
KA CHAK
MILO, WHAT THE FUCK?!
BEEP
BEEP
BEEP
BEEP
FUMP
BEEP
OH, MILO MILO MILO... RULE NUMBER ONE: **NEVER** DRINK AT WORK, RIGHT?

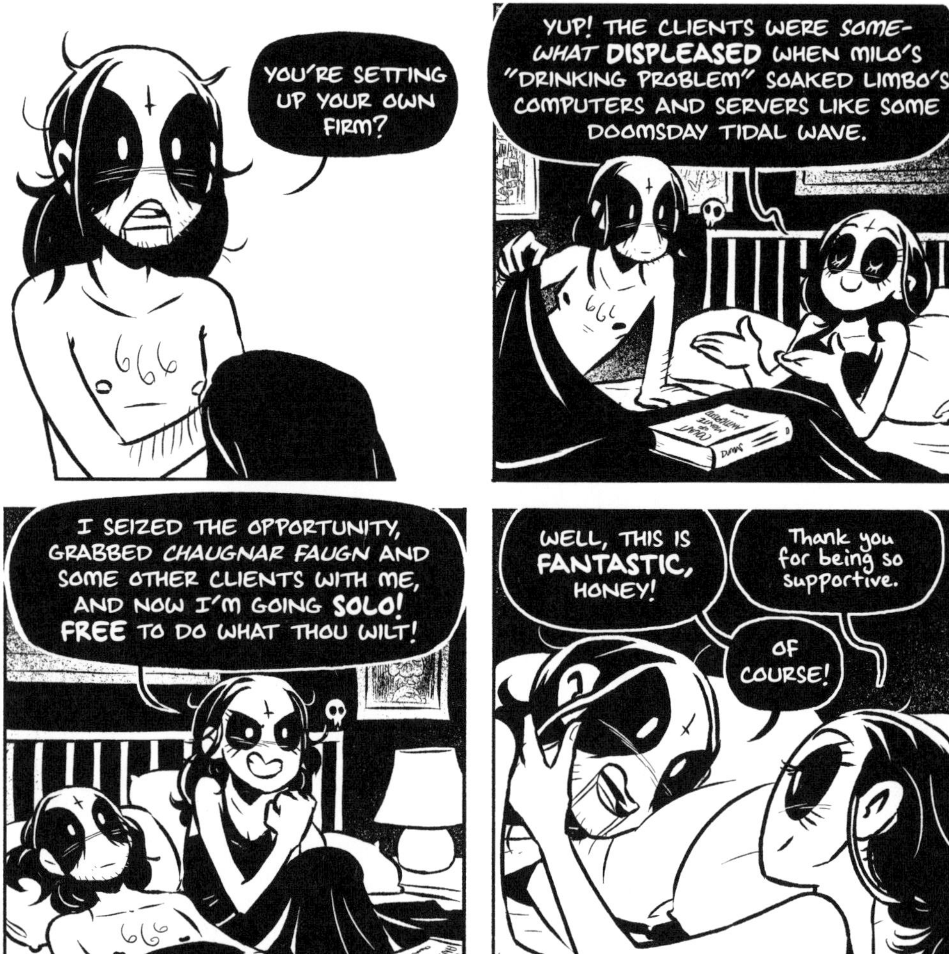
YOU'RE SETTING UP YOUR OWN FIRM?
YUP! THE CLIENTS WERE SOME-WHAT **DISPLEASED** WHEN MILO'S "DRINKING PROBLEM" SOAKED LIMBO'S COMPUTERS AND SERVERS LIKE SOME DOOMSDAY TIDAL WAVE.
I SEIZED THE OPPORTUNITY, GRABBED *CHAUGNAR FAUGN* AND SOME OTHER CLIENTS WITH ME, AND NOW I'M GOING **SOLO! FREE** TO DO WHAT THOU WILT!
WELL, THIS IS **FANTASTIC,** HONEY!
Thank you for being so supportive.
OF COURSE!

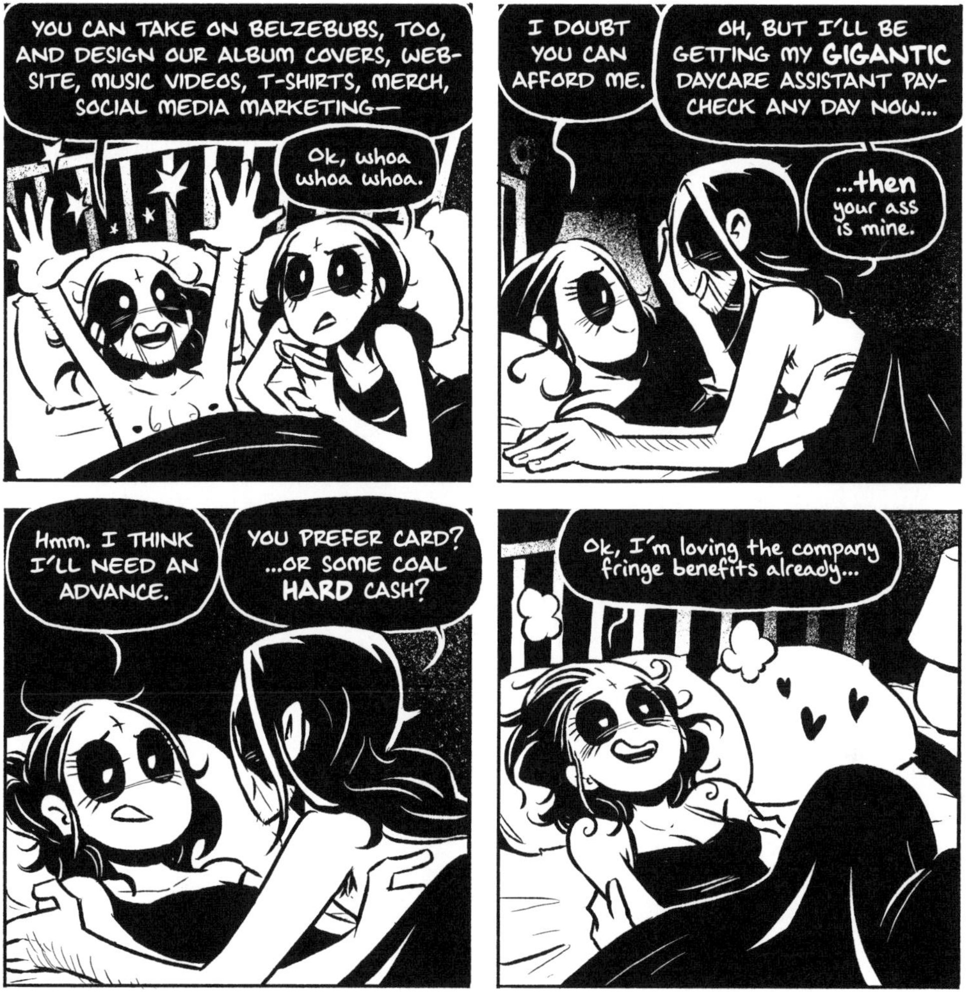
YOU CAN TAKE ON BELZEBUBS, TOO, AND DESIGN OUR ALBUM COVERS, WEB-SITE, MUSIC VIDEOS, T-SHIRTS, MERCH, SOCIAL MEDIA MARKETING—
Ok, whoa whoa whoa.
I DOUBT YOU CAN AFFORD ME.
OH, BUT I'LL BE GETTING MY **GIGANTIC** DAYCARE ASSISTANT PAY-CHECK ANY DAY NOW...
...**then** your ass is mine.
Hmm. I THINK I'LL NEED AN ADVANCE.
YOU PREFER CARD? ...OR SOME COAL **HARD** CASH?
Ok, I'm loving the company fringe benefits already...

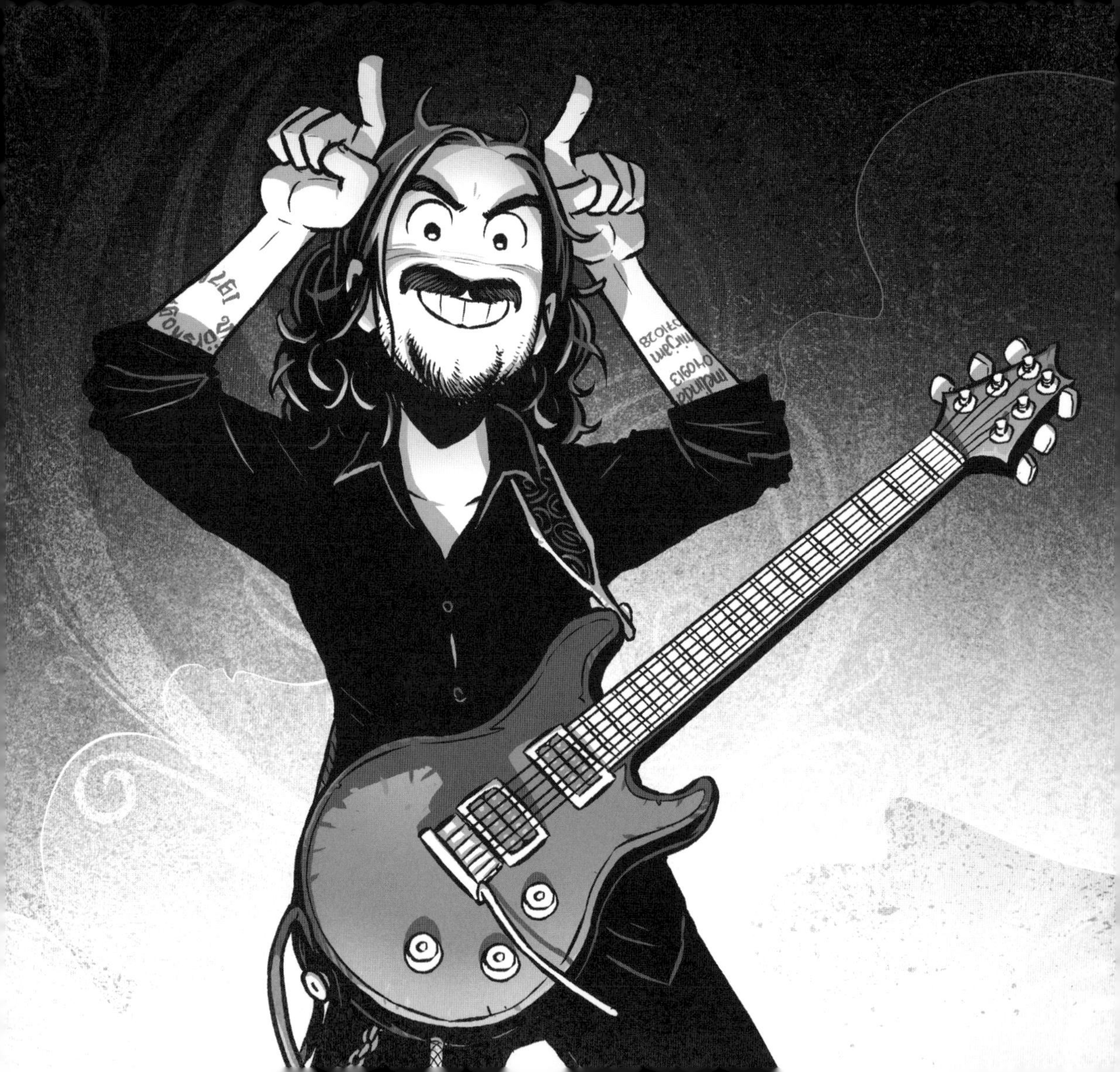

AFTERWORD *by Mikael Åkerfeldt*

JP Ahonen & KP Alare's graphic novel *Sing No Evil* first fell into my lap some ten years ago. Attached to the book was a Post-it note with a message from JP himself, thanking me for "all the inspiring music and art" I've participated in producing with Opeth. Most notably, JP pointed out our record *Ghost Reveries* as the main influence behind the realization of his vision for the book.

I'm a jaded old geezer now, and I was a jaded (slightly-younger) geezer then. I receive a lot of gifts from admirers of the band in the form of records, t-shirts, memory sticks (with music), hot sauce, wine—you name it! It is highly appreciated always, but they...pile up, for lack of a better term. Rarely am I gifted books, let alone comic books. And as the book in question had a Post-it note stuck to it, saying our music inspired its making, I took notice. I flicked through it quickly at first, but ultimately found myself slowing down, gazing at the pages and illustrations within.

The protagonist, Aksel Åkerlund, kinda looked like me (as in me, the slightly-younger geezer) and he cradled a guitar similar to the brand I'm using. And lo and behold! On the wall of Aksel's rehearsal room hangs an Opeth poster! There's even a scene in the book where I'm "talking" to Aksel from the poster, saying "We're nåt all meant tå be singer-våcalists, Aksel. Suck it up" in a faux Swedish/English accent. Fantastic! What's even more interesting is that Aksel's musical trials heavily resemble those I have (and have had) myself throughout my career. *Sing No Evil* holds a lovely story, and together with the outstanding illustrations of the talented JP Ahonen, it's really something of a page-turner.

So when JP emailed me asking if I'd be willing to put together an afterword for the second volume of *Belzebubs,* it was a no-brainer, and I quickly accepted. I must add, I'm quite humbled by the inquiry.

Certainly, I will continue following JP's future endeavors with great interest, and I'm looking forward to receiving a copy of this collection for my "efforts" writing this.

And please, JP...don't forget the personalized Post-it note.

— Lars "Old Geezer" Mikael Åkerfeldt
(Sunny) Stockholm, September 14, 2023

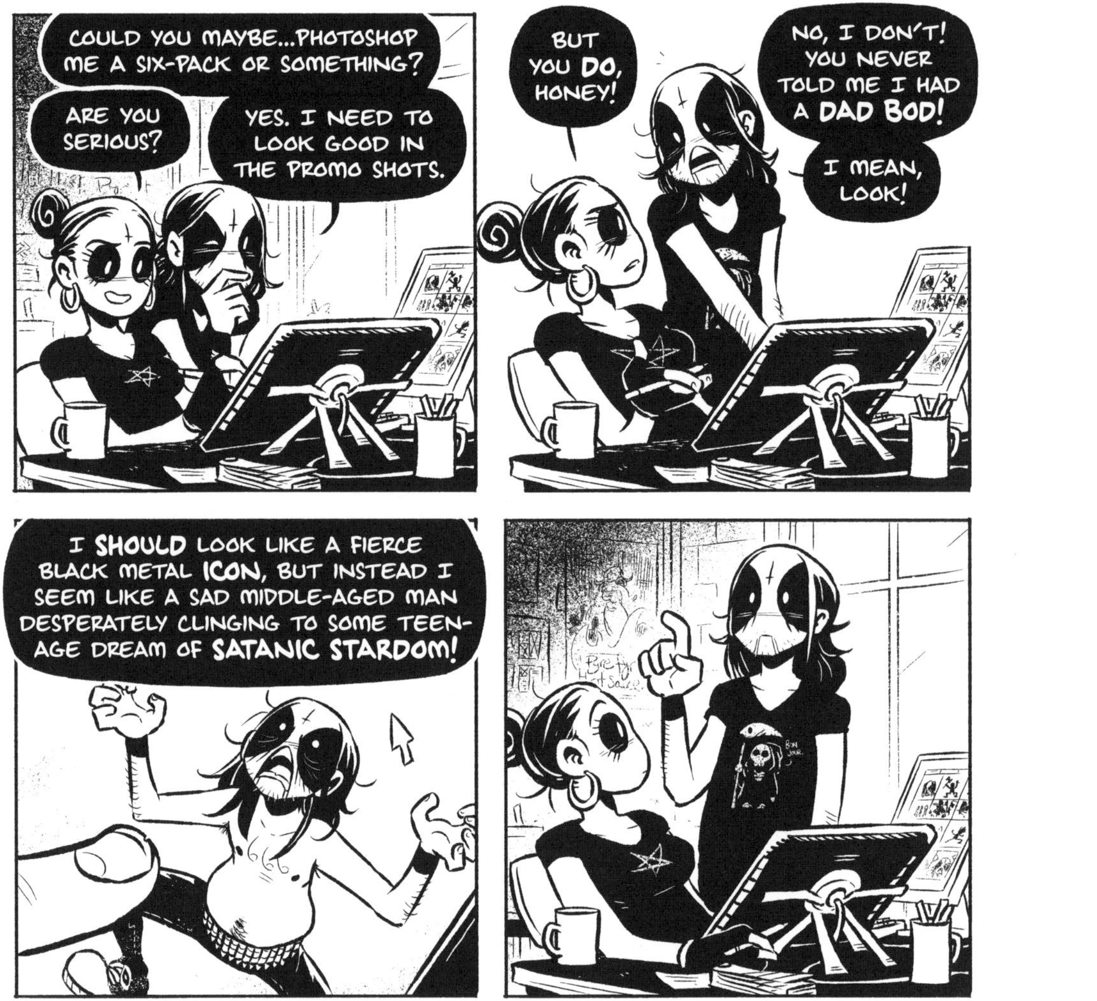
COULD YOU MAYBE...PHOTOSHOP ME A SIX-PACK OR SOMETHING?
ARE YOU SERIOUS?
YES. I NEED TO LOOK GOOD IN THE PROMO SHOTS.
BUT YOU DO, HONEY!
NO, I DON'T! YOU NEVER TOLD ME I HAD A DAD BOD!
I MEAN, LOOK!
I SHOULD LOOK LIKE A FIERCE BLACK METAL ICON, BUT INSTEAD I SEEM LIKE A SAD MIDDLE-AGED MAN DESPERATELY CLINGING TO SOME TEEN-AGE DREAM OF SATANIC STARDOM!

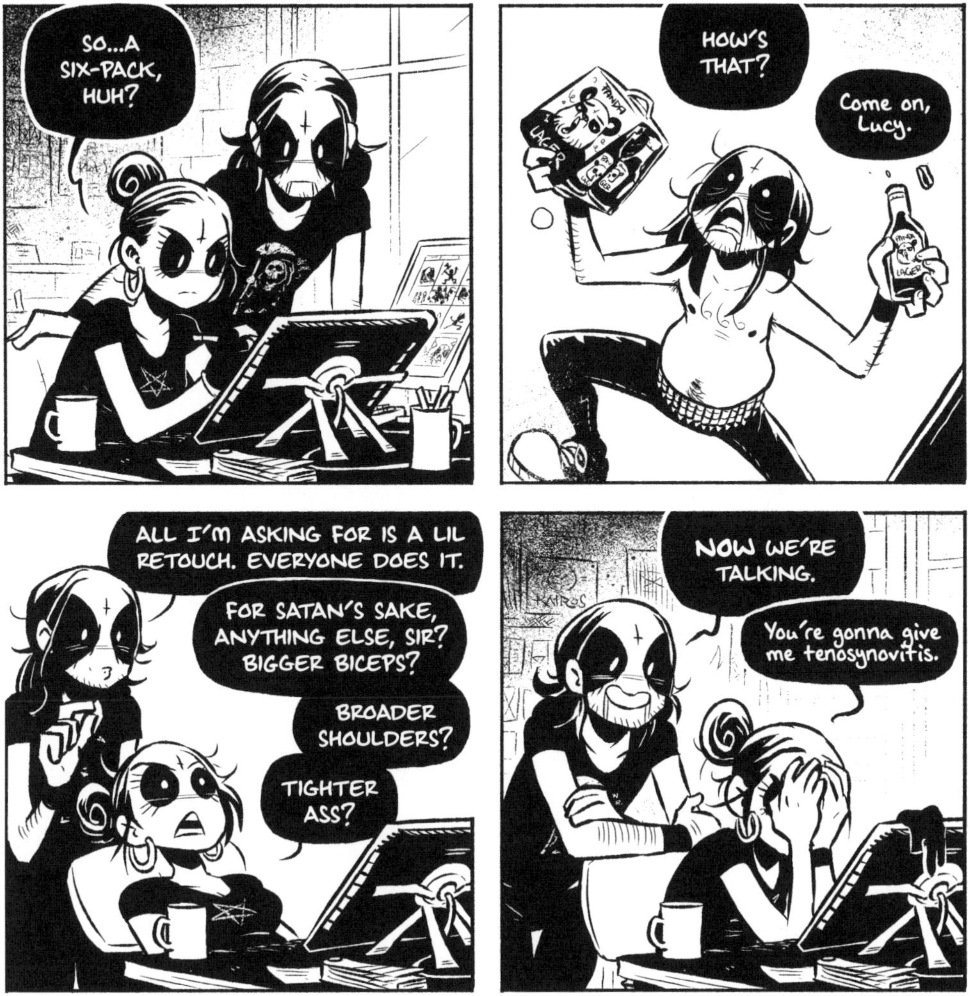
SO...A SIX-PACK, HUH?
HOW'S THAT?
Come on, Lucy.
PANDA LAGER
ALL I'M ASKING FOR IS A LIL RETOUCH. EVERYONE DOES IT.
FOR SATAN'S SAKE, ANYTHING ELSE, SIR? BIGGER BICEPS?
BROADER SHOULDERS?
TIGHTER ASS?
NOW WE'RE TALKING.
You're gonna give me tenosynovitis.

JP AHONEN is a Finnish comic book artist and author. He is best known for his black metal mockumentary **BELZEBUBS**, which has evolved from a humble self-therapy project into a cross-media beast, mixing together webcomics, music and animation. The first *Belzebubs* book and the debut LP, *Pantheon of the Nightside Gods,* both garnered wide critical acclaim across the globe.

JP is currently adapting *Belzebubs* into an animated series with Finland's national broadcaster Yle and Pyjama Films.